THE EUROPEAN SPORTS HISTORY REVIEW

Volume 2

Editors and Advisers

Pieces appearing in this collection are abstracted and indexed in *Political Science Abstracts, Historical Abstracts and America: History and Life* and *Physical Education Index*

THE EUROPEAN SPORTS HISTORY REVIEW

Volume 2

MAKING EUROPEAN MASCULINITIES
Sport, Europe, Gender

Editor

J.A. Mangan
University of Strathclyde

FRANK CASS
LONDON • PORTLAND, OR

First published in 2000 in Great Britain by
FRANK CASS PUBLISHERS
Newbury House, 900 Eastern Avenue
London, IG2 7HH

and in the United States of America by
FRANK CASS PUBLISHERS
c/o ISBS, 5804 N.E. Hassalo Street
Portland, Oregon 97213-3644

Website: www.frankcass.com

British Library Cataloguing in Publication Data

Making Europe masculinities: sport, Europe, gender. –
(European sports history review; v. 2)
1. Men – Europe – Identity 2. Masculinity – Europe 3. Sports –
Europe – History 4. Sports – Europe – Sociological aspects
I. Mangan, J. A. (James Anthony), 1939–
306.4'83

ISBN 0-7146-5089-7 (cloth)
ISBN 0-7146-8030-X (paper)
ISSN 1462-1495

Library of Congress Cataloging-in-Publication Data

Applied for.

Printed in Great Britain by
Antony Rowe Ltd, Chippenham, Wilts

Contents

Prologue: 'With spirits masculine'[1]

J.A. MANGAN

Woolworths, the celebrated commercial store of the common man, woman and child, in a television commercial for the Millennium festive season had two excited children watching in eager anticipation as a large Christmas decoration in the shape of a shining ball or bubble spiralled towards them and burst, dropping into the boy's hand a muscular Action Man, and clothing the girl in a pretty dress! *Plus ça change: plus c'est la même chose?*

The unbroken thread woven into the fabric of the chapters of *Making European Masculinities* is the fitness of the male – physical, moral, social and political – for confrontation with enemies, temptations and circumstances. It is not the single thread but it is the central thread.

In European history, the making of men has carried the explicit and implicit message that men faced outwards to the world and confronted its problems, while women faced inward to the home and its demands. Has it been different elsewhere? Whilst that has been the past, the future may well be different. This point will be considered in the Epilogue.

In recorded history there have been few exceptions to this arrangement. This state of affairs has ensured a basic continuity in the making of masculinity. The fundamental concept of masculinity, whatever sophisticated subsidiary concepts there have been, has changed little. It is hardly surprising, therefore, that the chapters of *Making European Masculinities* reflect this continuity. Of course, they reflect change in response to changing political, social, cultural and psychological imperatives but continuity looms larger than change down the centuries.

The key concept in any explanation is 'fitness' for struggle. The facts of male freedom from pregnancy, greater explosive power and greater expendability, has resulted in cultures devoting considerable effort to prepare the boy to be a man in an atmosphere of aggressive competition, personal assertion and inculcated self-sacrifice – to the perceived advantage of the group, the team, the nation. This is true in and beyond Europe. As David Gilmore has noted of the cultures he investigated in *Manhood in the Making: Cultural Concepts of Masculinity*, authentically neuter or androgynous cultures are relatively rare 'on a global scale'[2] and 'wherever "real" manhood is emphasised, even lightly, and for whatever reasons, three moral injunctions seem to come repeatedly into focus',[3] namely, 'Man-the-Impregnator-Protector-Provider'.[4] These roles recur repeatedly in the chapters of *Making European Masculinities*. Gilmore also makes the important point that these 'three male imperatives are either dangerous or highly competitive. They place men at risk on the battlefield, in the hunt, or in confrontation with their fellows'.[5] Nevertheless, for the majority of men there is no escaping from these imperatives and therefore, since 'boys must steel themselves to enter into such struggles, they must be prepared by various sorts of tempering and toughening. To be men, most of all, they must accept the fact that they are expendable'.[6]

All this is to be found in the chapters of *Making European Masculinities*. None of it is to deny the complexity of masculinity, the social or individual variations and the absence of a monolithic stereotype. There is 'a consortium of manly images and codes, a sliding scale or polychromatic spectrum'.[7] Nevertheless, the fundamental cultural image of the continually applauded male as aggressive, competitive, confrontational and dominant *when necessary* has been a constant phenomenon in the period under review in *Making European Masculinities* and is recorded in the following pages.

Gilmore remarks, 'we can safely say this: when men are conditioned to fight manhood is important; where men are conditioned to flight, the opposite is true',[8] and he adds with undeniable truth, that most societies choose at some time or other to fight possibly due to a general scarcity of resources and the inability for societies to simply run away, so whatever the sliding scale of masculinity, men virtually *everywhere* are prepared for war, *inter alia* in the modern world indirectly by an emphasis on school and post-school sport partly in readiness for military crisis or directly through integrated schemes of sport and military training in school and after school. The reason is clear. One constant masculine imperative throughout history has been 'a moral commitment to defend the society and its core values against all odds'.[9] Thus, in history, 'manhood codes seem to be derivative rather than arbitrary,[10] for this primary reason: 'Manhood is a social barrier that societies must erect against entropy, human enemies, the forces of nature, time and all the human weaknesses that endanger group life.'[11] What the socialisation of the male has amounted to, therefore, has been an attempted training in control.

It is for this reason that Gilmore argues that manhood like womanhood, is 'a nurturing concept',[12] and 'men nurture their society by shedding their blood, their sweat, and their semen, by bringing home food for both child and mother, and by dying if necessary in faraway places to provide a safe haven for their people'.[13] Underlying much cultural reflection, planning and implementation associated with making men out of boys, therefore, has been training, both direct and indirect, for readiness for battlefields, on playing fields or similar venues. A further and associated concern of the educator has been to develop a sense of community through an emphasis on the social virtues of loyalty, obedience, cooperation and discipline. Crucial qualities perceived as inseparable from success in war, politics and commerce have also received careful attention: aggression, persistence and endurance. Far less of a priority has been an education for marriage, domesticity and parenthood.

This pattern of strong and weak emphasis is reflected in the chapters of *Making European Masculinities* which, whilst it spans Europe geographically and historically, makes no pretence at comprehensiveness. However, in the space available, it does bring into sharp focus a masculine heritage that is both challenged *and* sustained at this time of revolutionary change in gender construction. Whilst change in history is not to be foolishly ignored, continuity in history is not to be naïvely overlooked!

NOTES

1. John Milton, *Paradise Lost*, bk II, 1, 547.
2. David D. Gilmore, *Manhood in the Making: Cultural Concepts of Masculinity* (New Haven, 1990), p.222.
3. Ibid.
4. Ibid., p.223.
5. Ibid.
6. Ibid.
7. Ibid., p.222.
8. Ibid., p.221.
9. Ibid., p.224.
10. Ibid.
11. Ibid., p.226.
12. Ibid., p.229.
13. Ibid., p.230.

The Ephebia in the Ancient Hellenic World and its Role in the Making of Masculinity

EVANGELOS ALBANIDIS

The size of the ancient Hellenic world varied at different times in its history and reached its peak during the Hellenistic period. During the great colonising period from the second half of the eighth century BC onwards, a large number of colonies were founded in Gaul, the Italian peninsula and North Africa as well as along the coastlines of Thrace, Euxeinos Pontos and Asia Minor.[1] After Alexander's famous expedition the Hellenistic regions extended from the Ionian Sea to the river Indus and from the Red Sea to Euxeinos Pontos.[2]

Wherever the Hellenes founded new towns, they established educational, political, military and religious institutions and remained faithful to their customs.[3] They were devoted to gymnastics, and physical education became part of their everyday education.[4] It played a more important role in Hellenic life than in the life of any other nation before or since.[5] Physical education was organised around the Hellenic gymnasium[6] which typified Greek life.[7] Gymnasia spread far and wide throughout the towns and communities of Hellenistic countries, in particular those conquered by Alexander and his successors and settled by Hellenes. Gymnasia are known to have existed in nearly 140 Hellenic localities.[8]

During Hellenistic and Roman times, national and cultural cohesion of Hellenes was based on the education of the young, just as it was in classical times and the gymnasium played a distinctive socio–political role in Hellenistic cities. In it Greek language as well as the moral, political and social education of the young was promoted. The gymnasium was closely associated with the ephebia since it was the place where the education of the ephebes was organised.[9] In the cities where there was more than one gymnasium, one was used exclusively for educating the ephebes. The word *ephebus* in the Hellenic language means adolescent. The ephebia was a school that provided military, gymnastic and intellectual education for young men of 18–20 years of age. Ephebia was also the term for the period of training in the school.

This chapter is based on the collection and analysis of data related to the foundation and expansion of ephebia all over the Hellenic world. It examines the general goals of this institution as well as its specific role in the making of masculinity. The main sources are inscriptions and in particular:

1. Ephebic lists which include the names of the ephebes who officially entered the ephebia.
2. Inscribed honour resolutions of the municipality and any other honours inscriptions. At frequent intervals, the municipality honoured the director of the institution for his generosity and faithful duties.
3. Ephebarchic laws and ephebic oaths containing information about the duties of the officials and the aims and curriculum of the institution.
4. Epitaph inscriptions on the tombstones of ephebes.

EPHEBIA IN ATHENS

For young males there was invariably compulsory training in the use of weapons and martial arts in all the ancient cities which were in constant conflict. The ephebia in Athens seems to have been the model for the formation of similar institutions in other cities. The earliest evidence refers exclusively to the Athenian ephebia.[10]

The date of the origin of the Athenian ephebia is uncertain. Even today, the exact year of the foundation of the Attic ephebia is disputed. There are two conflicting views. Both put forward strong arguments.[11] One maintains that the ephebia was founded in Athens in 335 BC by Epicrates,[12] and the other claims that its origins are much older. It seems that the latter view is much closer to the truth. From the available sources, it is impossible to be precise about the actual origin of the institution or the exact century. The most important source regarding the function of the Attic ephebia is Aristotle's *Athenian Republic*[13] which contains a detailed description and analysis of the institution.

The ancient Attic ephebia provided military training.[14] In Athens it was an institution for all youths aged between 18 and 20 and, according to the records of the city state, councils annually drew up a list of most young men reaching adulthood (that is 18 years of age). They were required to attend the ephebia. During their first year of attendance, the ephebes stayed in Piraeus (Mounichia and the Coast) and underwent physical education and military training. The local authorities elected two paidotribes and instructors to give them lessons in physical exercise and in hoplomachy, archery, javelin and catapult throwing.[15] The following year, after they had displayed their skills before the city assembly, they were given a shield and a spear as weapons. During this second year, they exercised in the open and guarded and patrolled fortified positions on the border. At that time, the ephebes were supported by the state, and wore a uniform which consisted of a large hat (*petassos*) and a *chlamys*.[16] After completing their two years of training, the ephebes became citizens.

In the year 269–268 BC[17] or even earlier in 305–304 BC,[18] the exact date is unclear, and only 30 years after the publication of Epicrates' law,[19] the attendance of the ephebes in the ephebia was reduced to one year and was no longer compulsory. The worldwide changes which occurred as a result of the campaigns of Alexander the Great and the establishment of the Hellenistic kingdoms, clearly influenced the evolution of the ephebia. Since the independent city states no longer existed, the army of Athens (as well as of other cities) was abolished. Consequently, the ephebia gradually lost its military emphasis which was replaced by an emphasis on physical and intellectual education during Hellenistic and Roman times. In fact, even from the third century BC there had been a dramatic decrease in the number of ephebes.[20] Only after the establishment of the Roman Empire, did the Attic ephebia flourish again.[21]

As mentioned above, the ephebate was originally compulsory in Athens. During the third century BC it became voluntary and exclusive to the aristocratic classes, whose sons alone could spare the time and support the incidental expenses, which included uniforms, subscriptions to special lectures, library expenses and funds for crowns, statues and other dedications. Oil was an additional expense which was not provided by the city or the magistrate in charge at the time.[22] The ephebate now spread through the Greek-speaking world, as a kind of university training for the sons of the well-to-do. It seems to have been open to any one who could afford it.[23]

EXPANSION OF THE EPHEBIA

Ephebic training thus originated in Athens and spread rapidly to the countries all over the Hellenic world. The ephebia were to be found in towns on the Hellenic mainland, on the Aegean islands, in Thrace and in Macedonia. The institution also spread to remote areas such as Asia Minor, the Eastern region, north east Africa, Euxeinos Pontos, the Italian peninsula and Gaul. Ephebia existed in a total of 124 places.[24] In fact, the expansion of these ephebic institutions was greater in Asia Minor than on the mainland of Hellas. In all, ephebia were adopted by 48 localities in Asia Minor,[25] Pergamum,[26] Miletus,[27] Ephessos,[28] Teos[29] and Cyzikos.[30] Information about the content and the goals of the ephebia in Asia Minor are therefore available from a great number of inscriptions.

Most Hellenic cities had a system of ephebic training. The Thracian ephebia were to be founded in ten cities, all of which were old Hellenic colonial centres.[31] The adoption of the institution in Odessos,[32] Dionysopolis,[33] Sestos[34] and Philippi[35] is of particular importance. The Macedonian ephebia were founded in the cities of Edessa,[36] Derriopos,[37] Orestis,[38] Thessaloniki,[39] Verroia[40] and Amphipolis.[41] Here the majority of the inscriptions belong to the Roman period. As well as the Hellenic mainland, the ephebia was to be found in 15 Aegean islands. The most important epigraphical evidence comes from Euboia,[42] Naxos,[43] Ceos,[44] Paros,[45] Cyprus,[46] Thera,[47] Delos,[48] Thassos[49] and Samos.[50] In Egypt, gymnasia were founded in Naukratis, Alexandria, Luxor, Philadelphia, Ptolemais, Theadelphia, Aphroditopolis and in non-Greek cities such as Ombi and Elephantine.[51] There is evidence of ephebia in the Ptolemaic period in the first half of the second century BC. According to inscriptions ephebia also existed in Alexandria,[52] Hermopolis[53] Oxyrynchus[54] and Arsinoe (Fayum).[55]

It is important to note the remarkable spread of the ephebia to Babylon[56] and Massilia.[57] Babylon was more than 3000 kilometres from Athens, and marked the eastern limit of ephebic institutions; Massilia marked the western limit.

The duration of ephebic service was not the same in all towns. As in Athens in the third century and thereafter[58] the usual ephebic period covered only one year, from age 18 to 19, but the duration of the service could vary from one to three years.[59] In most towns, the customary time spent in the ephebia, it seems, was one year, as was the case for example, in Cyzicus, Priene and Iasus.[60] In Halicarnassus[61] and the Pontic Heraclea,[62] however, there were classes of younger ephebi, a fact which suggests a two-year period of ephebic service. In Apollonis of Lydia,[63] there were three classes, one for the first semester, one for the second, and one for the second year. The difference in the numbers of youths attending the first and second year suggests that the second year was voluntary.[64] In Tomi, the ephebi were divided into two classes. From this evidence we may deduce that the duration of ephebic service varied from place to place and that the ephebia existed not only in big Hellenic cities, but also in small villages and communities.[65] Finally, analysis of the inscriptions has revealed the existence of ephebia not only in Hellenistic times but also in Roman times.

OFFICIALS OF THE EPHEBIA

The most important official of the ephebia was the gymnasiarch,[66] the principal of the gymnasium[67] (according to the initial definition of the term). He was responsible for all the activities which took place in the gymnasium including the ephebia, and was considered the director of the ephebi.[68] As suggested earlier, the authority of the gymnasiarch in Hellenistic and Roman times was given to the most honest and generous of all the citizens. He was responsible for supplying oil, organising games, providing the prizes and paying the teachers.[69] He was expected to spend his own money freely on the facilities. In some instances he paid for improvements and provided fuel for the furnaces of the hot baths. The gymnasiarch seems to have been a kind of local director of education.[70]

However, in Athens the most important role in educating the ephebi was that of the *kosmetes*. He was the principal of the ephebia and was elected by the citizens.[71] He was responsible for organising and supervising all activities of the ephebi. The kosmetes supervised the work of the ephebi in the gymnasia, organised lectures on rhetoric and philosophy[72] and accompanied the ephebi to sacrificial rituals, religious processions and torch races.[73] He was assisted by the *sophronistai* – discipline masters. One sophronistes was appointed from each tribe. The fathers of the ephebi in addition, chose three nominees each year. Out of a total of 30 nominees, ten were elected. All assembly members voted for the ten candidates. Direct responsibility for the education of Athenian youths lay on the shoulders of the sophronistai; by law, all nominees had to be over 40 years of age. Aristotle reports that the candidates were men of the most exemplary character and thus considered the most suitable to take care of the ephebi. Their salary was one drachma a day.[74]

In Egyptian and Bithynian towns (Alexandria, Hermopolis, Arsinoe, Oxyrhyncus, Fayum, Nicaea, Illium) as in Athens the director of the ephebi was a kosmetes.[75] All the other Hellenic cities called the head of the ephebes gymnasiarch or *ephebarch*.[76] The use of the term ephebarch was common. This title was often used in the northern parts of Hellas (Thrace, Macedonia, Euxeinos Pontos), in Asia Minor and in the Aegean islands (Lesbos, Ikaria, Euboea and Cyprus). Ephebarchs were to be found in 24 towns, assistants of ephebarchs in two towns and archephebes, a Peloponesian equivalent of ephebarch, in four towns.[77]

Knowledge of the function of the ephebarch is scanty and conflicting. The ephebarch was a magistrate and the head of the ephebi. He was chosen by the ephebes. The ephebarch was not an honorary title (*princep epheborum*) but a real public office for rich men or ephebes who offered part or all of their fortune to the ephebia.[78] It is important to recognise that the ephebarch was often an assistant to the gymnasiarch. Where the ephebarch and gymnasiarch existed side by side,[79] the former directed the ephebi, and the latter had a higher position and was in charge of the gymnasium or gymnasia.[80] Wherever the gymnasiarch directed the ephebi, he played the same role as the Athenian kosmetes. This is clear from an inscription of Priene[81] which states that he 'maintained orderliness, obliging all the teachers to co-operate with him'.

FOREIGNERS IN THE EPHEBIA

Admission of foreigners to the ephebia was not uncommon in the Hellenic world. In many cities, the local inhabitants, as well as the Hellenes, could attend the ephebia and often Romans, Asian settlers, *paroikoi* and Hellenes from other places composed the student population. In the Athenian ephebia, foreigners were admitted freely from 119 to118 BC and, especially during the Roman period, were more numerous than ever.[82] Consequently the Attic ephebia gradually lost its national character as the ephebi came from all over the Mediterranean world. Most came from Miletus and Rome; others came from Syria, Thrace, Euxeinos Pontos and from many islands in the Aegean.[83]

A vast number of inscriptions found on the island of Delos[84] makes it clear that the ephebi came from many countries, since Delos was a thoroughly cosmopolitan centre. Nothing prevented a foreigner from getting a position as an ephebic paidotribe; two such paidotribes came from Alexandria.[85] According to other inscriptions every foreigner was allowed to exercise in the gymnasium of Pergamum.[86] Among 178 ephebes on an ephebic list[87] dating from 147–146 BC, there are three ephebes with barbarian names. According to another ephebic list, Misoi and Masdiinoi were also enrolled in the ephebia of Pergamum.[88] Three more cities of Asia Minor (Lampsacus, Priene, Cyzicus)[89] complete this list of educational centres which accepted foreigners to the ephebia.

The gymnasia in Egypt, which developed after Alexander's conquest, were centres of Hellenic life, and it seems certain that only Hellenes and the most aristocratic Egyptians were allowed admission to them.[90] In Egypt, however, during the Ptolemaic period, there is evidence that native Egyptians were allowed to participate in some of the ephebic groups. The synod of *neaniskoi* at Theadelphia had one or perhaps two native officials and the leader of an ephebic section in the Fayum had a name which may have been Egyptian.[91] It is not particularly suprising to find names of Jews and Persians as well as Egyptians during the Ptolemaic period.[92] On an ephebic list of Kyrene, one hellenised Egyptian name[93] is to be found.

During the Hellenistic period, the local inhabitants of the eastern regions were able to build a gymnasium and found an ephebia with royal approval. The high priest Jason, for example, built a gymnasium and organised the ephebia for Jews in Jerusalem. Gymnasia for Phoenicians and Syrians were also founded in Tyros and Gadara, respectively.[94]

The most important findings concerning the admission of foreigners to the ephebia are the ephebic lists of Odessus and Dionysopolis in Thrace. These include the names of the ephebes who officially entered the ephebic institution. In Odessus, archaeologists have found eight ephebic lists.[95] The most important is that found in the Roman thermes.[96] The elaborate decoration at the top of the inscription, the athletic content of the decorative relief at the bottom and the wide range of names are very impressive. Out of 221 names on the eight Odessus lists, 167 are romanised (76%), 18 Roman (8%), 12 Asiatic (5%) and 24 are hellenised Thracian names (11%).[97] It is clear therefore, that Hellenic colonists, Romans and Asian and native Thracians were the members of the ephebic institution of the town. The Dionysopolis list,[98] has an important decorative relief (similar to the ephebic lists of Odessos) and a similar mix of names. Out of 30 names, five are hellenised Thracian (17%), three Asian (10%) and two Roman.

CURRICULUM AND GOALS OF THE EPHEBIA – THEIR ROLE IN THE MAKING OF MASCULINITY

Attica

Athenian ephebes commenced their service with a pilgrimage to the most important shrines of the city and towards the end of their first year took the famous oath[99] which reflected the goals of the ephebia. It is clear, that preparation for war was the basic goal.

> I will never bring reproach upon my hallowed arms, nor will I desert the comrade at whose side I stand, but I will defend our altars and our heaths, single-handed or supported by many. I will not leave the heritage of my native land poorer but greater and better than when I inherited it.

Military education was a necessity as war was common. After their defeat in the battle of Haeronia in 338 BC by the Macedonians, the consequences of a deficient military education which had been critisised by the Athenian historian, Xenophon,[100] were fully brought home to the Athenians. Plato, too, had recommended an adequate military education.[101] The Athenians decided, therefore, to organise ephebia more effectively according to the law of Epicrates. Their first goal was the defence of their nation and the second goal was submission to the laws and democratic institutions of the city which was also part of their oath:

> I will obey whoever is in authority and submit to the established laws and all others which the people shall harmoniously enact. If anyone tries to overthrow the constitution or disobey it, I will not permit him, but will come to its defence single-handed or with the support of all.

From this oath, it may be reasonably assumed that the commitment of the ephebes to their democracy was of major importance. Their political education was almost as important as their military education. The oath required that the ephebes should submit to the laws of the city and fully obey the authorities. Social restraint and compliance with the laws of the state were, of course, the obligations of free and responsible citizens. For the ancient Greeks, the law was binding on everybody, the gods, the people, the authorities and their subjects. The laws were considered as a gift of the gods and not submitting to the law was to disobey the gods.[102] The third goal of the education of the ephebes can be found in the last line of the oath. The ephebes promised to respect the religion of the nation:

> I will honour the religion of my fathers. Let the gods be my witness Argaulus, Enyalius, Ares, Zeus, Thallo, Auxo, Hegemone.

In short, the Athenian ephebes of the fourth century BC were citizen-soldiers. The ephebia basically prepared men to defend their nation in war but although its purpose was predominantly military, it had other aims, including moral and religious preparation for the full exercise of their rights and duties as citizens.[103]

The general purpose of the ephebic college is well described in one of the inscriptions:[104]

> The people, being ever most zealous for the training and discipline of the ephebi and desiring to have those who are leaving boyhood and entering manhood, become worthy successors of their fathers in the duties of citizens, enjoined by law that they should become acquainted with the land, the fortresses, and the borders of Attica and that they should perform in arms the exercises appertaining to war. On account of the aforesaid training, the people have adorned the city with trophies most beautiful and august; for which cause, likewise, it chooses the Kosmetes from the men who have led the noblest lives.

From the middle of the third century (262–261 BC) when the period at the ephebia was limited to one year, its purposes remained threefold. However emphasis was now given to spiritual development, moral behaviour and socialisation.[105] In a less militant climate military preparation was no longer so essential. The ephebia of Athens now provided a general education by offering lectures on philosophy, rhetoric and academic studies. Apart from the acquisition of knowledge and skills, the ephebia aimed at improving the moral behaviour of the ephebes, and instilling qualities such as decency, orderliness, discipline, integrity, submission to the laws and obedience to the authorities.[106]

In Hellenistic and Roman times, friendships made during their education were greatly valued by the ephebes and were retained after graduation by means of the so-called 'clubs of young men'. Life in the ephebia was organised like a miniature state with committees, elected authorities, officials (archon, general herald, king, polemarch),[107] debates and voting. All these elements encouraged the ephebes to play a full part in politics and public affairs after graduation and gave them a grounding in politics.[108] During the period of the Roman Empire, the ephebia became a school of politics and citizenship rather than of war. Ephebes called themselves 'citizens' and even had an Areopagus council of their own.[109]

When youths from many cities of the East and the West entered the Athenian ephebia[110] in Hellenistic times, national education naturally gave way to an emphasis on co-operation and peace among the ephebes, qualities essential for social co-existence. Living together, eating together and above all exercising together, as well as taking part in various social events in the city led to the development of a cosmopolitan team spirit.

However, the martial arts were not completely neglected, not even in the late Hellenistic period.[111] The military education staff was limited[112] but exercising with arms continued and remained one of the basic activities. Hoplomachy (fighting in heavy armour) and training in the use of the kestrosphendone (a kind of artillery engine) still existed during the Roman period.[113]

However, physical education increasingly played a more important role. The paidotribe became an increasingly significant and honoured figure. From the second century BC he was employed for life and was assisted in his task by 'hypopaidotribes'.[114] This state of affairs came about because physical exercise in the ephebia changed. The 'Republican ideal' had developed in the pre-classical era (late seventh to early sixth century BC) and a new relationship between the individual and the state had prevailed.[115] Under no circumstances, therefore, could the individual exist outside the state. Physical education in the ephebia no longer aimed at success in sport events and the development of the individual, but had a more collective 'political role'. Citizens exercised not only in order to satisfy their personal ambition, but also to learn to be members of a team so as to be able to deal effectively with public affairs.[116]

Of course, physical exercise was still considered an appropriate preparation for war. To Greeks under Roman control, it was through sport that they hoped to acquire their freedom.[117] Boxing, wrestling and the pancratium, in particular, prepared soldiers for war.[118] This is the reason why during the Roman period, races of various distances (*stadion*, *diavlos*, *dolixos*), wrestling and the pancratium were the most popular forms of exercise.[119] Riding, too, was popular,[120] a clear indication of how aristocratic the institution had become. The ephebia now became the university of the Roman Empire; wealthy young men came from everywhere to study in Athens. Ephebic training, with its recognisable archaic features from the classical period, originated in tribal age groups, started as a formalised rite of passage from youth to citizen, but later developed into a system of advanced education.

The Rest of the Hellenic World

In the course of its evolution, the ephebia changed in many ways. The economic and political situation of each town as well as its traditions influenced the curriculum. It is not possible, therefore, to make reliable generalisations for the whole Greek world. In many towns, especially during the Roman period, political education prevailed. In others, emphasis was still given to the military and athletic preparation of the ephebes. With the abolition of autonomous city-states during the Hellenistic period, there was no compelling reason to continue the military education of the ephebes. Nevertheless, it was kept alive and in a few cities it played a primary role in preparing the future mercenaries of royalty or the Roman army.[121] Through this military education, cities formed the men of the future and secured their own future.

At the same time, as well as providing military education for the ephebes, the Hellenes, who in their view, were surrounded by barbarians, expected the ephebia to initiate these youths into the Hellenic way of life, the most important feature of which was athletics. Through the athletic preparation of the ephebes, the Hellenes publicised, promoted and perpetuated their own identity as well as their own culture, and ensured fitness for war.

The curricular aims of the ephebia beyond Athens were as follows: physical, intellectual, political and military education, enculturation, inculcation of moral behaviour and the formation of cosmopolitan citizens. In one inscription there are ephebic paidotribes, military instructors and athletic contests and contests in armour. This suggests that athletic and military education remained important goals of the ephebia. The ephebarchic law of Amphipolis[122] (dating from about the first century BC) provides invaluable information on physical and military education. There is information on the teachers (paidotribe, trainer in javelin-throwing, trainer in archery, tamer of new horses). The training of ephebes in different sports (archery, javelin throwing, *sphendonismos, lithobolia*, riding, mounted javelin) and their participation in contests are also mentioned. Remarkably, in the ephebarchic law there is no reference whatsoever to non-athletic activities in the gymnasium. There is no indication of sophists, rhetoricians, schoolmasters and musicians. It seems that some ephebia concentrated on the athletic and military preparation of ephebes rather than their intellectual education.

The long inscription from Sestos[123] (107 verses) dating from about 120 BC provides a fascinating insight into the gymnastic activities of this town on the Hellespont. The gymnasiarch Menas Menitos conducted tactical exercises for both ephebi and *neoi* and organised contests in javelin-throwing and archery at his own expense. Fighting in armour (hoplomachy) and the long race in armour were also practised there. The whole inscription reveals an emphasis on the physical and military education of the ephebes. The ephebia in Tegea, in contrast, focused more on gymnastics than on military training as can be seen in the repeated mention of the 'oil-furnisher', a reference to the paidotribes.[124] No military instructors of any sort are named. In Delos, although the ephebic paidotribe[125] was not as grand a personage as the gymnasiarch, he meant a great deal to the ephebi, and frequently remained in office several years in succession, whereas a new gymnasiarch came from Athens every year. The paidotribe taught all the exercises himself since no other physical education teacher existed.[126] In Eretria, according to an inscription,[127] the gymnasiarch was not only in charge of young boys and ephebi, but was also responsible for the oil and the organisation of many long races. He also employed at his own expense an instructor in rhetoric and one in heavy armed fighting.

There was, therefore, variety to be found among the ephebia. In Pergamum, ephebi had exclusive use of their own gymnasium.[128] The gymnasiarch supplied an abundance of arms and brought in a teacher at his own expense.[129] In Teos, the ephebia had more of a military character than in most parts of Asia Minor, since three separate military teachers seem to have been employed; this can be found nowhere else.[130] In the third century BC, in the small city of Coressus, on the island of Ceos, the gymnasiarch himself was expected to train the ephebes in archery, javelin throwing, and firing the catapult three times a month.[131]

Samos had not only the ephebi, but also two preparatory groups, the *parephibi* and *pallekes*.[132] Several victor lists found in Samos give a full picture of the various kinds of gymnastics and sports used there. The pallekes trained in the use of the catapult, the lithobolos (an artillery engine for hurling stones; not identical to the catapult), the javelin and the bow and arrow; they also trained in hoplomachy and fighting with a large shield. In addition, they practised the stadium race, the double race, and the long race.[133] An inscription from Babylon[134] names a gymnasiarch and mentions the ephebi who had won various contests: archery, javelin throwing, hoplomachy with the round shield and the oblong shield, the long race and the one-lap race.

The last ephebic record dating from 323 AD, from Oxyrynchus, is a proclamation by a worthy citizen named Dioskurides who makes reference to an approaching gymnastic display.[135] This inscription is mainly concerned with physical exercise. It seems that wherever there were ephebi, there was physical education. The close connection of the gymnasiarchs with physical education and the ephebi is demonstrated by the disappearance of both simultaeneously during the same century.[136] Throughout their existence, clearly, physical and military training in the ephebia both developed the fitness of the body and imparted qualities such as courage, decency, discipline, orderliness, courtesy, integrity and *esprit de corps*.[137]

In the Thracian town of Sestos,[138] the gymnasiarch gave prizes of arms to ephebes who excelled in discipline, diligence, and physical fitness. There were similar competitions in Samos and a physical fitness competition with the list of winners in the gymnasium of Gorgippia.[139] In Thassos[140] and Massilia[141] there is evidence of an ephebic discipline contest. In Pergamum,[142] the ephebi were divided into three groups: the orderly, the industrious, and the fit, on the basis of their past record and an entrance examination.

Finally, the term s*ynephebi* was frequently employed to indicate the bonding that came from membership of the ephebia. During their attendance in the ephebia, close friendships were formed and in later years, adults were known to refer to each other as synephebi.[143]

In summary, from the extensive inscriptions throughout the Hellenic world it is clear that the ephebia was used by the state to form the men of the future out of the youth of the present. Military training, in particular was an education for responsible manhood and developed required masculine characteristics such as courage, endurance, diligence, self-control and physical and technical fitness for war. During their attendance in the ephebia, the ephebes also prepared themselves to become good citizens, obedient to the laws and the sovereign. This is especially clear from the ephebic oaths of Miletus,[144] Ephesos[145] and Dreros.[146] The ephebes of Miletus and Ephesos especially placed a strong emphasis on allegiance and obedience to the laws as well as to the Hellenistic king.[147]

Finally, religious education had an important place in the ephebia, but consisted of ritual practice rather than study of dogma and doctrine. Ephebes participated in the worship of gods and heroes and were also active in the worship of the Hellenistic princes and, later, of the Roman emperors.[148] Parades, processions, sacrifices and many other corporate social events were all part of ephebic life[149] and promoted a sense of *esprit de corps*.

Undoubtedly, the ephebes were effectively socialised since the gymnasium was the most important social centre of the city.

CONCLUSION

It is certain that the ephebia became virtually universal in the Hellenic world. It originated in Athens and spread through the Greek world from Massilia to Babylon. It was regularly seen in the gymnasia of Ptolemaic Egypt and even Jerusalem had its ephebes under Antiochus IV. Moreover, it continued to flourish under Roman rule.

The ephebia had a crucial role in the making of Hellenic masculinity. The original aim of the Athenian ephebia was the formation of a soldier; a man was prepared for war but submissive to the laws and obedient to the archons. In the course of its development, the objective of the Athenian institution became the formation of active citizens who were well educated, possessed of an ecumenical spirit, disciplined, strong and fit. In most of the other cities of the Hellenic world, more isolated and often set among barbarians, ephebic military and athletic training was strongly maintained during the Hellenistic and Roman periods as a form of practical insurance.

The Hellenistic-Roman city élite had little to do with war in the period of the Pax Augusta in an empire where professional Roman legions had ousted the old amateur citizen militiae. These upper classes could now afford to spend their lives in comfortable idleness: '... the scheme of life of the class is, to a large extent, a heritage from the past, and embodies much of the habits and ideals of the earlier barbarian period'.[150] The ephebes of the Hellenistic-Roman gymnasium provided the channel through which the old values could be carried through to later periods.[151] In the paramilitary atmosphere of the gymnasium and in athletic contests, which were replete with the old warriors' ideals, the upper classes re-enacted the civilisation of the antique warriors who did not need to earn their living since slaves did it for them, but lived as gentlemen of leisure, as warriors on the battlefield and as athletes training for war in periods of peace.[152]

In the ephebia it is clear that military preparation was used by the state to form the men able to protect it in an unsettled world. Military training developed the militaristic masculine characteristics of the ephebes. Through this preparation, as has already been made clear, the ephebia grew into men imbued with qualities such as courage, endurance, orderliness, diligence, obedience and the physical fitness required for war. The importance the Hellenes accorded the development of those virtues can be gauged from the competitions they organised. In addition, the ephebia was an in-patient social centre, which prepared young men for citizenship, formed them as citizens and helped their socialisation.

It should not go unrecognised that when an ephebe completed his training and formally became a 'young man' (*neos*) he frequently did not wish to abandon his exercises and studies altogether, but continued to attend the gymnasium. From quite an early date, such young men formed a club[153] under the patronage of the city, which often provided them with a gymnasium of their own and elected a gymnasiarch to direct their activities. These societies became, in the course of time, a regular feature of city life. The members pursued similar activities to the ephebes, though no doubt in a less strenuous and systematic fashion. A major reason for forming groups of *neoi* was to keep an interest in sport alive.[154] The existence of neoi is the most substantial proof of how effective was the education of the ephebes.

Finally, it should not be overlooked that in many cities the ephebia served as meeting place not only for Hellenes but also for Romans, Asian settlers and other foreigners as well. It was a cosmopolitan centre which played an important role in the Hellenisation and assimilation of men of diverse origin. During the Hellenistic and Roman periods the term 'Hellene' came to mean a man who had accepted Hellenic culture, irrespective of his origin.[155] National education gave way to an ecumenical and cosmopolitan spirit.[156] A national masculinity thus became an international masculinity.

NOTES

1. M. Sakelariou, 'The prosperity of archaic Hellenismus', Vol.B (Athens, 1973), 202–77 (in Greek); J. Boardman, *The Greek Overseas* (Athens, 1996) (in Greek).
2. F. Walbank, *The Hellenistic World* (Thessaloniki, 1993), pp.363–6 (in Greek).
3. M. Rostovtzeff, *The Social and Economic History of the Hellenistic World* (Oxford, 1986), pp.1057–71.
4. C. Forbes, *Greek Physical Education* (New York, 1971), p.180.
5. Ibid., p.3.
6. M. Rostovtzeff, *Hellenistic World*, pp.1058–9.
7. W. Tarn and G. Griffith, *Hellenistic Civilisation* (London, 1952), p.96.
8. See the useful list by J. Oehler, 'Gymnasium', *Realencyclopädie der Classischen Altertumswissenschaft*, 7 (1912), 2005–8; C. Forbes, *Greek Physical Education*, p.179, f.1.
9. E. Pavlinis, *The History of Gymnastics* (Athens, 1927), p.289 (in Greek); J. Krause, *Die Gymnastik und Agonistik der Hellenen* (Leipzig, 1841), pp.122–6.
10. For the Athenian ephebia see Chr. Pelekides, *Histoire de l'éphébie attique des origines à 31 av. J.C.* (Paris 1962); O.W. Reinmuth, *The Ephebic Inscriptions of the Fourth Century AD* (Netherlands, 1971); O.W. Reinmuth, 'The genesis of the Athenian ephebia', *Trans and Proc Amer Phil Assoc*, 83 (1952), 34–50; I. Marrou, *History of Education in Antiquity* (Athens, 1961) (in Greek); C. Forbes, *Greek Physical Education*, pp.109–78.
11. For the two different views and their arguments see: C. Forbes, *Greek Physical Education*, pp.109–26; A. Gianikopoulos, 'When did the institution of ephebia begin?', *Archaeologia*, 35 (1990), 64–73 (in Greek); A. Gianikopoulos, *The History of Hellenic Education (Hellenistic period)* (Athens, 1993), pp.195–213. O.W. Reinmuth, 'The genesis'.
12. Many researchers believe that the founder of the ephebia was Epicrates. Our sole source of knowledge about him is a fragment of the orator Lycurgus, preserved by Harpocration (*s.v.* Epicrates), from which we learn that a statue of this man was cast in bronze 'because of his law concerning the ephebi'.
13. Aristotle, *Athenian Republic*, 42.
14. The character of the Athenian ephebia had many similarities with the Spartan and Cretan system. In Sparta, as in Crete, ephebic training was organised by the state and it was certainly not organised primarily for intellectual pursuits – at least in the classical period. The general structure and the content of the education of the ephebes in Sparta and Crete were, however, very different. R.F. Willetts, *Social Aspects of Greek Physical Education* (s.a & s.l), p.29.
15. Aristotle, *Athenian Republic*, 42, 5.
16. *Inscriptiones Graecae*, Vol.2 (Berlin, 1873), 2090, 2606; Aristotle, *Athenian Republic*, 42, 5.
17. According to inscription, *Inscriptiones*, 665. See also I. Marrou, *History of Education*, p.165.
18. According to J. Oehler, 'Ephebia', *Realencyclopädie*, Vol.5 (1905), 2738.
19. See above, f.12.
20. J. Oehler, 'Ephebia', pp.2738–9. I. Marrou, *History of Education*, p.166.
21. Chr. Pelekides, *Histoire*, p.279.
22. *Athenische Mitteilungen* (1908) p.380; *Inscriptiones*, Vols.2–3, 1009, 1029–1030, 1041, 1043.
23. A.H.M. Jones, *The Greek City from Alexander to Justinian* (Oxford, 1940), p.224.
24. J. Oehler, *Ephebia*, 2737–46. C. Forbes, *Greek Physical Education*, p.263.
25. C. Forbes, *Greek Physical Education*, p.231.
26. *Mitteilungen des Deutschen Archaeologischen Instituts*, Athenische Abteilung, Vol.29 (1904), pp.170–3, no.14; Vol.29 (1907), pp.274ff, no. 10, 243f, no. 4; Vol.25 (1910), pp.422–5, no. 11.
27. W. Milet, *Ergebnisse der Ausgrabungen und Untersuchungen seit dem Jahre 1899*. Vol.1, 3, no.139; Vol.1, 47ff; W. Dittenberger, *Sylloge Inscriptionum Graecarum*, Vol.3 (Leipzig, 1915–24), p.577.
28. E. Zierbarth, 'Zum griechischen Schulwesen', *Jahreshefte des österreichischen archeologischen*

Instituts, Vol.13 (1910), p.108.

29. Dittenberger, *Sylloge*, 578.
30. Ibid., 798.
31. E. Albanidis, 'Educational athletic institutions in Thrace during the Hellenistic and Roman periods', *Australian Society for Sports History, Bulletin*, 27 (1997)' pp.15–20; E. Albanidis, 'Athletics in Thrace during the Hellenistic and Roman periods', *International Journal of the History of Sport*, 15 (1998), 163–72.
32. G. Mihailov, *Inscriptiones Graecae in Bulgaria repertae*, Vol.1 (1956), 47–50, 51 bis. 51 ter
33. Ibid., No. 14.
34. A. Dumont and Th. Homolle, *Mélanges d' archéologie et d' épigraphie*, Vol.3 (Paris, 1892), No. 111 c7.
35. *Revue de Philologie, de Littérature et d'Histoire anciennes*, Vol.13 (1939), p.147.
36. M. Demetsas, *Macdeonia*, Vol.1, 1 (Athens, 1896), p.31; *Supplementum Epigraphicum Graecum*, Vol.43, No. 381 (1993), p.124.
37. Ibid., Vol.1, No. 261, pp.304–5.
38. Ibid., pp.234–5.
39. Ibid., No. 372, pp.433–4; *Supplementum*, Vol.43, No. 381, p.124; *Inscriptiones*, Vol.10, No. 214, p.135.
40. Ibid., Vol. 53, pp.64–5.
41. Ph. Gauthier and M.B. Hatzopoulos, *La loi gymnasiarchique de Beroia* (Athens, 1993), pp.161–2, f.3.
42. *Inscriptiones*, Vol.12, 9, No. 20, 191A, 234, 235, 240, 243, 904, 916.
43. Ibid., 5, No. 39.
44. Ibid., No. 620, 621, 647.
45. Ibid., No. 144, 145, 1173, 132.
46. W. Dittenberger, *Orientis Graeci Inscriptiones Selectae* (Leipzig, 1903–5), No. 583; IGRom. Vol.3, p.935. See also C. Constantinou-Hadjistefanou, *Athletics in Ancient Cyprus and the Greek Tradition* (Nicosia, 1991), pp.59–60.
47. *Inscriptiones*, Vol.12, No.3, pp.327, 339, 340.
48. *Bulletin de Correspondance Hellenique*, 15, 1 (1891), p.252; 15, 17 (1892), p.159; 32, 2 (1908), p.414.
49. Ch. Dunant and J. Pouilloux, *Recherches sur l'histoire et les cultes de Thasos*, Vol.2, *De 196 avant J.C. jusq'à la fin de l' antiquité* (Paris, 1958), pp.254, 261, 337.
50. W. Dittenberger, *Sylloge*, No.1061; Ch. Michel, *Recueil Inscriptions Grecques* (1976). no.899.
51. For Egyptian gymnasia see T. Brady, 'The gymnasion in Ptolemaic Egypt', *University of Missouri Studies*, 3 (1936), pp.9–20; M. Ibrahim, *Grecoroman Education in Egypt* (Athens 1972), pp.22–8, 240–51 (in Greek).
52. *Archiv für Papyrusforschung*, Vol.2, 44 (1903), p.560.
53. C. Forbes, *Greek Physical Education*, p.263.
54. Grenfell and Hunt, *Oxyrhyncus Papyri*, Vol.9, 1202 (London 1898-), pp.232–4; Vol.1 (1898), 42, p.87–89.
55. C. Forbes, *Greek Physical Education*, p.263.
56. *Klio*, 9, 1 (1909) p.353.
57. *Inscriptiones*, Vol.14, No.2444, 2445.
58. C. Forbes, *Greek Physical Education*, p.201.
59. A.H.M. Jones, *The Greek City*, p.223.
60. C. Forbes, *Greek Physical Education*, p.232.
61. *Sitzungsberichte der Akademie der Wissenschaften in Wien*, 132, 2 (1895), 29.
62. *Bulletin*, 22, 2 (1898), 493f.
63. Ibid., 11, 6 (1887), 86f.
64. C. Forbes, *Greek Physical Education*, p.232.
65. *Archaeologisch-epigraphische Mitteilungen aus Oesterreich, 1877-97*, 6, 47 (1882) 24.
66. E. Pavlinis, *History of Gymnastics*, p.289; J. Krause, *Die Gymnastik*, pp.122–6.
67. For details of the role and the goals of the gymnasium in the Hellenic city, see Pausanias V, 15, 8; and Plutarch, *Symposium*, 2, 4; J. Krause, *Die Gymnastik*, pp.107–10; N. Gardiner, *Greek Athletic Sport and Festivals* (London, 1910), p.468; I. Marrou, *History of Education*,

p.193.

68. The different opinions of historians about gymnasiarchia presented in J. Oehler, 'Gymnasiarch', *Realencyclopädie*, Vol.7 (1912), No.1975–6.

69. For the duties and the activities of the gymnasiarch see J. Oehler, 'Gymnasiarch', pp.1969–2004. J. Krause, *Die Gymnastik*, pp.191–2; M.P. Nilsson, *Die Hellenistische Schule* (Munich, 1955), pp.55–6; N. Gardiner, *Greek Athletic*, pp.501–2.

70. N. Gardiner, *Athletics of the Ancient World* (Oxford, 1930), p.89.

71. Aristotle, *Athenian Republic*, 42, 2.

72. *Inscriptiones*, Vol.2, No.1028, 1030.

73. Ibid., No.1028.

74. Aristotle, *Athenian Republic*, 42, 3; C. Forbes, *Greek Physical Education*, p.127.

75. C. Forbes, *Greek Physical Education*, pp.233, 253.

76. About the rule of the ephebarch see J. Oehler, Ephebarch; *Realencyclopädie*, Vol.5 (1905), No.2736; I. Marrou, *History of Education*, p.171; N. Gardiner, *Greek Athletic*, p.503; C. Forbes, *Greek Physical Education*, pp.185, 189, 194, 196, 234.

77. J. Oehler, Ephebarch; *Realencyclopädie*, Vol.5 (1905), No.2735–6.

78. I. Marrou, *History of Education*, p.171; J. Oehler, Ephebarch, *Realencyclopädie*, Vol.5 (1905), No.2736; C. Forbes, *Greek Physical Education*, p.234.

79. The gymnasiarch and ephebarch existed side by side in many towns such as in Cyzicus. (Dittenberger, *Sylloge*, No.798) and Apollonis in Lydia (*Bulletin*, 11, 6 (1887), p.86).

80. C. Forbes, *Greek Physical Education*, p.236.

81. Incr. Priene 113, I, 26f.

82. C. Forbes, *Greek Physical Education*, p.159; I. Marrou, *History of Education*, p.116ff.

83. For relevant tables with a list number of foreign ephebes see I. Marrou, *History of Education*, p.499, f.7; Chr. Pelekides, *Histoire de l'ephébie Attique*, pp.184, 186, 187; C. Forbes, *Greek Physical Education*, pp.172–6.

84. *Bulletin*, 15, 1 (1891), 252; 17 (1892), 159; 32, 2 (1908), 414.

85. Ibid., 15, 3 (1891), 261; 32, 2 (1908), 414f.

86. *Mitteilungen*, 25, 11 (1910), 422–5.

87. Ibid., 29, 14 (1904), 170–3.

88. Ibid., 25, 11 (1910), 422–5; *Supplementum*, 38 (1988), 383–4.

89. C. Forbes, *Greek Physical Education*, pp.236–7.

90. M. Rostovtzeff, *Social and Economic History*, p.1071; C. Forbes, *Greek Physical Education*, pp.251–2,f.1.

91. *Bull. Soc. Alex.* n.s. 7, 3 (1929), 277.

92. About 20 per cent of these men have non-Greek names. T. Brady, 'The Gymnasion', 3 (1936), 17.

93. *Supplementum*, 42, 1666 (1992), 483.

94. A. Mehl, 'Erziehung zum Hellenen – Erziehung zum Weltbürger. Bemerkungen zum Gymnasion im hellenistischen Osten', *Nikephoros*, 5 (1992), 64.

95. G. Mihailov, Vol.1, No.47,47bis, 48, 49, 50, 51, 51bis, 51ter.

96. Ibid., 47bis; M. Mirtschev, 'Inscriptions', *Bulletin Musée National Varna*, 14 (1968), 151–62 (in Bulgarian).

97. The analysis of names is according to D. Detschew, *Die Thrakischen Sprachreste* (Vienna, 1957); V. Besevliev, *Untersuchungen über die Personennamen bei den Thrakern* (Amsterdam, 1970); G. Bakalakis, 'Thrakische Eigennamen aus den Nordagäischen Küsten', *Thracia*, 2 (1974), 261–79; K.-M. Apostolidis, 'About the language of Thraceans', *Thrakika*, 3 (1932), 181–235 (in Greek); D. Samsaris, *The Hellenisation of Thrace during the Hellenic and Roman Antiquity* (Thessaloniki, 1980), pp.285–93.

98. G. Mihailov, Vol.1, No.14.

99. Lycurgus, *Leokratis*, 77; Polydefkis, VII, 105; Stoveos, 93, 48. The English translation of the oath is by C. Forbes, *Greek Physical Education*, p.149.

100. Xenophon, *Lacedaemonians' Republic*, 2, 1.

101. Plato, *Laws*, IIX, 829.

102. C. Bowra, *The Greek Experiment* (Cleveland and New York, 1957), p.68; M. Andronikos, *Introduction to Olympic Games in Ancient Greece* (Athens, 1982), p.9 (in Greek).

103. I.Marrou, *History of Education*, p.164.

104. *Inscriptiones*, Vol.2, 2, No.1106, 1, 52ff.
105. A. Gianikopoulos, *History of Hellenic Education*, p.230.
106. *Inscriptiones*, Vol.2, 2, No.1006; A. Gianikopoulos, *History of Hellenic Education*, pp.230, 238.
107. J. Oehler, 'Ephebia', *Realencyclopädie*, Vol.5 (1905), No.2740.
108. I. Marrou, *History of Education in Antiquity*, pp.167, 168.
109. C. Forbes, *Greek Physical Education*, p.170.
110. Ibid., p.159.
111. *Inscriptiones*, Vol.2, 2, No.1043.
112. C. Forbes, *Greek Physical Education*, p.164.
113. Ibid.
114. I. Marrou, *History of Education*, No.167.
115. Thucydides, *Pericle's Epitaph*, 40: 'whoever does not participate in public affairs is considered useless'.
116. Isokrates, *Panathenaekos*, 45.
117. Lucian, *Anacharsis*, 30.
118. Philostratos, *Gymnastikos*, 9, 11, 43; Plutarch, *Symposium*, V; cf. M. Poliakoff, *Combat Sports in the Ancient World* (London, 1987), pp.94–9.
119. C. Forbes, *Greek Physical Education*, p.171.
120. Ibid., p.162.
121. I. Marrou, *History of Education*, p.169.
122. The ephebarchic law was excavated in 1984 and unfortunately has not been thoroughly analysed until now. Only a part of the law was presented in *Ergo* (1984) 23. Ph. Gauthier and M.B. Hatzopoulos, *La loi gymnasiarchique de Beroia*, pp.161–2, f.3.
123. A. Dumont and Th. Homolle, *Mélanges*, 111c7; Dittenberger, *Orientis*, 1 (1903–1905), 537–544, No.339.
124. *Inscriptiones*, Vol.2, 50, 1, 77.
125. *Bulletin*, 32, 2 (1908), 373, 414 f.; Vol.15, 1 (1891), 252; 3, 261.
126. C. Forbes, *Greek Physical Education*, p.214.
127. *American Journal of Archaeology*, 11 (1896), 175–6, 189.
128. C. Forbes, *Greek Physical Education*, p.216.
129. *Mitteilungen*, 33 (1908), 376ff.
130. *Corpus Inscriptionum Graecarum* (Berlin, 1828–77), No.3085; C. Forbes, *Greek Physical Education*, p.228.
131. A.H.M. Jones, *The Greek City*, p.224.
132. Dittenberger, *Sylloge*, No.1061.
133. Ch. Michel, *Recueil* (1976) no. 899; C. Forbes, *Greek Physical Education*, p.206.
134. *Klio*, 11 (1909), 352–63.
135. Grenfell and Hunt, *Oxychyncus Papyri*, Vol.1, 42, pp.87–9.
136. C. Forbes, *Greek Physical Education*, pp.256–7.
137. The term *synephebi* was frequently employed to indicate their fellowship. *Archiv für Papyrusforschung*, 2, 44 (1903), 560. Dittenberger, *Orientis*, No.188, 189; C. Forbes, *Greek Physical Education*, p.253.
138. A. Dumont and Th. Homolle, *Mélanges*, 111c7. The inscription is also translated in J. Krauss, *Die Inschriften von Sestos und der Thrakischen Chersones* (Bonn, 1980).
139. B. Latyschev, *Inscriptions Antiquae orae septentrionalis Ponti Euxini Graecae et Latinae*, Vol.2 (1965), No.432; M. Kublanov, 'Agone und agonistische Festverastaltungen in den antiken Städten der nördlichen Schwarzmeerküste', *Altertum*, Vol.5/6 (1959/1960), pp.131–2.
140. M. Launey, *Le sanctuaire et le culte d'Herakles à Thasos* (Paris, 1944), p.44.
141. *Inscriptiones*, Vol.14, 2, 2445, p.646.
142. *Athenische*, 33 (1908), 384–400, 376.
143. T. Brady, 'The Gymnasium in Ptolemaic Egypt', pp.11–12.
144. W. Milet, *Ergebnisse*, 1, 3, n. 139, 47f.
145. *Jahreshefte*, 13 (1910), 108.
146. E. Zierbarth, *Aus dem Griechischen Schulwesen* (Berlin, 1914), pp.163–4.
147. A. Mehl, 'Erziehung zum Hellenen', *Nikephoros*, 5 (1992), p.63.
148. M. Nilson, *Die Hellenistische Schule*, pp.61–6; C. Forbes, *Neoi: A Contribution to the Study of*

Greek Associations (Middletown, 1933), pp.54–5.
149. M. Nilson, *Die Hellenistische Schule*, pp.78–80.
150. Th. Veblen, *The Theory of the Leisure Class: An Economic Study of Institutions* (London, 1924), p.246.
151. H.W. Pleket, 'Games Prizes, Athletes and Ideology', *Stadion*, 1, 1 (1975), 77.
152. Ibid., p.78.
153. On the expansion of associations of *neoi* in the Hellenic world see C. Forbes, *Neoi*.
154. Ibid., p.45.
155. Isokrates, *Panigirikos*, p.50.
156. A. Mehl, 'Erziehung zum Hellenen' pp.63, 70. A. Gianikopoulos, *History of Hellenic Education* (Athens, 1993), p.11 (in Greek)

Fighting Bulls in Southern European Culture: Anthropomorphic Symbols of Aggression and Mythical Male Heroes

FRÉDÉRIC SAUMADE and
JEAN-MICHEL DELAPLACE

If bullfighting is marked by a paradoxical, emotional, humanised relationship between the animal and its opponent – the two heroes of the dramatic spectacle of the arena[1] – can we see anthropomorphism in the biographies of fighting bulls? It is clear that the language associated with the spectacle uses the terminology of dominant social values to describe the animals' technical qualities. For example, Spanish *aficionados* say of a fighting bull that it complements the matador's 'artistic' expression if it is 'noble', 'suave', has a 'good temperament', that is, if it bows to the game to the extent of accepting the glorious kill reserved for it.

In fact, the balance of the ritual depends on a certain anthropomorphic representation of the animal, established by inbred characteristics of this so-called 'wild' species. From the eighteenth century in an Andalusia consisting mainly of *latifondia* (estates), certain members of the upper middle classes in search of prestige, and a few aristocrats of fairly ancient stock, have developed a breeding programme to improve the characteristics of the *toro bravo* (wild bull) for the arena. Responding both to the demand for a commercialised mass spectacle and to their own ostentatious nature inspired by the nobility, they created and passed on a pattern for the classic animal, intent on displaying its inherent wildness in the harmonious order of the *corrida*. Anxious to preserve the integrity of this animal 'aristocracy', breeders established family trees of the livestock. We have previously shown[2] that from the late eighteenth century close matrimonial and politico-economic relations between the Spanish court and the dominant classes of Betis province had contributed to a common Andalusian bullfighting culture, promoting the *fiesta nacional* at the expense of other forms of fighting and of breeding bulls, notably in Navarre. The culmination of this imperialist process, the image of the matador in his apparel associated with the *toro bravo* caste, has become today part of Spanish folklore known the world over. Bull and matador are symbols of maleness.

TAURINE RELATIVISM

Despite the popularity of the Andalusian *corrida* with death as the outcome, comparative anthropology reveals the existence of different versions of bullfighting localised in scattered regions of south-west Europe, which have in common no public execution of animals in the arena.[3] Around the Camargue, for example, principally between Saintes-Maries-de-la-Mer, Montpellier and Avignon, namely, between Languedoc and Provence, not only is the bull not ritually killed but it becomes a living hero, a performing animal whose spectacular male exploits excite the collective passion. In the eyes of the *Bouvino* people,[4] cattle of Camargue stock are clearly distinguished from the Andalusian *toro bravo*; moreover, connoisseurs admit that its generic characteristics differ completely from those of its Spanish counterpart. The former is recognised by its upright horns, haughty carriage, slender body and uniformly dark brown coat, the latter by its horizontal horns, low carriage and thickset body, and its coat can vary widely in colour between individuals.

In fact, far from being natural, the zootechnical type of the Camargue bull was fixed at the end of the nineteenth century by the impetus of the *manadiers*[5] *Félibres* of the Languedoc. Both breeders and poets, these people rejected the practices of their Provençal counterparts who crossed native cattle with breeds imported from Spain, giving rise to the so-called Spanish-cross breed. Under the iron rule of the Marquis of Baroncelli-Javon, disciple of Mistral who had joined the *Bouvino* 'as one joins the church', it was a question of re-establishing the purity of the Camargue race and the integrity of this local emblem in the face of intrusion by 'foreign blood' and Spanish cultural imperialism. This undertaking was in effect attempting the impossible because, according to the specialists, the entire herd was to a greater or lesser degree marked by this crossbreeding. Yet, under the pretext of bullfighting, the radical regionalism of the Félibrige was the real undercurrent here.[6] This tendency was explained by the need to produce a fighting bull whose 'wild identity' contrasted with that of the Iberian *toro bravo*. Only such a distinctive animal could be held to represent this *race d'oc* (Languedoc line) that Mistral's followers wanted to restore in all its pride. Baroncelli decreed in writing what the perfect regional bovine form should be: selection theoretically excluded specimens whose two-coloured coat or low horns were a little too suggestive of the animals used in *corridas*. Thus appeared the figure of the Camargue bull, still revered to the present day by *manadiers* (herders).

CAMARGUE AND ANDALUSIAN BULLFIGHTING RULES

How did the *Bouvino* people assess the combative qualities of beasts selected for the Camargue fights – the *cocardier*[7] bulls? Protagonists of the spectacle, *cocardiers* (bulls) must dominate their human opponents the *raseteurs* (fighters), wearing white jumper and trousers which contrasted with the pomp of the famous 'clothes of light' worn by *toreros*. In the Carmargue, the fight posters proclaimed the animals' names in big letters, especially if their viciousness made them particularly brilliant individuals; more often than not, the *raseteurs*' names were in small letters. Certain *cocardiers* had such an effect on the crowds over the course of their long careers that, as with the great personalities of the Republic, the municipalities of Beaucaire (Gard) and Lunel (Hérault) erected statues of them in the town. Others, just as famous, died natural deaths and were buried under a commemorative pillar. However, contrary to what heroic symbolism might suggest, the heroic *cocardiers* had nothing of the super male, since in reality they were castrated! Ironically, connoisseurs called them 'fighting bulls' in French but *biòus* (bullocks) in *langue d'oc*, the two terms being applied at random.

In the fight *raseteurs* armed with a metal hook would attempt to grab prized emblems – *cocardes* (cockades), 'tassels', 'frontals', 'strings' pieces of ribbon and cords that the breeders attached to the animal's forehead. Central to the action, the *cocarde,* reduced to a 5cm long red ribbon, symbolised the spirit of republicanism.[8] All the interest for the *afeciounados*[9] depended on the *cocardier*'s capacity to defend these emblems against the venality of the *raseteurs*, destabilising agents seen as veritable ritual thieves. Local worthies (councillors, businessmen) indulged in betting on the contests announced over the loudspeaker by the president of the fight as if to put the bullfighters in their place by openly showing their support for the bull. In fact, the latter knows its business well. In the course of the bullfighting year from March to November the crowd's support for the bull would grow in proportion to its performance if during the fight it showed evidence of 'intelligence' and 'viciousness', adopted defensive postures to discourage the *raseteurs* and chased them, expelling them violently from the ring or tossed them against the barricade that marks the area of combat (an action called a barrier blow).

A bull can live on average 20 years. Between the age of eight and ten, a good *cocardier* must exhibit the personality and style of a star. Reputedly purposeful, obstinate, the bull must show bravery and a determination to charge the *raseteurs* who taunt him. In short, the animal combines masculine qualities comparable to those of a human being, above all its *manadier*, who is associated with the glory of the animals he hires out to the fight organisers for a price that reflects the fame of each animal. Over and above the selective breeding by which he builds his herd,[10] recognisable by the behaviour and physical formation of his animals, the breeder must know how to protect his interests by influencing as much as possible the behaviour of each bull in the arena. If a *cocardier* is weak, lacking in spirit, the breeder must plan its appearances carefully; if, on the other hand, a bull is excessively spirited, a wise *manadier* would tend to hire him out often to calm his reckless ardour and increase his self-confidence. The *manadier* is thus both the father of his herd and the trainer of individual animals descended from it. In conversation, certain *afeciounados* even go as far as comparing the man and his animals: 'he's a hard case, like his bulls'. Bull and man share esteemed male virtues.

Nothing could be further from this idea of an intelligent and dominant animal than the Andalusian-based Spanish bullfight in which the *toro bravo* performs only once. After three or four years in the pastures of an estate,[11] where the ranges are a 'wild' open space,[12] it is sold to an impresario only to be executed in the arena by the matador, after about 20 minutes' active fighting. During this single performance, the bull is judged on various criteria, especially its combativeness. If cowardly, the *aficionado* calls it a *manso* (domestic bull). On the other hand, if it fights mercilessly to the death, the public acknowledges, by giving its mortal remains a standing ovation, the true worth of the *toro bravo*, of 'good stock'.

A 'willing victim', the bull takes part in the execution of a highly orchestrated ritual, authorised by state legislation.[13] Masters of the ceremony, *toreros* on foot and *picadors* on horseback, must demonstrate their ability to dominate the animal by employing, with grace and lightness, a lethal artistic technique. The ideal *toro bravo* fights in a relatively predictable manner, for which it is classed as noble: ideally, it charges, head low, into a fabric lure (*muleta*, cape) that the *toreros* hold out for it. With no previous experience, it has acquired no malice, which would not suit the nature of the spectacle. Paradoxically, the good 'wild bull' must collaborate in man's sophisticated plans; its submissive attitude, indicated by the way it 'nobly' lowers its head before its adversaries, sets it apart from the arrogant Camargue *cocardier*, which aggressively charges the *raseteurs* from behind, in the 'barrier blow' action. This is summarised in Table 1.

TABLE 1

CAMARGUE AND ANDALUSIAN BULLS COMPARED

Camargue bull	Andalusian bull
Individual hero at the heart of a breed	Hero representing a line
Vicious, intelligent, dominating	Noble, stylish, submissive
Protagonist of regional bullfighting in which man celebrates the bull while it is alive, by erecting a monument to it	Non-protagonist of national bullfighting which recognises the man who puts it to death

In the Camargue and Spanish traditions, the bulls are clearly opposites. Whereas the *cocardier* bull becomes a hero as a result of the fight, a true individual in the *manadier*'s herd, indeed a real public personality, the *toro bravo* is more of an ordinary animal, whose innate qualities, only acknowledged after it has been put to death, are the basic characteristics of its breed. Selection criteria are the direct result of these different ideals of bullfighting. But both bulls demonstrate the classic male qualities of courage and aggression.

THE PRODUCTION OF GREAT BULLS

Breed and Individual Selection and Initiation of the Cocardiers

In the Camargue, the purist ideal of bull breeding still holds sway although it does not actually correspond to reality. Resolutely individualist, the *manadiers* cultivate their own idea of breeding stock; most experimentally mate their own animals with those of their neighbour. With one exception, a supporter of interbreeding, they admit that crossbreeding is beneficial to maintaining their herd and are not really worried by possible effects of Spanish blood.

Selection is based on fights which permit evaluation of the combativeness of young cows and bulls. These fights may take place as part of a traditional village festival; every day in the arena, exceptionally open free to the public, young cows are let loose for the benefit of youths wishing to demonstrate their courage or their sense of humour in public.[14] This is a sort of male initiation in a popular atmosphere, where the *manadiers* choose the cows which will be used as the breeding stock of the herd. The bulls are selected according to their performance in minor 'protection' fights, in which where they are offered less able *raseteurs* and beginners.

Coming from this somewhat uncontrolled system, the bull calves follow a 'biographical' path which will progressively prove their aptitude for fighting. At one year old, in May, June or October, they are branded and their ears nicked with a knife with a pattern unique to the herd. These *ferrades* are often the occasion for festivals organised by private individuals or by associations who hire an entire *mas* (farmhouse) for the day from the *manadier*. The introduction of young animals into the social life of the herd thus takes place amid the festivities of spectators unfamiliar with the breeding activity.

The adult bulls are castrated at the time of the first trial fights, in order to flesh them out physically but more importantly, according to the *manadiers*, to train their character to the conditions of the bullfight. The operation *bistournage* is carried out when the animal is three years old, with the exception of specimens that the *manadier* wants to be outstanding. Theoretically, these are preserved intact for two or three years longer and are then castrated in order to follow a career in the arena. Curiously, the Camargue castrato becomes not inoffensive but more dangerous; he concentrates better his combative energy because he is free of the disturbing effects of cows in season. His habitual behaviour, improved with fighting experience, gains consistently in 'reliability' the connoisseur says; the bull is 'done', and qualified as very *cocardier* if it shows itself to be superior in the fight.

Although emasculated, the *cocardier* is qualified to be a 'fighting bull'. A real fighting bull would be classed as 'whole', or *tau* in *langue d'oc.* A whole bull is qualified as a stud, even if it does not fulfil this breeding role. Thus, certain fights of anonymous cadet bulls, not castrated, are called 'stud fights', or even 'new studs' (never having fought in the arena). We have therefore

biòu (bullock) = fighting bull = *cocardier* = initiated

tau (fighting bull) = whole = stud = non-initiated.

Cocardiers can be baptised (named) at a very young age if they have a particularly remarkable allure in the herd, or due to an anecdotal adventure that the *gardians* (herdsmen) want to remember, but the majority of them are named after the *bistouriage* and the first formal fights. Up to now, they have been described as 'beasts'; the name, left to the breeder's imagination, confers the title of *biòu*. It is worth noting that certain breeders of fighting bulls have a system of naming by descent – for example, the sons of a cow called Saladelle all take the name of a wild plant – but its free application is limited to their individual progeny.

Status of the Cocardiers: *The Untouchable and the Inedible*

The profitability of a Camargue bull farm depends on the regular production of *cocardiers* good enough to present to the public. Apart from lucrative profits which are his right, a *manadier* in possession of a star bull benefits from an enhanced prestige among the *afeciounodos* and a greater political stature than the majority of his colleagues in as far as negotiation with fight organisers is concerned. That is why *cocardiers* – there are barely 20, of which one or two are outstanding, even in the most classy *manades* – occupy a privileged status expressed in the spatial organisation of the farm. A fencing system separates them from the main body of the herd (which averages 200 head) in a 2–3 hectare enclosure situated close to the farm buildings. Supervised by the *gardians*, fighting bulls are given a special feeding regimen: lucerne in winter plus a ration of oats during the active season (*temporada*) to give them increased vigour, 'blood' the 'bull people' say. The other animals are grouped according to age and sex, and dispersed throughout the ranch.

Even if the grazing areas rarely exceed 100 hectares for one ranch, and the barbed-wire fences are a constant reminder of man's control, breeders happily say that the cattle living there are wild and in their natural element. Close to human habitation, the *cocardiers* receive respectful attention. They are called 'the big boys', as if to underline not only their presence but also their importance. Although peaceful in their enclosure, they establish their own pecking order. Thus, the 'S' *manadiers* and *gardians* are happy to note that their *cocardier* Samouraï, star of the farm but now 'retired', remains the chief because he eats before the others. Nevertheless, the one they call 'the old boy' has always been docile with his keepers – 'because he is very intelligent' they say at the *mas*. The *cocardier* enclosure is considered more protective than repressive. The men feel they are better able to care for their bulls and prevent confrontation with young whole bulls, which are capable of causing injuries or a fatal accident. However, in summer, the 'big boys' join the herd in order to take advantage of the new growth that rainstorms bring to the pastures. Despite the risk of fighting, it is accepted that these variations in the everyday food ration are good for the *cocardiers'* morale.

In A.G. Audricourt's phrase[15] good fighting animals are 'part of the family or the clan, there is no question of killing or eating them'. Theoretically, a great *cocardier* will die naturally in the fields. It may be buried under a tombstone adorned with an epitaph, following the example of Joffre, Rami or Cosaque, who remain in the very heart of the *mas* where they were born. However, and here is the inevitable ambiguity, an ordinary *cocardier* is always killed when it is no longer capable of a guaranteed performance and is of no further use. Moreover, some *manadiers* are rather partial to the meat of their animals. An anecdote along these lines is as juicy as it is suggestive. Breeder S. wanted to try an experiment between blood relations and had his best cow served by his best bull who was no other than the son of this cow. The product of this mating was a beast devoid of *cocardier* qualities. Disappointed, he decided to have it killed to supply the family table. Unfortunately, the meat was so tough that it was impossible to eat, even as shepherd's pie! Told half-jokingly, this story reveals the underlying bull classification system that exists in the mind of the *manadier*. At the top are the great *cocardiers*, with which the men have a relationship that hovers between carnal and mystic. The other members of the herd, on the other hand, end up on the fork without the slightest concern. Mentioning the inedible meat, a sorry postscript to a terrible bullfighting experience which broke fundamental cultural taboos is an example of the lowest level in the order of Camargue bulls: an animal from an incestuous mating, useless in a fight and definitely totally unfit for consumption.

Breed and Lineage, Selection and Exclusion of the Toro Bravo

From the nineteenth century, breeders of Spanish fighting bulls have directed their enterprise towards the exclusive exploitation of the

Andalusian breeds, which showed themselves better suited to satisfying the demands of the public. Motivated by powerful corporatist sentiment, today's *ganaderos* will still confirm, with the support of family trees, that they hold and develop the various lineages of these cattle of privileged origin. Guarantors of good breeding, they strive to maintain a system of breeding based on selection trials, *tientas*, where the heirarchic organisation of their business is devoted to the different roles given to cowherds, grooms, stewards, chief cowherds (*mayoral* or *conocedor*) and children of the *finca* (farm) who are initiated into contact with cattle.[16] Here, we are a long way from the reckless popular character of fights where Camargue beasts are selected: in the small private arena, a *finca* outbuilding, and with the help of examination by invited hand-picked *toreros*, there is scientific testing of the combativeness of young cows or males descended from the best sires. If shown to be 'sound', the latter will be kept for siring. However, a good *toro bravo* can become a perfectly bad stud and produce offspring unworthy of the *ganadería*'s reputation. Only studs that 'link', passing on their temperament down the line, are kept alive for several years. Sometimes, errors in choice or flaws due to excessive interbreeding lead the breeder to 'refresh the blood' by buying in a stud or a few cows, in spite of the dominant ideology of homogenic lineages that everyone would like to maintain.

Calves produced from 'quality' parents are identified and supervised for reasons of integrity. In contrast to the *cocardier*, named with reference to an individual character represented in the pastures or to the *manadier*'s pure imaginative creation, the *toro bravo* is baptised from birth with the masculinised name of its mother. As a general rule, the son of Bodeguera is called Bodeguero, to link it to an ancestral (matrilineal) chain. Branded on the hindquarters, shoulders and ears during its first year, it begins a life apart from its peers. If it is not kept for the *tientas* (stud), it is deprived of all contact with cows until the day it is brought to the arena. This isolation aims, moreover, at guaranteeing the bull's indisputable innocence; before public killing, they know no other milieu than the *finca*'s 'wild' pastures.

Animal as an Object: Animal as a Subject

The system in force in Spanish *ganaderias* implies the existence for breeders of a certain relationship with the animals destined for the arena. A member of the Seville aristocracy, Don Luis is the proprietor of an 850 hectare latifundium, half agriculture (wheat, sunflowers) and half pasture in which 400 head of cattle graze. He lives in town, where he is a practising lawyer, and occasionally comes to the *finca* to take part in *tientas*. Work in the herd thus exclusively concerns residential employees, the *conocedor*, cowherds and *pienseros* who produce and distribute (*pienso*) food for the cattle Here, like the Camargue *cocardiers*, the fighting bulls are penned in enclosures close to human habitation. One of these enclosures is reserved for *cabestros* (tame), *media casta* (half-caste) bullocks, animals descended from the crossing of a domesticated line with a *brava* line.

The bulls are destined to be sold in lots of eight for a price that depends on the line's reputation. In the last six months of their existence, they receive a daily ration of wheat and barley meal so as to 'perfect' their presentation in the arena. Spectators would not like to see animals run in their natural appearance. Even though excess weight reduces their aggressiveness, they must be glossy and well-covered.[17] In Don Luis' *finca*, herds of 20 bulls in 50 hectare enclosures calmly accept the daily intrusion of *pienseros* who bring them prepared food. Despite this obvious domestication, there are many bulls who show bravery in the fight when their turn comes. Sometimes, their wild instinct is awoken when inside the enclosure as a result of isolation. Affected by cows in season or irritated by climatic changes, bulls fight amongst themselves, until the death of one of the duellists results. The cowherds cannot always intervene in time and accept such events as part of the risks of the business. They show neither excessive sorrow nor secret pleasure, although a fight to the death is the sole occasion when bulls are eaten at the *finca*. Only the *ganadero* is concerned because he then suffers the loss of the sale of a bull worth around one million pesetas.

The uncertainty as to the *corrida* animals' future behaviour to a certain extent explains the impersonal relationship of the *conocedor* and cowherds with these animals. In contrast to the *cocardiers*, named as if implying an emotional relationship with the *manadier* and the *gardians*, *toros bravos* are recognised by the colour of their coat, the shape of their horns or the number marked on their side rather than by the name under which they are registered from birth. Condemned to an anonymous death, they are grouped together under a uniform status. They may become personalities posthumously: the name of a 'great corrida bull', celebrated by the press and the public who demand a lap of honour for the hide, confirms the glory of the *ganadería* and thereby its profitability. Occasionally, the animal's head is stuffed and given to an association of *aficionados*, a bull museum, or even preserved by the *matador* or *ganadero* in their trophy room as a paragon of the breeding line. But there is no taboo about eating the heroic bull. At the end of the *corrida,* it is cut into joints at the skinning house, just like its fellow creatures, to end on the butcher's stall, sold as 'fighting bull meat'.

EXCEPTIONAL BULLS OR THE CREATION OF MYTH

In Andalusia the *toro bravo* symbolises the virtues of aristocratic breeding, devoted to maintaining the lustre of the *fiesta nacional*, the bull fighting festival of all Spain: in the Camargue the *cocardier* represents individualism and regionalism. Of the two, only the latter can enjoy a long life and even acquire a certain immortality, but at the price of the irreversible loss of its sexual power after *bistournage*. The former is also necessarily deprived of all contact with cows and arena experience.

However, these opposing bullfighting principles, which allow social identification and the presentation of the 'wild bull' to the world seem no longer to apply when men are confronted with an exceptional subject, an animal whose unprecedented combative spirit eludes the usual classification. Disregarding the norm, breeders create a regimen relative to the extraordinary status of the chosen bull. Such an animal becomes a universal myth.

Llorón and Civilón

In Andalusia, studs can live much longer than ordinary *corrida* bulls. To achieve that, they have passed the *tienta* test, rare in itself, and have normally been presented in a *corrida* and shown great courage before the public and the authorities.[18] An agent for the *ganadería*, the stud enjoys special treatment comparable with that reserved by *gardians* for the *cocardiers*. Generally, he is easy to domesticate because the painful experience of the *tienta* has weakened of his character. The cowherds call him by his name, know his ways, and stroke him or sometimes even tame him, like the bull Guitarrista from a famous breeder in Seville who remained tied up in the stable in the company of horses, its natural enemies as we are reminded, *corrida* after *corrida*, by the *picadors'* violent performance.

According to *ganadero* A. Domecq, a good stud normally lives to the age of 15 or 17 years and is then killed because with old age performance decreases. However, if he has sired remarkable sons, he has the right to particular consideration: and he finishes his days accompanied by a harem reduced to 12 cows, so that he does not wear himself out. Domecq recalls his dear bull Llorón, who died in the peace and sweetness of the pastures. He had the head stuffed and put it in his dining room 'as a totem to breeding'.[19] Symbol of the breed and of excellent breeding selection, Llorón thus became the intimate myth of the aristocratic Domecq family and its line of *toros bravos*, whose products have been the glory of taurine Spain and the breeder's fortune.

Over and above the breeding family circle, certain bulls have been immortalised in the arena. Particularly edifying in this respect, the biography of the famous Civilón was related by the encyclopaedist J.M. de Cossío.[20] First submitted to the *tienta*, the animal was chosen as a stud. Later, in the enclosure, he demonstrated a particularly 'noble' and docile character: the cowherds fed him by hand and the children of the *finca* climbed on his back to play. One fine day, however, his breeder decided, contrary to all the traditional rules, to send Civilón to fight in the Barcelona arena. The bull still showed great bravery against the *picadors* but, extraordinarily, 'at the very moment where the fight was at its hardest' (*sic*), the *conocedor* of the *ganadería* called him from the inside barricade. Then, Civilón calmly approached the *gardian* and, as if he had become a tamed bullock, a *cabestro*, he let himself be stroked to the delight of the public. The animal was reprieved, then the *conocedor* twice again made this 'trial of gentleness' with the same success, a reversal of the trial of pain that is the *tienta*.

Civilón was kept in the arena's corral, far from the pastures of his birth, in this northern town poor in bullfighting tradition, 'until the first moments of the civil war' (*sic*).

Sanglier and Vovo

In the Camargue in the early 1920s, the *cocardier* Le Sanglier impressed the public by his extraordinary behaviour.[21] Breaking with the tradition of the area, his prestigious owner, Fernand Granon, did not castrate him. Presented on the publicity posters as 'King of the Cocardiers' or even 'The terrible and incomparable Sanglier', this animal was, according to its *manadier*, a perfect specimen of the pure Camargue race. Like his colleague Baroncelli, Granon was loyal to the integrist concept of rearing: he lived in the Languedoc village of Cailar, dubbed the 'Mecca de Camargue tauromachie' because every summer the Camargue bull herds moved to the pastures there.

Contrary to usual practice, Le Sanglier was named as soon as he was born, in 1916, when the *gardian* found him with his mother well away from the herd, near a litter of wild boar. Spared, by a miracle, the story says, from the carnage the cattle farms suffered until 1918, the animal began its career the day after the end of the First World War and became the idol of the rediscovered peace. An exemplary result of progress in rational selection, in the arena he represented a totally new style that earned him the title of 'first modern *cocardier*' (he was certainly the first capable of inflicting 'barrier blows' on the *raseteurs*). For the *afeciounados*, he represented a sort of achievement, a model of balance and 'seriousness', even though he was not castrated like the others.

Nevertheless, this singular state, beyond the norm, exposed Le Sanglier to all the dangers inherent in the basic bullfighting institutions, to breeding and to fighting. One day, he fought one of his fellow creatures who tore off one of his testicles; he kept half of his genitals but, as a precautionary measure, Granon decided to take him out of the fields and to house him in a shed by his house. Far from fights and cows – he had no descendants – Le Sanglier was also protected in his public appearances. Due to the huge influence he exerted in bullfighting circles, the *manadier* was able to manage a limited programme of fights. It was a question of tactfully handling the animal's strengths, sensitive as he was to the natural mood swings that would have upset a normal career. But Granon's opponents, linked to the Provençal *manadiers* and their Spanish-cross bulls, contested the merits of Le Sanglier, too popular not to triumph easily.[22] In reaction, his supporters, his *gardians* and Granon himself had acquired the habit of giving him the surname Lou Biòu (the bullock), ironically affirming that he was the *cocardier par excellence*.

Le Sanglier died in Granon's shed and, legend has it, Granon had him wrapped in the best pair of sheets in the house and buried under a commemorative pillar with an epitaph. Placed at the crossroads from Cailar to the Camargue delta, Languedoc to Provence, this monument reminds today's *afeciounados* that Lou Biòu remains the paragon of classicism and purity handed down by the ancestors. As such, Le Sanglier is a homologue of the bull Llorón, immortalised in the dining room of the Andalusian bull rearer Domecq. Both animals personify their own culture, the submissive bull and the dominating bull. Llorón is a god whose existence, far from the arena and the outside world, was spent in pastures and on furthering a good line; Le Sanglier is a public god whose existence, far from pastures and females, was spent in the popular spectacle of the Camargue bullfight.

After the Second World War, a new whole *cocardier*, Vovo, won the *afeciounados'* hearts. After running away, his mother, from the Baroncelli cattle ranch, had been covered by a stud of distant Spanish origins belonging to the neighbouring farmer, Reynaud. The calf was born in his father's pastures and lived his first few months there, but at the time of going for branding, Reynaud decided to send him back home. As if considered undesirable, his ears were given the Baroncelli mark, whereas in such cases tradition holds that ownership of the calf be accorded to the bull's *manadier*.

Acquired irregularly and considered a bastard, the adult Vovo behaved aggressively both in the ring and in the pastures where he even attacked the *gardians'* horses in the manner of a *toro bravo*. The *afeciounados* who followed him from fight to fight recall an uncontrollable *cocardier*, which even smashed the terrace planks and support posts so that the whole arena was caught in a wave of panic.

Vovo's career was managed quite differently from that of an ordinary *cocardier*, but his treatment was in fact the opposite of that accorded Le Sanglier. The owner and his impresarios exploited and abused his frightening strengths. He was presented without respite to a public hungry for his destructive outbursts and between each performance, far from letting him recover, the rearers shut him in enclosures which the cows of the three great cattle farms passed. Prematurely exhausted by his attacks while fighting and by siring, Vovo ended his career without having assimilated what a *cocardier* needs to become a lasting figure of social standing. 'He was crazy ... he was not intelligent ... he was too vicious', those who knew him said. He died isolated from the herd, in winter, in the depths of the Camargue. No public monument was erected to commemorate his glory.

The sad fate of a cursed *cocardier* contrasts Vovo with the model bulls Sanglier and Llorón, but brings him somewhat closer to Civilón. In fact, the latter's history is also marked by the outrageous treatment by humans who knowingly mixed the two principal dimensions of the bullfighting world – the wild space of the ranches pastures and the cultural space of the arena where this 'wildness' is presented. Civilón, like Vovo, was at the same time sire and performer. Both, moreover, had similar ends: they disappeared, the first in an arena far from his native soil where he left the undying memory of the reconciliation of innate wildness and domestication through human contact, the second on the fringes of the Camargue pastures, far from his fellow creatures who had learned how to reconcile their instinct and the bullfighting business.

These symmetrical opposites are revealed not only within the same culture (Llorón/Civilón, Le Sanglier/Vovo) but also by crossbreeding (Llorón/Vovo, Le Sanglier/Civilón). Thus the logic of the myth, based on the inversion of norms for the production of great bulls – submissive virgin animal, dominant castrated animal – reveals a coherent, semantic system despite intercultural differences. Although at first sight very different, the Andalusian and Camargue bullfighting cultures stem from a common set of values involving man and beast – the virtues of violence, aggression, courage and confrontation. For animal and man history is made mythology: for one in the bullring, for the other on the battlefield. In both male qualities are revealed, demonstrated, publicised and acclaimed – and the mythical hero is both.

NOTES

1. These themes have notably been developed by M. Leiris, *Miroir de la tauromachie* (Montpellier, 1981), and J. Pitt-Rivers, 'Le sacrifice du taureau', *Le Temps de la Réflexion* IV (1983), pp.281. In this respect, our own essay, *Des sauvages en Occident. Les cultures tauromachiques en Camargue et en Andalousie* (Paris, 1994), p.297, from which the information dealt with in this piece is drawn, follows the same tradition, although we do not follow our prestigious forerunners in their willingness to consider the *corrida* with death as a sacrifice. See F. Saumade, *Des sauvages en Occident*, pp.1113, 265.
2. F. Saumade, *Des sauvages en Occident*, p.31.
3. These are the Landes, Portuguese, NavarroAragon and Camargue events. For comparative analysis of all the southern European forms of bullfighting, see F. Saumade, *Les tauromachies européens. La forme et l'histoire, une approche anthropologique* (Paris, 1998), and E. Désveaux and F. Saumade, 'Relativiser le sacrifice ou le quadrant tauromachique', *Gradhiva*, 16 (1994), 79–84.
4. *Bouvino* – 'bovine race' in the *langue d'oc*. It is clear that, here, men directly empathise with their emblematic animal.
5. *Manadier* is a specific term for herders of fighting bulls in the Camargue.
6. For the history and ideology of the Félibrige, see P. Martel, 'Le félibrige', in P. Nora (ed.), *Les lieux de mémoire, 3. Les France, 2, Traditions* (Paris, 1992).
7. *Cocardier*: 'chauvinistic', an allusion to regional symbolism.
8. F. Saumade, 'Le taureau cocardier', in M. Agulhon (ed.), *Cultures et folklores républicains* (Paris, 1995), pp.171–83.
9. *Afeciounado*: 'devoted, impassioned, zealous, ardent, having a taste for, amateur', F. Mistral, *Lou tresor dou félibrige* (Raphèle-les-Arles, 1979), p.37. (Equivalent to the Castellan *aficionado*.)
10. The generic concept of the Camargue breed is that there are as many lines as there are breeders. For analysis of the concept of breed in Languedoc and Provence, see F. Saumade, 'L'hispanité en Languedoc et Provence. Une image de "l'autre"', *Ethnologie française*, 24, 4 (1994), 728–38.
11. *Novillo* bulls, reserved for bullfights with apprentice matadors, *novilleros*, are fought at three years old, whereas *toros* are fought at four.
12. F. Saumade, *Des sauvages en Occident*, p.50.
13. Until the beginning of the twentieth century in Spain, the *corrida* was controlled at provincial

capital level, as is still the case in the Mexican states, for example. In 1930 General Primo de Rivera decreed the first national legislation, renewed in 1962, then in 1991.

14. In votive festivals, the relationship of the people to the bull (or the cow) is presented as derisory. As, for example, the game *toro-piscine*, a selection test for young cows, is a reversal of the seriousness of the *cocardier* fight. On this point, see F. Saumade, *Des sauvages en Occident*, pp.124–32.

15. A.G. Haudricourt, 'Note sur le statut familial des animaux', *L'Homme*, 99 (1986), 119–20.

16. F. Saumade, *Des sauvages en Occident*, pp.162–71.

17. D. Fournier and F. Saumade, 'L'artiste, le boucher, le sacrificateur', *Etudes rurales* (1989), 113–14, 203–20.

18. In Spain until the promulgation of the new law on *corridas* (1991), 'gracing' the bull (*indulto*) was only permitted in the exceptional case of a breed competition, where similar to the *tienta*, the matador aims to show the bravery of the animal merely as a spectacle. Since 1991, the *indulto* has been permitted for all *corridas* taking place in arenas of the first and second category (notably provincial capitals), on the joint opinion of the president of the bullfight (representing the civil authorities), the matador in the ring, the *ganadero* and the public. This measure aims to improve the breeding process by increasing the supply of good breeding bulls; the graced bull is then recovered by the *ganadero* and chosen for breeding. This has reduced the importance of the kill. We have recently on many occasions seen a matador triumph after having worked to perfection, then spared, a very brave bull: enactment of the death-blow (without sword, or using a banderilla) sanctions the 'grace' of the animal and is welcomed by the enthusiastic public as a contribution to bullfighting. It should be noted that almost all *toreros* are enriched by their exploits in the arena and buy a *ganadería*, which they have wanted since the start of their career, and launch themselves into the breeding business.

19. A. Domecq y Diez, *El toro bravo. Teoría y práctica de la bravura* (Madrid, 1986), p.274.

20. J.M. de Cossío, *Los toros. Tratado técnico e histórico*, 1 (Madrid, 1951), pp.346–7.

21. The principal source used here is a beautiful exegesis. M. Salem, *A la gloire de la Bouvino* (Nimes, 1965).

22. On the 'conspiracy' against Le Sanglier, organised in the Arles arena by the Provençal *raseteurs* and *afeciounados*, see F. Saumade, 'Mythe et histoire dans une société du spectacle tauromachique', *Ethnologie Française*, 21, 2 (1991), 148–59.

Asserting Male Values: Nineteenth-Century Fêtes, Games and Masculinity – A French Case Study

REMI DALISSON

Prior to the gradual inclusion of women in sport and the acceptance of mixed sports, both to any significant degree phenomena of the twentieth century, sport was widely viewed as a male activity,[1] with the role of inculcating and underlining masculine values, serving as an affirmation of masculinity,[2] and reinforcing the segregation of the sexes to the advantage of man.

Of course, this assertion must be qualified.[3] Certainly well before the twentieth century some games and sports reserved for the middle and upper classes, such as real tennis and hunting, clearly had as one purpose the provision of opportunities for the intermingling of the sexes.

Nevertheless, how general was the traditionally held view of sport as the domain of the male in France *before* the Third Republic? And was any link between games and masculinity displayed and conveyed?

In France one venue worth consideration because it throws a clear light on this question, was the public fête. It was both popular and institutional, a perfect link between the ideological policies and values of the central authority and the social and cultural common realities of everyday life. It constituted a public space where sexual segregation and claimed masculinity could be displayed in front of the whole community united under the controlling aegis of those in power. In fact, it is for this reason that games and contests, more or less codified, took place in a rural département such as Seine-et-Marne[4] at *all* fêtes between 1815 and 1939. These athletic activities shaped masculine and feminine relations[5] in favour of the former.

Seine-et-Marne, a department east of Paris, is an excellent location for inquiry as it remained politically stable throughout the nineteenth and twentieth centuries. It was wholly representative of the evolution of a nation that moved progressively towards a moderate republicanism, always legalistic and mostly temperate. In addition, the region combined the urban and industrial and was republican in its northern urban part and monarchist in the more traditional rural and agrarian central and southern parts. Finally, from the Revolution on, as it was close to the capital city[6] it was witness to, sometimes even a location for, experiments in all those cultural, including athletic, innovations which were thought up in Paris and carried out in the departments. These innovative practices, their implementation and the associations they generated through the fête to a lesser or greater degree enabled the different social and sexual groups to assert themselves in political, symbolic, cultural and recreational domains. The fête had the advantage of continuity and permanence as no regime or community, even the smallest, failed to see how valuable it was. It flattered the authorities and entertained the people.

Thus, through the various fêtes, their games and their 'proto-athletic' activities, it is possible to discern the constitution and assertion of masculinity among players and spectators and its evolution through *four political regimes* (two monarchies, a republic and an empire) in the period 1815 to 1870 (see Figure 1), before this masculinity was called into question during the Third Republic which witnessed 'the emancipation of women, one of the most striking consequences of the Great War, which contributed greatly to popularising athletic activities'.[7]

At all fêtes, festive masculinity took on specific aspects. Indeed it was a policy at fêtes to assert strongly the masculine values of the day, mostly depicted in games and contests. Paradoxically at the same time, as will be discussed later, these festive activities played a large part in the questioning of an increasingly archaic conception of the masculine as the country became more democratic.

POST-NAPOLEONIC FETES AND GAMES:
MASCULINE POWER TRIUMPHANT, 1815–1848

In 1815, after Napoleon's defeat at Waterloo, the conservative Ultras, who were now back in power, were determined to sweep away a 25-year heritage of revolutionary changes. But they were quickly brought face to face with reality and had to compromise. Consequently, they set up a restoration, and a charter that retained liberal elements even though it remained authoritarian, and embraced a belief in absolute monarchy, which gave priority to a Christian-based triumphant masculinity.

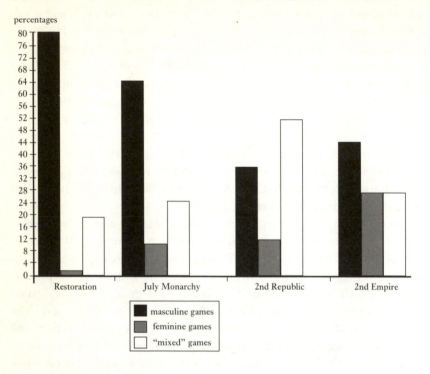

FIGURE 1

EVOLUTION OF THE SEXUALISATION OF GAMES, 1815–70, SEINE-ET-MARNE

TABLE 1

	Restoration	July Monarchy	2nd Republic	2nd Empire	Average
Masculine games	80	65	36	45	56.5
Feminine games	1	10	12	27.5	12.5
'Mixed' games	19	25	52	27.5	31
Total (%)	100	100	100	100	

TABLE 2

	Restoration	July Monarchy	2nd Republic	2nd Empire	Total
Number of games studied	102	186	70	210	568

Public fêtes made possible the assertion of masculinity through mass activity, an assertion generally reinforced by each successive government. Unsurprisingly, therefore, between 1815 and 1870, the 865 public fêtes in Seine-et-Marne organised recreational programmes and political activities that reinforced masculine assertion. Indeed, 502 of the programmes (60 per cent of the total number) of the fêtes closely analysed[8] in this essay could not be understood without an appreciation of this clearly apparent gender dimension (see Tables 1 and 2).

Fêtes, Games and Gender Activities

From their introduction public fêtes ensured an 'original sociability'.[9] It was first and foremost masculine in order to perpetuate a ruling masculine order. However, in time, it became an 'open sociability' and included activities which were characterised as purely feminine. The public fête, whether a regular or occasional ceremony ordered by a central or local authority, presented for the whole community in a codified way various themes and values. These were representative of both sexes. Masculinity may have been prioritised, but it did not totally exclude femininity or activities ostensibly reserved for the 'fair sex'. Sharing tasks among the sexes certainly existed at fêtes. Indeed, it was noted that 'in the countryside, sexual segregation diminishes mostly during fêtes; women take part as well as men, even though they may be confined to the role of spectators'.[10] Nevertheless, at the same time their tasks were 'processes of preserving sexual and athletic identities'.[11] And this process of preservation, heavily masculine in emphasis, existed in fêtes and their entertainments which included *both* traditional rural and modern urban activities.

From 1815 to 1870 the organiser of the fêtes was always male; sovereign, mayor or prefect, or even parish priest. So everything in the fête reinforced masculinity, especially the military qualities that were demanded in the sports – virility, endurance, strength, martial skill, sacrifice and victory. Indeed, even feminine functions were given a masculine interpretation. A birth, for example, could not be celebrated unless the heir was a *male*, and even the *'maternal'* dates such as the Assumption of the Blessed Virgin, were used to glorify a manly and sovereign warrior, Louis-Napoleon Bonaparte. Also the dates selected for public fêtes often commemorated the anniversary of a masculine patron saint, Philippe, Louis or Charles, or the memory of a revolution that honoured the sacrificial citizenry – *'distinguished men'* who had died

for their homeland. In these manifestations the exclusive triumph of a
dominant masculinity was evident.

The prefects and the parish priests also underlined the idea of
masculine superiority in the festive locations, ceremonials and liturgy.
For example, at the start of the parades the women remained in the
churches and later left the front ranks to men in the parades that then
crossed the parishes. The precedence that ruled the parades during
festivities further marked the triumph of masculinity by excluding the
wives of the civil servants from walking with their husbands, with a view
to relegating them to a position of secondary importance and demanding
that they walked with the professional representatives of the 'fair sex' –
at best in the sixth rank (secondary school teachers), most often in the
twentieth and last rank of the parade (primary school teachers). In the
same way, the prefectorial proclamations[12] that announced the public
fêtes and their games mostly used words and values people assumed to
be the prerogative of men. In short, virtually all aspects of festive
sociability remained substantially masculine, and in all regions, but
notably in rural ones such as Seine-et-Marne; it was 'very seldom
feminine'.[13]

At all the essential stages of public fêtes, morning mass to parades,
dances and banquets, men, on average, accounted for more than two-
thirds of the guests,[14] while traditional reviews of the national guards,
firemen or soldiers, symbolised a dominant masculinity. As for the
games and activities, these were always clearly divided into masculine
and feminine contests. Of a total of 65 *types of games* recorded in the fêtes
from 1815 to 1870, more than two thirds were reserved for men so that
they could demonstrate their domination of female activities which,
incidentally, were less well resourced than those of their male
counterparts. The most popular game during these fêtes was always the
very phallic greasy pole,[15] and the best prizes honoured strength (a
manifestation of virility), courage and shooting[16] which was a men–only
activity. Even the bands were composed of male musicians. In short, the
lion's share of the fêtes' prizes always went to the male sex.

Women were not excluded from public fêtes. They were just
subordinate and subject to the approval of the ruling body that
reproduced to perfection the wider gender rules prevailing at the
beginning of the nineteenth century. Theirs were the obscure and minor
tasks such as making flags[17] to deck the houses, supplying and preparing
food for children's parties (particularly during the Second Republic),

taking the census of the poor who were to be issued with rations (an activity reserved for feminine charities, the only associations that were not exclusively masculine, such as the 'ladies of charity' in Meaux or the 'sisters of charity' in Melun). Theirs were the games that reminded people of their domestic vocation (the games of scissors, of flowers, of rings, sewing…). Theirs was the role of the passive (and, of course, enthralled) spectator watching the physical activities (or shooting matches) of their male companions. Theirs was the presentation of awards to the male winners. Their only restrained active appearance was at the evening dances much criticised by the Church which strongly advised against the presence of single women (or girls) who had to be invited to dance by men if they did not want to be labelled 'loose women'.[18]

Thus at first sight the organisation of public fêtes both reproduced ancient patterns of masculine domination which could only confirm and 'reinforce the masculine/feminine opposition'[19] while it flattered the masculinity of the competitors. In practice, however, things could be rather more complex, and this masculinity which seemed rigid was over time more flexible than it first seemed, depending on the political powers in charge and their festive arrangements.

REGAL CELEBRATIONS AND MALE DOMINATION DURING THE RESTORATION, 1815–1830

The festive system of the Restoration which aimed at breaking away from the innovations and the ideology of 1789[20] directly adopted traditional values, among which, as already mentioned, an assured masculinity came first. Official national festivals thus both re-emphasised a historic masculine domination and simultaneously reasserted the historic sexual distinctions of public and private activities.

The Saint Louis festival, an official festival celebrated on 25 August was the regime's *central festival*. It was to remind people of the warlike virtues of the regime and above all of the triumph of a sovereign who was the 'father' of all his subjects. This enhancing of fatherhood, while motherhood was denied or reduced to its sole function of producing male heirs, was a factor common to all authoritarian regimes. However, under this regime, two more ceremonies celebrated the birth of the prince of royal blood, and yet another two honoured deceased male relatives of royal blood.[21] The queen, who was only celebrated for her male children, was never granted any personal ceremony.

The only breach in the thematic emphasis on masculinity was the acknowledgement of so-called feminine 'sentimental' qualities, in a ceremony in remembrance of Marie Antoinette's death which, along with that of Louis XVI, was to manifest every October the act of penance of the French, who had to face up to the 'that disgraceful period' and the revolutionary 'crimes'[22] (royal beheadings). This celebration consisted in reading 'moving and highly emotional'[23] letters written by the queen, demonstrating virtues that were allegedly feminine; at the same time, however, the courage and the 'male confidence' of her husband, were praised. All other regal ceremonies glorified virile values, notably war – the Spanish War and the Algerian Campaign – and the king's stamina in 1825 after his attempted murder. They stressed a festive royal masculinity which was made up of strength and self-confidence. For this reason the themes in *all* festivities were mostly military (the warrior King), reactionary (the cult of an absolute and masculine, due to Salic law, monarchy) and administrative (a masculine prerogative). This masculinity was also strongly underlined by the *vocabulary* used in prefectorial proclamations in which there is a huge number of words containing sexually connoted values such as 'the soldier', 'strength', 'glory' or 'gentlemen'.

Needless to say, at the fêtes of the reinstituted regime, women were marginalised. The clergy, self-evidently masculine, upholders of the theological justification for the belittling of women, had become the organisers of fêtes again and relegated women to the role of passive 'bigots' confined in the darkness of churches while the army and the guards who were inspected in daylight, were living symbols of the strength of armed men that all could admire. The assertion of this male superiority was further proclaimed by the exclusion of women from parades. Furthermore, in the 100 ceremonies investigated for this essay, women never carried the busts of sovereigns; strong soldiers undertook this august task. Only once were women allowed to parade and they had to be dressed in white, a symbol of virginity as well as royalty.

The songs that were written for the festivities[24] popularised masculine values. One out of two referred to the 'saving father' of France. In these songs while men waged noble war, women were attributed passive and sexist attributes. In the song entitled 'L'élan du coeur' which was sung for the first time at the Royal Celebration in Meaux in 1816, it was a question of having 'our girls humped by our valorous boys' to revive a sort of *jus primae noctis* and ensure masculine prerogatives since 'all mothers will have boys'.[25] This martial and authoritarian masculinity would not tolerate any exception to tradition. For this reason the games reproduced to perfection the humiliation of women by a masculinity that could be termed as of the 'ancient regime'.

The *games or 'proto-athletic' activities*[26] were indeed the public, and thus fully manifest, incarnation of the triumph of the virile male. Indeed, when designating the games 'for boys only' from those 'for girls only' on all the programmes under all political regimes, the edge was of course given to the former. Of the 102 games under the Restoration, studied for this chapter,[27] more than 80 per cent were entirely masculine. The greasy pole accounted for 25 per cent of them. The mast which, in one third of cases was coated with grease to increase the physical exertion, was erected in a blatantly phallic and provocative way in the village square, sometimes opposite the church. It evoked the picking of fruit (pleasure) reserved for male physical effort under the eyes of passive and excluded women who were not allowed to climb it. Far behind with 18 per cent of the games, came races (with or without hurdles) reserved for boys and then shooting matches (7 per cent) which were always exclusively for men and performed by ancient companies such as the 'Fontainebleau Archers'.

All the games served to reinforce the image of a robust, natural and innate superior masculinity. For this reason sham fights collectively ranked high in the list of games (15 per cent were 'sabre games', and 3 per cent were archery games). Men and boys had to demonstrate their physical and 'military' abilities and reveal their 'muscular capacities'[28] before being rewarded at the end of the day. As mentioned earlier, only a few games were reserved for women (or young girls), including the traditional games of scissors and the tray which symbolised their domestic virtues characterised by patience and endurance in contrast to the strength and swiftness of men. Mostly it seems that they participated very little and remained spectators who admired the manly performances that represented the masculinity of a monarchy which yearned for the ancient values of 'a strong sex' represented as symbolic of 'a strong power'. In this era males staged their 'raw strength, the strength of a phenomenal man'[29] to assert the superiority of their sex in a masculinity that was both sportive and political. At the same time, it is necessary to make it clear that games did not dominate these fêtes. They took up only 18 per cent of the programme.[30]

MASCULINITY: QUESTIONS AND HESITATIONS

The new political power which was born in 1830 in Paris on the barricades and which witnessed the dramatic reappearance of women,[31] revived earlier revolutionary traditions and also in its early years, anticlericalism, and produced a timid questioning of masculinity.

The new *festive system* in these new political circumstances aimed at being the exact sporting expression of the new liberalism and, influenced by England, could not ignore the questioning of traditional masculinity that was spreading notably in sports. This system now coexisted with the earlier one. Once more there were two national festivals, one rather rigid and intolerant, celebrating sovereignty (Saint Philippe's day on 1 May) and the other, rather more open and tolerant, celebrating liberalism (on 27, 28 and 29 July each year). The latter was dedicated to all the 'victims of the days of July'. If men were still predominant among favourite heroes, women were no longer largely excluded. In 1833 a prefectorial statement referred to *all* the victims of July, thus including all social classes and both sexes. Even more to the point, in the 18 official proclamations which dealt with the fêtes of the survey for this chapter, the number of 'feminine' words increased for the first time (by exactly 8 per cent), with a feminine use of the term 'indigents' and even once of the word 'citizens' (*indigentes* and *citoyennes*). Even though administrative, sexless, religious, military and masculine words remained in the majority in all proclamations (some 60 per cent), less 'masculine', less contrasting notions appeared with the use of affective and 'family' words (14 per cent) which had more 'feminine' connotations such as 'heart', 'affection' and 'love'. They nicely complemented liberal words (13 per cent) which evoked democracy. Thus at least on paper women were now taken more into consideration through the use of words such as *'citoyennes'*.

In the same way, even though the monarch, a man full of 'very fatherly good will'[32] remained the father of the 'nation' (then composed of 'the French' and no longer of 'France'), even if the Duke of Orléans' death marked 'the death of the male heir to the throne of France'[33] and the Count of Paris' birth brought the hope of a quiet royal succession in 1838, masculinity was no longer the sole value that was celebrated. Nevertheless, in spite of these developments, the stamp of dominant masculinity remained on the essentials. The king's physical resistance was celebrated after the failure of the July 1835 'cowardly' attempt 'to overthrow him', and the dynastic continuity was assured thanks to the birth of male heirs after the death of the Duke of Orléans – 'a highly popular and admired man'.[34] And the army remained an honoured part of society.

Festive practices reflected slight changes in attitude but at no time was masculine superiority called into question. The loosening of the power of the clergy enabled women to leave the churches and sometimes to take part in the parades and the festive events. However, for the most part, they most certainly remained in the background but the fact that they were now mentioned was an advance on the past.

Indeed, they were not merely mentioned, they were active. In 1831, in Meaux, they threw flowers at the processions; in 1830, in Melun, they read part of the new Charter and in July 1843 they took part in the community processions during the Lagny fête. In other places such as Meaux or Fontainebleau, they were draped in tricolour flags, a far cry from the virginal white synonymous with feminine submission they used to wear under the Bourbons. That very same year, in La Ferté-sous-Jouarre, they stood *beside* the boys during the school fête which paid unprecedented homage to its women schoolteachers (*institutrices*). Furthermore, what was previously women's work became more equitably shared. Contributions to the poor were no longer exclusively carried out by religious and female organisations but also by 'social' services such as the Meaux or Jouarre councils. In addition, more women were welcomed to the dances that were more numerous than under the Restoration.

At the same time, much remained the same. During the few processions for children that took place outside schools, the boys were always *in front* of the girls such as in Lagny (1845) or Buissière (1847). Only national guards or soldiers carried the busts as they guaranteed an aggressive and protective masculinity. Precedence never altered and politicians and official representatives always came first under the Restoration. As before, men wrote the songs for fêtes and the lyrics remained as sexist and chauvinistic as ever. They praised the image of the 'father-sovereign' (in Coulomniers in 1835), the old martial values in new hands such as the duty to confront the enemy – 'the new warriors were French, men worthy of their elders',[35] religion, 'which protected our nation' and a highly 'virile' authority. Nonetheless, a small breach had been opened in the long-standing walls of a triumphant masculinity. And games were to widen it.

Games in liberal-controlled fêtes were more numerous in those than under the Restoration. They increased from 18 per cent to 30 per cent in the 186 programmes studied. The extended pleasures of outdoor activities, which enabled women to participate more, were clearly more appropriate to a liberal than to a 'conservative' regime. Conditions were favourable to those of a liberal disposition. There was an increasing English influence and 'sports ... were slowly establishing ... their autonomy and cultural and beneficial specificity'.[36] Nevertheless, although games were more numerous and more varied than under the Restoration, they retained their main characteristics. They were still segregated and more than two thirds of the games were still reserved for men or boys. Among them was the ubiquitous greasy pole (40 per cent), and shooting matches (18 per cent) – virile activities.

The other male games mostly stressed competition and strength and included races, ball contests, archery and sabre competitions. They amounted to some 18 per cent of all male games and put a premium on agonistic activities, 'whose socialised aspect is sport'.[37] In these games all the rewards, self-evidently reserved for men, were particularly appreciated since they included, for example, a full set of military equipment, gun and powder included, as in La Ferté-sous-Jouarre. As before the women demonstrated their domestic skill by playing the scissors game!

However, things were slowly moving forward, even though 'triumphant masculinity' apparently remained substantially unchanged. For the first time, games that were explicitly *mixed* appeared. They amounted to 26 per cent of all the games and involved various races during the July ceremonies in Nemours (1832) or Ferrolles-Atilly (1833). Also for the first time, *specifically* female athletic games are now mentioned. They amounted to 9 per cent of all games. Things, while not all that different from before, were still not quite the same as before.

By the 1840s, however, a backlash was evident, and 'triumphant masculinity' asserted its authority. New freedoms were curtailed. References to 'women' in both programmes and official instructions disappeared after 1840. However, there was to be a further twist to this lion's tail. The 1848 Revolution was to provoke a new sexual as well as political upheaval that the Second Empire could not minimise.

FETES, GAMES AND THE QUESTIONING OF MASCULINITY, 1848–1870

The period that was born on the barricades in February 1848 died with the coup in December 1851 but it had cultural and sociological ramifications that survived until the collapse of the liberal Empire in 1870. Indeed, whereas the Second Republic emphasised education, including that of women, logically as it wanted to be the worthy heir of 1789, the Second Empire after an authoritarian start had to take liberal evolution into account and the need for emancipation that the growth of an industrial society entailed.

This interest in education, along with the consequences of the second industrial revolution and English influence, changed the way masculinity was seen. As society was slightly opening itself up to consumerism, as the right for women to be educated was claimed, as industry required more workers, including women, the door was open not to a direct challenge to triumphant masculinity but to less segregative practices which would still allow the retention of what were considered 'virile values in a society that was considered far too effeminate, in which women are now beginning to invest sectors so far reserved for men'.[38]

REPUBLICAN MASCULINITY, CIVIC FETES AND SPORTING REALITIES, 1848–1851

The Second Republic, once again a regime born on the Parisian barricades erected by both men and women and in which the place of women was not a taboo subject, immediately ordered its festive system according to the principles of pluralism, and social as well as cultural democracy.

By choosing to celebrate *principles* rather than important men, the Republic reversed the order of the values that had been so far celebrated. The absence of a tutelary figure, naturally masculine, made it possible to question the far too masculine image of power and those fêtes, such as the new national festival, the 'anniversary of the proclamation of the Constitution', on 4 May which praised the fact that a masculine national assembly was back in business but failed either to praise the emancipation of the population or to glorify 'the Republic, which guaranteed the freedom we had recovered'.[39] Fêtes now celebrated the innovatory February happenings. To these events should be added the occasional fêtes such as the 'remembrance fête' in June 1848 and the fêtes for the constitution in November 1848. They, too, stimulated the growth of the seeds of liberal principles and raised questions regarding the liberation of the individual, in all probability including women.

The celebration and exaltation of those *political and democratic principles* which excluded the feminine *less* than before was to be found at all levels of power to the extent that during the debates about the restoration of universal suffrage, which became effective on 4 March 1848, a few men suggested the unthinkable: giving women the vote. There was no ruling family to be celebrated, so no birth of a male heir to be welcomed, no royal fecundity to be praised. Now, it was the celebration of the freedom of expression, pluralism involving the multiplication of clubs including women's clubs, and the replacement in the Republic of the doctrine of property by that of fraternity which meant reduced masculine power.

Above all, for the first time, there was a huge increase in local fêtes controlled by municipal councils which diminished the projection of male power typical of past festivities. There was, for example, the famous 'planting of trees for freedom' where the whole village community, women included, would gather under the reassuring protection of the Republic and of the clergy in order to bless the trees. There were also the very new musical entertainments and the 'Republican banquets' where women accounted for nearly a third of the guests.

New festive themes were also created such as those that praised community values (local societies, progress, education) or republican values (freedom, secularism), which celebrated human rights and granted women opportunities to express themselves. The *vocabulary* used in prefectorial proclamations confirmed this liberal trend as there was a large number of words which referred to democratic and local powers (10 per cent), to the rights of the French with a special emphasis on the values of the enlightenment (24 per cent with words such as '*citoyennes*', '*freedom*') or to affective and allegedly more feminine words such as 'children', 'love' or 'happiness'.

Ceremonies were also more emancipatory in the way they *took place*. Since, at least during the first two years under the regime, the Church sided with the Revolution, it immediately became more relaxed. It allowed women to join processions (which nevertheless remained extensively masculine) and to take part more often in banquets. It also became more tolerant of balls, allowing females at dances, as the mayor of Pécy put it during the celebration of the constitution: 'shortly after mass, dances united all the citizens in a spirit of fraternity'.[40] Last but not least, schools participated in festivities more extensively – seven times more than previously – and symbolised the new emancipation. The pupils, boys *and* girls took part in fêtes by reading extracts from the constitution or original poems.

Of course, masculinity was still dominant in guards or army parades; indeed, processions were still codified by the Messidor year XIII male decree but these ceremonies now sometimes contradicted this masculine reality. They used emblems inherited from the 1789 Revolution that were more feminine than yesteryear royal images.

Thus the Republic became a woman, 'a republican goddess, dressed in wreathes',[41] who foreshadowed the Marianne who was to come later. Schoolgirls were allowed to sit in the second row of platforms, just behind high officials, as in Melun or Meaux in 1848. In places a few delegations of female workers (*travailleuses*), proudly wearing their flags, paraded with their male colleagues, notably in the northern part of the département where the women working in the china factory participated in the Magny, Meaux or Melun fêtes in 1848. Finally, women were to be seen in processions again, carrying civic busts, listening to the reading of the constitution, surrounding the 'altars of freedom' in Fontainebleau and Egreville in 1849, draped in the tricolour and wearing laurel wreaths synonymous with victory, thus paying homage to revolutionary activities between 1789 and 1793.[42] Women also appeared in a more positive light in the songs written for celebrations as a consequence of the role they had played during the revolution. They were still kept in the background, and presented only as victims (see for instance, the fatal fate of girls and wives in the *Marseillaise*), but male workers and their 'faithful wives'[43] were united and women even dared compose a 'Marseillaise des cotillons' (*Marseillaise* of the petticoats) in which they were as martial as their husbands.[44]

In short, even though 'triumphant masculinity' quickly reclaimed its rights when the Prince-President came into office and despite the fact that his celebration in January 1852 praised the success of 'France's saviour whose sword was covered with blood',[45] festive games over time had a paradoxical evolution. Indeed, while Republican *games* themselves marked the assertion of a less dominant masculinity they kept their distance from practices that were too innovative without, however, keeping a complete distance. For the first time since 1815, mixed games were the *most* numerous, comprising half the total number of games and there were twice as many 'women only' games (14 per cent) and the use of the greasy pole, archetype of the 'men-only game' fell by a third. And yet the male events still dominated the whole programme with 36 per cent of the games, and the sexual segregation that still existed revealed the weight of a sexist cultural heritage. However, the existence of feminine games which were tolerated alongside masculine games, illustrated a relative loss of masculine preference, a loss that sportsmen and representatives of the 'stronger sex' dreaded greatly. For this reason, although there were fewer games during the new fêtes (one third less than before) paradoxically the 70 games listed under this regime seemed to fall back on the most traditional masculine values as if to counterbalance the moving forward of women under the early days of the regime. Thus contests that were unequivocally masculine kept increasing, notably races that eventually comprised 10 per cent of all games.

This state of affairs ensured that the limit of feminine progress had been reached and resulted in the continued predominance of masculine games. Reconstituted shooting matches, for instance, amounted to a good 11 per cent of all games. Above all, manly activities including military activities such as archery or sabres doubled as if men had to assert their ultimate and muscular specificity. At the same time, feminine games – 'parlour (salon) games' that were inspired by domestic activities, such as the scissors game or the ring – also doubled. The segregation of the sexes was clearly re-established. These two increases illustrated both the cultural resistance and resilience of masculinity. Female socialisation was 'a way to reinforce men's supremacy and its control in our society'.[46] Interestingly, mixed games remained for children (blindman's buff, whirligig, scarf) – a clear statement that the awakening of masculinity could not take place during the powerless period of childhood but only during adulthood, the age of responsibility and power, a power reserved for the stronger sex.

Thus under the Republican regime, there were indeed a few practical and philosophical breaches in the walls of the fortress of 'triumphant masculinity', in education events and symbolism. But with regard to the fêtes and their games there was an effort, but hardly a significant effort, to capitalise on the creation of a breach.

THE IMPERIAL TURNING POINT: DREAMT VERSUS EXPERIENCED MASCULINITY, 1852–1870

The Second Empire – 'matrix of modern France',[47] was caught between social and sexual realities – modernisation and the Emperor's vision of worker control and the authoritarianism of an essentially undemocratic system. Fêtes and their games illustrated perfectly this dichotomous dilemma as they restored to texts a 'triumphant masculinity' and yet tolerated some questioning of the historic virile monopoly, which foreshadowed quite accurately the developments of the Third Republic.

Virility, Wars and Show Fights: A Protective Masculinity

Immediately on coming to power, the Prince-President and Emperor-to-be followed in his virile uncle's footsteps, for whom fêtes were to represent 'the everlasting signs of all the important things brought about by Bonapartist genius'.[48] He thus chose as a national festival 'Saint Napoleon's day' on the very holy 15 August.

Each year, this ceremony praised 'the French and chivalrous virtues'[49] of a sovereign who was once again the father of the Nation and it depicted Napoleon III as indeed 'a predestined man who had saved the country from anarchy'.[50] The other ceremonies reinforced this recovered masculinity as they praised the Imperial family; the wedding of the sovereign (March 1856), the birth of the male heir the 'offspring ... which guaranteed a security and greatness that everybody was waiting for',[51] his christening in June, and also Prince Jérôme on his soldier's death (1860). The strength of the king, who had survived the Orsini attempt, was also eulogised in 1858.

Above all, however, the fêtes for the armies' victories in the Crimea (1855 and 1856) and in Italy (four ceremonies between June and July 1860) saw a wave of martial and masculine passion in praise of 'the triumph of our brave soldiers, who represent the noblest tradition of our youth'.[52] Local fêtes also celebrated the passage of the armies on their return to France, for example, in Meaux, Melun, Fontainebleau, with many triumphal arches and male theatrical performances. This martial, virile theme accounted for nearly a third of all local celebrations of the survey for this chapter. Numerous historical fêtes praised masculine and established figures such as King Henry IV, François I or J. Amyot. Other themes referred more and more often to a mythical and masculine past, filled with heroic warriors – Napoleon I, King Henry IV, and even Joan of Arc who was celebrated not for her femininity but indeed for her virtually masculine and martial virtues, or Bossuet who was the guide of both monarchs and male Capetian heirs. The church and the army once again became the two great attractions at imperial ceremonies which were still codified according to the highly masculine (and imperial) text based on Messidor year III precedences. Even the words used in prefectorial proclamations reinforced masculinity as a great number of them belonged to the 'dynastic', military, Bonapartist and administrative worlds. In contrast, all affective and sentimental words sharply diminished by more than 10 per cent.

The *staging of ceremonies* confirmed a recovered masculinity as the presence of women was once more restricted in processions and at banquets (they now represented only 20 per cent of guests). There was a multiplication of unveiling of statues of local as well as national emblematic heroes, two-thirds of whom were male soldiers. Women no longer wore imperial flags; soldiers and firemen did so. The new festive fashion of commemorative emblems and medals created a whole set of strongly masculine images, mostly of the Emperor, his male children, generals, or the tutelary and virile figure of Napoleon I. The great number of triumphal arches and their ancient and military references seemed to mark the final victory of masculinity embodied by a Roman celebration of martial triumph that all men and women could admire.

Songs at fêtes also marked the return to masculinity as they belittled and instrumentalised women who were reduced to their original reproductive function. Thus the text entitled 'It's a boy, or the son of the Emperor' was sung to the tune *Homeland, honour for whom I am my hand*.

Men had to 'drink flasks empty', fight bravely for 'Mars wanted to recall this male hero's bravery',[53] sing about the army 'the soldier's choir' and recover a masculine honour that had been threatened by the disastrous and permissive Second Republic.

Indeed, masculinity seemed, both on paper and in reality, to have recovered its former lustre and to be marked by 'the great period of games of strength'.[54] Sham fights had never been more numerous and they seemed to reject republican and liberal sexual progress. But matters were in fact more complex and both games and society represented, paradoxically under such an authoritarian regime, a festive masculinity that was more open than the establishment almost certainly intended.

Liberalism, Democracy and Games: Limited Masculinity

Thus there were breaches in this reconstituted masculine uniformity. Thus, for the first time, a female sovereign was celebrated ('celebration of the Empress's regiments of the departments' in 1860) for her traditional feminine virtues such as motherhood and also for her new social role in creating Vésinet (mutual help societies). Of course, she was celebrated by men (soldiers) and the roles of a warring and conquering husband and a charitable wife who was concerned with social welfare were still clearly defined. This classical distinction was not particularly emancipatory but it had the virtue of making official an autonomous feminine function. In the same way, schools which participated in the fêtes never failed to get girls to represent Duruy's projects on the education of women. Schoolgirls and boys were again to be seen together in the second row of platforms as in Meaux or Lagny.

However, it was basically the *games* that best marked the evolution of sporting and festive masculinity. They increased by 50 per cent over those under the Republic and references to them in programmes increased by 15 per cent, thus showing that the expression 'Imperial fair' (J. Plessis) was not dead. Still segregated by sex and predominantly masculine (such games amounted to 50 per cent of all games, which represents a 25 per cent increase since the Second Republic), but they were less numerous than under the monarchies. And games 'for women only' increased considerably (27 per cent of the games) whilst mixed games diminished by half.

The increase in masculine games was due to new circumstances – 'after 1860, the emphasis was on a policy that encouraged the practice of sports'.[55] Masculine games were more and more often *contests*, notably races (15 per cent) and the virile shooting match (10 per cent). All men's games retained a virile, if not martial, aspect that complemented the warlike ideology of the regime. And yet, although it followed fashion, this masculine specialisation left the door wide open to games that were less overtly masculine. That is why the use of the greasy pole diminished by another fourth (it now only represented 25 per cent of all games) and, as a victim of its monarchic image, it gave way to other games. Among them, feminine games took the lion's share with games such as the scissors game (which represented 7 per cent of the games) or the pan.

The other contests were mostly mixed (sack races, blindman's buff (8 per cent), a type of snakes and ladders or skittles). It was a way to tolerate the presence of more women in the public space of fêtes without questioning the supremacy of warlike masculinity. We may indeed consider this sexual differentiation as a way to specialise, or even to 'ghettoise' women in their domestic abilities but it also meant giving them a place in fêtes and showing them to the whole community as was already the case for men.

In any case, men could tolerate such questioning of masculine dominance as they kept the exclusive rights[56] to *sports* that were fast-growing. The appearance of purely athletic activities such as soccer (1 per cent of the games), athletics events (2 per cent) and especially cycling (4 per cent), which women were highly advised against 'as violent movements impeded the good functioning of the organs of the fair sex',[57] enabled men to extend warlike games to activities expurgated of all feminine elements and thus to set limits to the return and entry of women into festive and sporting activities.

The rare athletics societies and clubs which, 'above all, remained a place where men gathered'[58] and were present during Imperial celebrations confirmed this new masculinity and counterbalanced the general trend of a society that was opening itself to women. Sport or games, 'which heated socialization white-hot',[59] opened up a new age in the sexualisation of sports and festive activities that the Third Republic was to codify.[60]

But the antagonism between the desire of ruling bodies for virile and warlike domination and the reality of games and local practices blurred the image of masculine predominance at a time when the economic evolution of the country was modifying relations between the sexes. The Second Empire, its fêtes and their games, were indeed a turning point which enabled women to question exclusive masculinity in games and 'sports' and made men react to this intrusion by confining each of the two sexes to their 'fated' and inflexible functions.

Fêtes and their games in Seine-et-Marne thus had a double function. On the one hand, they were perfectly in keeping with the general political evolution as they confirmed the dominant masculinity which had been claimed by most regimes between 1815 and 1870. Except for the Second Republic and the early days of the July Monarchy, sports practices, national festive decisions and staging always gave the lion's share to an aggressive and conquering masculinity. That is why masculine games were always dominant and represented 56.5 per cent of the games between 1815 and 1870.

On the other hand, while they were codifying and perpetuating this sexual division of the space allotted to sports at fêtes, they were assimilating the values of a French society which, due to liberalism and the industrial revolution, was opening itself up and becoming more complex even in rural départements such as Seine-et-Marne. Festive masculinity as it was experienced in the parishes gradually became different from the masculinity dreamt of by the establishment. That was the main contribution of games to public ceremonies as the share of feminine games kept increasing until 1896 or 1870, whereas specifically masculine games diminished in the same proportion. Far from 'ghettoising' women too much, these developments enabled the blooming of mixed games which moderated the exclusive masculinity of festive space. The presence, *side by side* of both men and women as well as the fact that feminine performances were tolerated constituted a sexual, social and cultural questioning of the masculine which held strongly to the reins of power.

If, on the one hand, national élites could still assert, at the dawn of the twentieth century, 'that there is nothing more hateful than what we call a sportswoman',[61] as they recalled nostalgically the masculinity of the fêtes of the nineteenth century, festive sports practices on the other hand had indeed given birth to a masculinity, tolerant and flexibile enough to open the way to slow sexual cultural mutations.

NOTES

1. In P. Arnaud and T. Terret, *Histoire du sport feminin* (Paris, 1994), p.1.
2. A. Davisse and C. Louveau, 'Sport, école, société, la part des femmes', *Féminin, masculin et activities sportives* (Joinville-le-pont, 1991), specify (p.222) that 'the field of athletic and physical activities ... could well be seen as the place where, above all, the distinction between the sexes is perpetuated, or even as the repository for a highly traditional masculinity and femininity'.
3. See, for example, M.A. Messner, *Power at Play, Sports and the Problem of Masculinity* (Boston, 1992), or P. Duret, *Les jeunes et l'identité masculine* (Paris, 1999).
4. This department was the subject of my history thesis (Sorbonne, 1997) 'De la Saint Louis au cent-cinquantenaire de la révolution. Fêtes et cérémonies publiques en Seine-et-Marne, 1815–1939' (Lille, 1999). We studied 1669 public fêtes and 1002 of their programmes, with in particular 568 games or sports, grouped into 65 different types, between 1815 and 1870.
5. See C. Louveau, 'Sport masculin/féminin, intérêt et apport de l'analyse couplée', in Arnaud and Terret, *Histoire du sport féminin*.
6. The prefecture (Melun) was only 65 kilometres away from Paris, and the biggest town in the department Meaux in the north was 40 km away. In addition, from the eighteenth to the twentieth century, the department was a traditional holiday resort for the Parisian élite.
7. J. Thibault, *Sport et éducation physique en France, 1870–1970* (Paris, 1972), p.162.
8. For the number of games studied under each political regime, see Table 2.
9. J.C. Farcy, 'Le temps libre au village', in A. Corbin, *L'avènement des loisirs, 1850–1960* (Paris, 1995), p.244.

10. A. Davisse and C. Louveau, *Sport, école, société*, p.111.
11. See, for example, the 24 Messidor year III decree which regulated all official parades during public fêtes until the 1907 reform of precedence.
12. We studied a sample of 40 prefectorial proclamations which codified public ceremonies, i.e. 2800 indicators (words of more than two characters).
13. J.C. Farcy, 'Le temps libre', p.256.
14. Statistics based on the 65 banquets organised between 1815 and 1870 during the 502 public fêtes studied.
15. See on the subject J.M.L Hotte, *Le symbolisme des jeux* (Paris, 1976), p.70.
16. In all the ceremonies from 1815 to 1870 we studied we found only four references to prizes awarded to women after games or athletic contests.
17. Between 1815 and 1870, in 600 programmes of the fêtes we studied, the only references to the origin of the flags, so rare as to be found in only 6 texts, were of course those of women 'sewing flags together for the new regime' as indicated in the programme for the regal celebration in Meaux in 1833 (A.M. Seine-et-Marne, series M 10171).
18. Docteur Rozier, for example, said in a study on dances on fête days published in 1855 that 'prostitution has spread to public dances'.
19. J. Durry and B. Jeu, 'La conquête du corps' in *Le sport dans la société française* (Paris, 1992), p.102.
20. See on the subject M. Ozouf, *La fête révolutionaire, 1789-1799* (Paris, 1976) and R. Sanson, *Les 14 Juillet, fête et conscience nationale, 1789-1975* (Paris, 1975).
21. The ceremonies for the birth of the Duke of Bordeaux, the 'miracle child', in 1820, his christening in 1821. As for the deceased, two ceremonies, one for the Duke of Berry in 1820, another for Louis XVIII in 1825.
22. Official instructions, Bulletin des actes administratifs, Seine-et-Marne records, série K 1824, n 51.
23. Official instructions for the October festival, A.D.S-M, 21 EDT 70.
24. We studied 15 of them, most of which had been created for the unveiling of royal busts.
25. Song for the Royal celebration in Meaux, 1825, Municipal Records, Meaux, série 1 1 15.
26. By 'proto-athletic' activities, we mean physical and games activities which had not yet been codified by rules (or ethics) and structured *sports* at the end of the nineteenth century, notably in England.
27. These are the words most often used in fête programmes between 1815 and 1839. See for example the programmes of Melun, Meaux or Lagny fêtes (A.D. S-M, M 6893 to 10105).
28. R. Caillois, *Les jeux et les hommes, le masque et le vertige* (Paris, 1967) Folio, p.51.
29. G. Andrieu, *L'homme et la forme; marchands de la force ou le culte de la forme (XIX–XXième siècles)* (Joinville-le-Pont, 1988), p.43.
30. See R. Dalisson, 'Activities sportives et Fêtes publiques, sociabilités et associationnisme dans la France du Nord l'exemple seine-et-marnais, 1815-1939', *STAPS* (1999).
31. See the famous painting by E. Delacroix, *La liberté guidant le peuple sur les barricades* and the central figure of Marianne who symbolises the action of women. See on the subject M. Agulhon, *Marianne au combat, l'imagerie et la symbolique républicaine, 1789–1880* (Paris, 1979), pp.55–9.
32. Official instructions, Bulletin des actes, Serie K., AD S-M, 1833.
33. Ibid., 1842.
34. J.P. Bois, *Histoire des 14 juillet, 1789-1839* (Rennes, 1991), p.117.
35. Song written by the chief of the national guard, Provins, King's ceremony, 1834, AD 10183.
36. G. Vigarello 'Le temps du sport' in *L'avènement des loisirs*, p.193.
37. R. Caillois, *Les jeux et les hommes*, p.99.
38. J. Durry and B. Jeu, *Le sport dans la société*, p.102.
39. Meaux fête programme. A-M Meaux, 1 1 23.
40. Letter written by the mayor and sent to the prefect, November 1848 AD S-M, M 10179.
41. Mayor's report to the prefect, Lagny, AD S-M, M 7069, November 1851.
42. See J. Ehrard and J. Viallaneix, *Les Fêtes de la revolution, Actes du colloque de Clermont-Ferrand* (Paris, 1977).
43. Song composed in Fontainebleau for the celebration of the Constitution, 1848, ADS-M, M 10179.

44. See M. Vovelle, 'La Marseillaise' in *Les lieux de mémoire*, dir. P. Nora, TI (Paris, 1984).
45. Song written in Coulommiers for the fête of the coup, January 1852 ADS-M, M 6893.
46. P. Fletcher, *Women First: The Female Tradition in English Physical Education, 1880–1980* (London, Dover, New Hampshire, 1984), p.2.
47. C. Nicolet, *L'idée républicaine en France, Essai d'histoire critique* (Paris, 1982), p.146.
48. Ministry of cults, on the subject of Imperial Fêtes, 1806. Quoted by J.P. Bois, *Histoire*, p.106.
49. Instruction from the prefect to mayors, 1852, AD S-M, M 6895.
50. Programme for the fair in Melun, 1853, AM Melun, 1 14 2/2.
51. Bulletin des lois, 1856, AM S-M, serie K, No.15.
52. Proclamation by the mayor of Meaux, 1860. AM S-M, 106 Edit. 30.
53. Song written in Melun, celebration for the Emperor, 1855, AD S-M M 10163.
54. E. Debonnet, *Les rois de la force* (Paris, 1910), p.45.
55. C. Pociello, 'Pratiques sportives et pratiques sociales', Colloque de St-Etienne, 1982, CIERC, p.293.
56. See A. Davisse and C. Louveau, 'Masculin, feminin, sport', in *Sociologie du sport*, Study and Research by GISS, No.5 (Geneva University, 1997).
57. Dr Tessier, who was, however, in favour of feminine athletic activities, in J. Durry and B. Jeu, *Sport et société*, p.103.
58. J. Durry and B. Jeu, *Le sport*, p.101.
59. G. Vincent and B. Camy, *Fêtes à Givors, Education, fête et culture* (Lyon, 1981).
60. See J. Thibault, 'Les origines du sport féminin', in *Les athlètes de la République, Gymnastique, sport et idéologie républicaine* (Toulouse, 1987), pp.331–9.
61. H. Desgranges, 'L'auto', 12 juin 1904, in Y. Leziart, *Sport et dynamiques sociales* (Joinville-le-Pont, 1989), p.85.

The Other Side of the Coin:
Victorian Masculinity, Field Sports and English Elite Education

J.A. MANGAN and CALLUM McKENZIE

The morality of field sports[1] and their purpose in élite education were contentious issues during the nineteenth century. Field sports now symbolised aristocratic privilege and sustained the traditional code of the gentleman in a period when middle-class sensibilities were reconstructing his image and redefining his masculinity on games fields. Field sports, therefore, were no longer unproblematic. The situation had become more complicated. Thomas Arnold's rejection of field sports during his headship at Rugby, for example, aimed at curtailing perceived anti-social behaviour. Although he succeeded in minimising the boys' poaching in the vicinity of the school, Arnold's efforts to reshape youthful sensibilities, however, faced a number of difficulties. The pervasiveness of the rural masculine ideal of the huntsman, and the associated moral imperatives of the country gentleman, not to mention his accustomed pleasures, remained strong throughout the nineteenth century and indeed long after.[2] This ideal found expression in literature, art and custom and represented for many an appropriate social training for middle- and upper-class boys. Furthermore, by the age of the New Imperialism killing wildlife for sport by the young had become part of an ideological conflict in which racial superiority, ethnocentric assertion and manly aggression were given priority over the Christian virtues of consideration, compassion and gentleness. This chapter considers the evolving relationship between masculinity, field sports and élite education during the nineteenth century and discusses field sports as both *complementary to, and in competition with* team games, in the making of period élite masculinity.

SETTING THE SCENE:
FIELD SPORTS BEFORE THE ERA OF ATHLETICISM

Before about the 1850s, there is no evidence to suggest that field sports took place in any organised way at the public schools. The rural location of some schools meant that their pupils were free to roam without restriction through the countryside during leisure hours. In the winter at Winchester, for example, badger-hunting was a favourite sport. Huntsmen were hired to keep badgers and provided terriers and dogs.[3] Winchester was described as a 'sporting school, in a very sporting county', where many of the boys hunted in the holidays.[4] At this time, too, 'not a few boys kept guns for hare and partridge shooting'.[5] Other activities at Winchester included bird-shooting, nesting, duck-hunting and beagling, but the most common and popular of all was 'toozling' or chasing and killing birds with hand thrown stones in the hedgerows. There were variations on this. One pupil spent all his free time killing squirrels and birds with a catapult, a practice which he later felt was useful for creating proficiency in other pastimes such as racquets, cricket, tennis and big-game hunting![6] At Harrow, one 'toozler' wrote in his diary,

> went out shooting over Hedstone fields and having no sport, put down the gun and found a Joe Bent in Hedge adjoining private road, which was killed after a splendid run by M. Tufnell. Found a robin in same hedge, which, after an exceedingly brilliant run, was killed by Mr Torre. Had an animated run with Joe Bent. Home by Church Fields. NB Game plentiful but blackbirds wild. First eggs taken, Mistle Thrushes.[7]

Bird-nesting was a widespread hobby.[8] The boys of Wellington College were occasionally lectured by Charles Kingsley on the manly merits of bird-nesting.[9] Pupils at Marlborough during this period also enjoyed the largely unrestrained hobbies of taking birds eggs from nests, as well as trespassing and poaching game. In addition, in the vicinity of the college, rabbits and squirrels were at constant risk from the 'squaler', a small cane with a lead head thrown with uncanny accuracy by some Marlborough boys.[10] Frogs fared no better when hunted by the Marlborian 'barbaric tribe' which 'collected in gangs to beat frogs with sticks in the wilderness and filled buckets with their bodies'.[11] Eton too provided many opportunities for the reluctant scholar to decimate local wildlife. Some students kept ferrets at 'Fishers' and hunted rats in the hedgerows; 'Nimrod's' autobiography notes how recreations such as rat-catching and rabbit and badger taking provided certain Eton scholars with the necessary skills for subsequent careers as Masters of Foxhounds.[12]

Poaching by public school boys at this time did not carry the stigma of dishonour. On the contrary, boys identified as poachers were often lauded by their peers.[13] Poaching by the sons of the aristocracy and gentry not only won public esteem, it provided excitement, hazard, entertainment and useful experience. Some, like Joby Minor, 'the most artful poacher in Eton', graduated in time to the respected position of kennel huntsman to the Eton Beagles in the 1860s.[14] Sir John Dugdale Astley (1828–94) chased deer and poached pheasant eggs in Home Park while at Eton, fully 'enjoying the excitement of dodging the gamekeeper'.[15] Poaching by upper-class boys, of course, was not born of necessity, nor was it an act of social resentment. It demonstrated a healthy sense of boyish daring, privileged resistance to conformity and the right to upper-class licence. Poaching as a marker of bravado, non-conformity and freedom lingered on into the twentieth century. In fiction, Rudyard Kipling's schoolboy heroes in his *Land and Sea Tales for Scouts and Guides*[16] were capable rabbit ferreters and had the 'poaching instinct', while in life, boys at Eton prior to the Great War were still poaching large amounts of game. Between October 1908 and July 1910, for example, six friends at Eton poached 2,260 head of game.[17]

ARNOLD, MANLINESS AND MIDDLE-CLASS MORALITY

For many mid-Victorians, Thomas Arnold was a focus for the desire for moral reformation.[18] His objective, at least according to C.L.R. James, was the development of a public-school system which provided a meeting place for the moral outlook of the dissenting middle classes and the athletic instincts of the aristocracy.[19] Perhaps. What is more certain is that within any alleged compromise between the aristocratic and bourgeois conceptions of culture, however, there was no place for field sports. Character-building was the main purpose of Arnold's Rugby, in which education was firstly an ethical and only secondly an intellectual process.[20] One aim, as is well known, was the creation of Christian gentlemen as the 'champions of righteousness especially selected to combat the ever watchful forces of evil'.[21] To this end Arnold wanted to reduce the difference in lifestyles between the middle and upper-middle classes.[22] His ambition was moral embourgoisement – downwards. The luxury and privilege of the 'sporting squire' without responsibility, and his associated recreational and social excesses, was anathema to Arnold.[23] Arnold's perception of the Christian gentleman was not that of the old chevalier, jealous of his paramilitary honour but otherwise indifferent to morality, but that of a new gentle gentleman, competing not in duels undertaken or foxes killed, but in consideration for others.[24] Field sports, a prominent part of this older culture, were considered by him as a feudal anachronism and at odds with his civilising mission for young gentlemen. Arnold's objections to field sports certainly derived from his evangelicism, a Christian doctrine which was antithetical to killing wildlife for sport, with its stress on moral earnestness and compassion for the weak. Masculinity for many of the aristocracy and gentry, on the other hand, still manifested itself in military prowess, and in codes of honour based on medieval chivalric martial values, in which field sports were essential training. The life of the feudal élite, of course, had been dominated by the essentials of war, hunting and the tournament, the last two being preparation for the first.[25] This domination, with the exception of the tournament, had by no means disappeared by the first half of the nineteenth century.

For his part, Arnold thought all field sports a 'waste of time'. At Rugby he was determined to secure their abolition. If Arnold's vision was to be realised, in his view he needed to abolish those recreations which reinforced cultural divisions and boundaries and traditional, unacceptable practices. Consequently, on arrival he attempted ruthlessly to end the former licence to roam the countryside at Rugby: in 1833 Arnold expelled six boys for fishing in the Avon, the local river, after complaints from a local landowner.[26] Then hunting became the target. It had been common practice prior to Arnold's arrival for boys to hire cottages from local countrymen for hiding dogs and sporting equipment. The use of dogs and guns were now forbidden and keeping to bounds firmly enforced.[27] He went further, actually destroying packs of hounds kept by the boys.[28] By edict, and by appeals to local farmers and landowners, Arnold gradually curtailed the traditional sports of hunting, shooting and fishing. According to Charles Kingsley, fishing was the sport of sports for those overworked businessmen, professional men, barristers, statesmen and merchants, who sought mental relaxation to ease the strain of excessive occupational pressure.[29] This argument did not work with Arnold. Even angling, that restrained, leisurely rural activity, was denied the boys. In a nutshell, Arnold's opposition to field sports of all kinds, was driven by idealism, pragmatism and humanitarianism.[30]

Arnold's deliberate efforts to exclude the landed aristocracy from Rugby formed part of his crusade against field sports.[31] It is interesting that between 1800 and 1850, the proportion of boys at Rugby from titled families never exceeded between five and seven per cent in any decade.[32] Subsequently the post–Arnold opposition to field sports was facilitated by the substitution of readily acceptable alternatives, such as cricket and football.[33] These were part of an emerging and increasingly powerful educational ideology, namely athleticism, incorporating tests of manliness and character formation without the need to kill animals or exhibit prowess on a horse.[34] Circa 1850, various headmasters brought about organisational and disciplinary reform in their schools.[35] These included an increase in indirect surveillance by the headmaster and assistant masters over the boys' recreational activities and pastimes,[36] a practice which contrasted with the earlier unrestricted freedom which allowed, among other things, shooting, beagling and ferreting.

Competence at team games now for many became the supreme expression of masculine moral excellence.[37] The result was the arrival of a process by which the public schools after the 1860s, increasingly produced a unified and standardised English educational élite,[38] and formulated a new concept of the English gentleman in due course nowhere better exemplified than in the image of the ex–public school cricketer, A.W. Hornby[39] or his superior at the 'game for gentlemen', C.B. Fry.[40]

These educational developments took place as Britain underwent at least some material embourgeoisement, involving a partial amalgamation of the established upper class and the rising middle class.[41] However, another social development was also taking place. Where the new commercial, industrial and business class sought assimilation with larger landowners, field sports were one expression of class parity. They were a form of recreational conspicuous consumption that demonstrated comparable, or ever superior wealth, especially when linked to the expensive honour of Master of Hounds. Arnold had a lonely victory. Field sports were not abandoned in the public school system at the onset of athleticism. The *two* means of making masculinity now co-existed. And it would certainly be an over-simplification to suggest, therefore,

that boys from well-established landed families pursued field sports at
school, whereas those from industrial middle-class families did not. Well
before 1850, cotton and ironmasters, for example, were buying land for
sporting purposes, indeed as early as the late eighteenth century.[42] The
new man of wealth sought to become part of the existing establishment
by buying land and playing by the rules of existing landed society; few
families, it has been argued, held out for long against its leisured, bucolic
delights.[43] The acquisition of a landed estate was one of the criteria for
the upward rise of the socially ambitious.[44] By about 1800, it had become
common practice to transfer wealth from commercial enterprises to
moneyed interests and then to landed estates.[45] Field sports were popular
amongst the new men of commerce and industry, despite the opposition
to killing wildlife by leading Dissenters during the early nineteenth
century.[46] Furthermore, the 1831 Game Reform Act quickened the pace
of democratisation in field sports. Not only the upper middle classes
could 'sport', according to one authority, but also the 'blacksmith, the
butcher, the hog jobber, the fisherman and the cadger ... all have
certificates'.[47] By mid-century, new money was being used to support
fox-hunting. According to a number of contemporary hunting
authorities, the middle classes were firmly established in the hunting
field. These included 'the *pater familias*, respectable householders and
responsible vestrymen, churchwardens and other parish administrators;
attorneys, country bankers, doctors, apothecaries – the profession of
medicine has a special aptitude for fox-hunting – maltsters, millers,
butchers, bakers, innkeepers, auctioneers, graziers, builders, retired
officers, judges home from India, barristers who take weekly holidays,
stockbrokers, newspaper editors, artists and sailors'.[48] The erosion of
class boundaries and the rise in the popularity of field sports was linked
then to the increased earning capacity of the business and professional
classes. *The Saturday Review* even suggested that the radical movement
against field sports, which began in the 1840s, was now ineffectual
because 'sport could not be represented as peculiar to the aristocracy, as
all men like to shoot, and men in trade bought estates and became game
preservers'.[49] The gradual erosion of social barriers in field sports was
noted by the old Etonian, Charles Milnes-Gaskell, who asserted that all
classes who had any leisure or money to spare could participate in field
sports. He added, sadly, 'it is humiliating to be obliged to acknowledge
that in spite of all the additional facilities afforded in this country for the
pursuit of a scientific or artistic career, the average Englishman's

conception of a leisured life is undoubtedly a life spent in the enjoyment of sport. The Englishman who has the means will spend those means on racing, hunting, fishing or shooting.'[50]

Arnold's well-meaning reforms, then, were taking place at a time when field sports were becoming as much the recreation of the business and the professional middle classes as of the aristocratic class.[51] This trend continued into the late nineteenth century.[52] In 1851 the population of England and Wales was 17,927,609 with 28,950 game licences issued; by 1866, 43,231 licences had been sold; the number of gun licences sold per thousand males in England confirmed the rise in participation: 9.7 in England and Wales, 7.8 in Scotland; by 1891, this had risen to 11.37 and 8.8 respectively.[53] In the light of this evidence, it is tempting and reasonable to suggest that class boundaries and their respective codes of masculinity were becoming increasingly blurred. Nevertheless, while the 'gradual emergence of the bourgeoisie as the ruling class ... their growing control of major institutions, and the consequent spread of their values through society' was particularly evident in games and athletics,[54] and despite the 'bourgeoisification' of aristocratic culture through these games, at Eton and Cambridge in particular, field sports remained powerful symbols of upper-class masculinity. And one other manifestation of the pursuit of a class 'caste mark' should be noted, the desire of the 'nouveau riche' to educate their sons at public school and university. Its relevance will be seen shortly.

BASTIONS OF RESISTANCE, INCLUSION AND EXCLUSION: ETON AND OXBRIDGE

Aristocratic refugees from Arnold's Rugby with their too frequent enthusiasm for field sports, were frequently advised that Eton would provide a more suitable education.[55] And there was sense in this. Field sports played a distinctive and influential part in Eton life throughout the Victorian period. In part, this reflected the social composition of the school, which contained about 20 per cent of boys from titled families in every decade during the first half of the century,[56] but it also reflected a keenness on the part of the *nouveau riche* on entry to display a hard-won caste mark. And it also reflected a propensity by both groups to cling tenaciously to a long-standing Etonian tradition.

Hunting at Eton College possessed a long history. From the seventeenth century onwards, Eton boys hunted, sometimes with rams as quarry.[57] The Founder, in fact, had stipulated that no scholar, fellow, chaplain or other minister of the College should keep dogs, nets for hunting, ferrets, falcons or hawks. These rules, however, seem to have been broken at will.[58] However, the Eton College Hunt, founded in the late 1850s by boys from the shires, familiar with and keen on field sports, represented a departure from past defiant and less formal modes of hunting, by virtue of the tacit approval given to it by the school authorities. The Oppidan Hunt, a separate group, began on 19 January 1858 with the formation of a beagle pack,[59] initiated by 'a manly country-loving boy, versed in the etiquette of hunting and devoted to a healthy open-air life, who loved horse and hound, and who spent every moment of daylight cultivating the instincts of a clean, country bred Englishman'.[60] Contemporaries recalled that this first pack of beagles was led by two influential senior pupils, Valentine Lawless and Eyre William Hussey, who had already attained high positions within the College, the latter being the Captain of the Boats[61] and the former being a member of Pop. The inspiration for a College Hunt clearly came from the desire to perpetuate the practices of the country gentleman in this school for gentlemen. Membership was open to all on payment of an annual subscription. It should not be overlooked that almost at the very moment when athleticism was establishing itself formally within the public school system, hunting too, at least at Eton, was also establishing itself with similar formality!

When Dr Goodford[62] resigned in 1861 at the prospect of the publication of the Report of the Clarendon Commission,[63] the new Headmaster, Dr Balston,[64] did not enforce the school rules against hunting. The then Captain of the Boats, Valentine Lawless, was invited to meet Dr Balston to discuss the question of 'Lower Boys frequenting Tap', which was a private room in a public-house beyond Barnes Bridge. Here, boys were prone to drink large quantities of beer and took part in customs such as 'drinking the Long Glass'. Dr Balston proposed that, in return for Lawless' assistance in keeping Lower Boys away from 'Tap', he would withdraw the rules against dogs in College, and authorise and recognise the Beagles Club. There was logic in Balston's offer, since field sports were widely seen as an antidote to degeneracy. 'What is a youth,' one observer enquired, 'without his shooting and his hunting, his gloves and his foil? – an inflation of tobacco and beer, of vice and folly. And what's a man without his recreation? – a miracle of inaptitude, of infirmity of purpose, and incapable of action'.[65] In *The Young*

Sportsman's Manual of 1867, one writer insisted on the superior moral status of the manly field sportsman, asserting that most sporting writers were united against mixing the pleasures of the field with alcohol. 'There was no place,' he argued, 'for drink in the field, covert or moor.'[66] At the meeting between Dr Balston and Lawless, clearly a deal was struck and beagling was officially sanctioned by the College, although there was some resistance, at least for a little time, in some official quarters. The *Eton College Chronicle* reported briefly in 1864 that 'our only regret is that the authorities do not seem well-disposed towards this fine and invigorating exercise'.[67] The exercise appeared to prove invigorating. In its first month, there were about one hundred pupils out following the pack. The Eton College Beagles, incidentally, were entirely financed, administered and organised by the boys. The construction of new expensive kennels on College land in 1872, for example, was wholly financed by them[68] and had an educational rationale. The development of appropriate masculinity was considered to be closely linked to self-reliance. The Public Schools Commission Report of 1864 alluded to the 'freedom of public school life', which promoted 'independence and manliness of character'. Goodford himself was described as 'unmeddlesome',[69] and argued that 'English gentlemen should not be excessively manipulated and shaped by the school'.[70] In Goodford's action there was not only purpose, there was precedent. In 1866 judicious action by the boys at Eton had resulted in an amalgamation between the Oppidans and Collegers[71] to strengthen the Hunt against the local farmers, some of whom were reluctant to allow meetings to trample their crops.[72] This was smiled upon by the authorities. The capacity of Etonians to successfully organise and administer hunting was one expression of a confident *and* competent masculine identity.[73]

The relationship between the Hunt and adjacent farmers deteriorated steadily in the 1860s. The successful management of conflict, which might require a superior attitude towards others, was an essential component of period upper-middle-class masculinity. In consequence, the continuation of the Eton College Hunt became a contest of wills. The first mention of school field sports in the *Eton College Chronicle* on 14 May 1863 had noted that local farmers had asked in 'a good-natured' manner for Eton gentlemen not to cross the young corn. *The Chronicle* opined that to accede to their request was a good idea as the farmers by and large were very helpful with regard to the Hunt, especially in finding hares.[74] This sound advice appears to have been ignored. By the mid-1860s it was reported that the Beagles had had a poor season owing to 'the extreme perversity of some farmers, who own the best land about the place. We cannot see what possible harm a few boys running over ground could possibly do to crops, and compensation is easily and readily obtainable.'[75] Difficulty with local farmers is also recorded in the boys' hunting journals. Clearly the farmers had persisted in their complaints, and the boys in their dismissal of them. The fact that the local farming community felt able to do so reflected developments at a national level. By the 1860s the capability of farmers to organise and improve their position was improved by the establishment of new farmers' clubs and associations. In August 1865 *The Field* remarked that such local groups were intent on publicising the issue of landlords' sport, a sure sign of farmers' growing self-confidence.[76] Local assertion was no doubt a consequence of this. In contrast to the period before the 1850s it is notable that Eton's young sportsmen now preferred negotiation rather than confrontation when dealing with the local farming community.[77] One Master of the Beagles, H.B. Creswel, noted in the *Hunt Diaries* that 'great care should be taken with regard to certain farmers, or my successor will get into serious trouble which may lead to the abolition of the Hunt'.[78] There can be little doubt that farmers' growing self-assertion nationally was reflected locally.

In the mid-1860s the Public Schools Commission found that intellectual standards were unsatisfactory at Eton and the other 'Great Schools'.[79] This fact, together with the growing popularity and significance of organised games as well as the formal acceptance of the Eton College Hunt during this decade, resulted in debates about education at Eton, and indeed at the other public schools. Nevertheless, athleticism went from strength to strength. During the 1860s, for example, there was a gradual admission of Collegers into Oppidan school sports in general: the lower club and lower college were now allowed into cricket, and athletics, a development which was seen as an extension of their privileges.[80] By the turn of the century these changes had become consolidated. For most boys games playing became *de rigueur*. In 1898 it was recorded that:

> There are fifty fives courts where before there was one; twenty games or thereabouts of cricket as against three; compulsory football for every house four or five times a week; to say nothing of beagles and athletic sports in the Easter Term, and rowing and

bathing daily through the summer. There are house colours for football and school colours for football, cricket, rowing, racquets; there are challenge cups, senior and junior ...[81]

The Hunt, however, remained strong in the face of major changes in sport at the school.

A.J. Pound, the first Master of the combined hunt in 1866 was 'thoroughly honest and straightforward', if intellectually below average. This was no liability. His virtues[82] were ordered correctly. Pound was fondly remembered as a spartan and spirited youth, frequently arranging to be early at the 'Saying Lesson, so as to be away from school at seven-thirty a.m., breakfasting on beer and biscuits, and hunting until eleven a.m.'[83] Prestige allocated to huntsmen was enhanced by their knowledge of, and interest in, sporting literature rather than Greek or Roman Classics, a practice not always condemned by the school.[84] Popular public school heroes and their many admirers, of course, preferred energetic sports to sedentary classwork, since all but the most material forms of intelligence were considered effeminate.[85] Etonians with no fondness for Greek and Latin, as noted earlier, were praised for their manly rowing and poaching.[86] At Eton, those who rejected the river, track or pitch could legitimately take part in ratting, poaching or fox-hunting. The distinguished Eton headmaster, Edward Warre[87] was concerned about the manliness of boys who were excessively academic, and was convinced that strenuous exercise was the panacea for associated youthful deficiencies.[88] He was reassured that Eton 'possessed in itself the antidote to effeminacy'.[89] It comes as no surprise, therefore, that Warre supported the Hunt. This antidote, in his view, *included* field sports.

The Trinity College Foot Beagles at Cambridge, like the Eton Hunt, was under the control of Matthew Arnold's 'barbarians', the unintellectual sons of country gentlemen. For these Beaglers, field sports were their preference, for both social and educational reasons. As with school pupils and beaks, so with students and dons. Both combined to make a success of the College Beagles. William Edward Currey,[90] for example, took the lead in setting up the Beagles in 1867, combining the duties of College don and Master of the Beagles, while W. Rouse-Ball[91] was an enthusiastic supporter of the Beagles as well as a loyal Fellow of the College. Field sports at Cambridge, of course, had long been a counter-balance to scholarship. One foreign visitor in 1602 noted that students 'perhaps keep more dogs and greyhounds that are so often seen in the streets, than they do books'.[92] Student preference for field sports over learning was again noted in the late eighteenth century.[93] In the 1740s Francis Coventry noted of Magdalene College that wealthy fellow-commoners and noblemen were indulged in by tutors who hesitated to oppose the inclinations of gentlemen. The allure of preferments and benefices in the gift of titled families ensured that the Dons allowed students to substitute hunting parties for lectures much as they pleased. Privilege and patronage eroded the authority, power and control of the school beak and the university don.[94] Generations of Cambridge undergraduates, therefore, had been noted sportsmen, who raced at Newmarket, shot throughout Cambridgeshire, and avoided lectures and chapel whenever possible. The pleasures of point-to-point and partridge shooting were frequently accompanied by heavy drinking and riotous behaviour, and the rights of local owners of land received little sympathy.[95] In passing, it might be noted that things were no different at Oxford. Local farmers and huntsmen were resentful of irresponsible undergraduates who paid little attention to crops or more heinously to the proper treatment of hounds,[96] while the famous George Osbaldestone, hunted for three days a week at Brasenose during the early nineteenth century and kept two hunters;[97] Captain John White, educated at Eton and Christ Church, hunted regularly on his three hunters and, after a catalogue of falls and broken bones, stupidly or bravely or perhaps both, he rode 'harder than ever'.[98] Christ Church, according to one observer writing in 1890, was open to anyone who 'could eat, drink and hunt, play cricket and punt'.[99] Not always, it appears. In 1885 the Dean of Christchurch wrote to Lord Bathurst in some exasperation, suggesting that his eldest son should find a more convenient hunting box for the following season than the 'House'.[100] Nevertheless, at the turn of the century, Christ Church, New College, Magdalene and Exeter all had their own beagle packs. And despite intermittent moral objections to hunting, Christ Church Beagles were formally supported by College Amalgamation Club subscriptions.[101]

In the last quarter of the nineteenth century Cambridge had the reputation over Oxford of giving even more latitude to sportsmen and placing even less emphasis on learning.[102] Old Etonians were the leading figures in the halcyon years of the Trinity Foot Beagles from the late 1870s to the early 1880s, when Lord Yarborough, Watkin Wynn, W. Warton, E. Mesey-Thompson and Rowland Hunt among others, 'graduated with the degree of Master of Foxhounds'.[103] Of course, some managed to combine classwork with 'fieldwork'. J.W. Larnach, educated at Eton and Trinity College, Cambridge, was a case in point. At Cambridge he hunted regularly with the Cambridgeshire and Fitzwilliam and raced at Newmarket. *Baily's Magazine* noted approvingly that immediately prior to his finals he raced during the day and worked through the night.[104]

Nonetheless, it is true to say that at Cambridge in the whole of the second half of the nineteenth century many students had little interest in serious study. Only 44 per cent of undergraduates took honours courses between 1850 and 1906,[105] and many who took the ordinary degree never bothered to graduate. Magdalene nicely illustrates both the licence and the laxity which too frequently prevailed at Cambridge throughout the nineteenth century.

During the 1860s Magdalene became the sanctuary for those unruly and ill-disciplined students rejected by other colleges.[106] Under the Mastership of Latimer Neville,[107] described as a 'thoroughgoing opponent of academic progress', Magdalene became a 'pleasant residential sporting club for the well-to-do or more or less well-descended young men'.[108] Superior social position demonstrated by access to field sports, particularly the costly activity of hunting, enabled students from the older landed families to set themselves apart. In this way they could, and did, flaunt an older tradition of masculinity, and distanced themselves from their inferiors. The growth of the public school system and the expansion of the ancient universities increasingly brought the commercial and professional middle classes into close proximity with the established landed classes in the second half of the nineteenth century.[109] Eton and Oxbridge, for example, were by this time receiving an ever-increasing number of solidly middle class entrants.[110] Field sports at Eton and Oxbridge, therefore, could be manifestations of social demarcation which heightened self-perceptions of superiority based on cultural heritage.[111]

No Cambridge college projected this self-perception more completely than Magdalene. Magdalene in the 1860s, it was observed, was occupied by 'decent chaps devoted to horse and hound, but unfortunately, there were also in residence a few undergraduates, mostly sons of monied parvenus from the north of England, who exhibited a cheap imitation of these very creditable gentlemen ... They tried to liken themselves to country gentlemen, and succeeded in looking like stableboys.'[112] According to contemporaries, hunting and riding were the most notable features of Magdalene at this time, when five or six couples of hunters were regularly to be found waiting at the College gate.[113] Between about 1850 and 1904 an undergraduate at Magdalene was allowed to count two nights towards his term if he was in college before 11 p.m. and did not leave before 6 a.m. on the following morning. This arrangement was intended to control the large number of Magdalene men who hunted two or three days a week with the Fitzwilliam Hunt or the Oakley, often staying overnight in Bedford. Absence from Chapel or Hall entailed the payment of fines, although when racing was on at Newmarket, Hall was cancelled.[114] In fact, the restrictions were pointless. Undergraduates frequently broke curfews and college regulations in order to pursue hunting.

After 1850 success on the games field, as already noted, was increasingly evidence of a proper masculinity. However, many undergraduates who hunted at Cambridge saw themselves as a male élite. They had no wish to embrace the fashion for modern sport – in any form. One member of the Beagles put this well:

> the truth is that we were extremely, almost morbidly, sensitive of being regarded as having any connection with any form of athletics, and the appearance of a stray member of the 'Hare and Hounds', a paper-chasing athletics club, set all our defensive bristles erect in half a minute. He might be a magnificent runner and keep with the hounds all the way, but we would observe that he knew nothing of skirting, or of saving himself by any knowledge of the shifts of the hunted hare: his running was fine running, but it wasn't running to hounds, so he was felt to be no sportsman and therefore to merit no trophy. Beagling is hunting ... the exercise of running was a subordinate consideration.[115]

The historian of the Trinity Foot Beagles, F.C. Kempson, stated bluntly that athletic contests, based on Hellenic morality, were an inferior way of establishing masculine and moral identity, and that in contrast, hunting, beagling and steeplechasing were clear evidence of the natural superiority of the 'barbarian' character with his masculine qualities of efficient organisation, control and negotiation. The appearance of a critique of hunting in the *Cambridge Review* in 1912, hardened Kempson's suspicions that middle-class athletics were not only inferior activities but the antithesis of virtuous field sports, which remained rightfully in the control of the country gentleman. He regretted the fact that the ancient universities were now under the control of the middle classes. The true sportsman, he asserted, matched himself *against* nature, and pursued no reward unlike the modern multi-coloured blazered and scarved game-playing 'blue'. To emphasise this point, dress for hunting was tweed jacket, breeches and a soft cashmere scarf. In this way, the values of the new 'blood' preoccupied with colours, and the old sportsman honouring tradition, were pointed up.

Of course, in reality *both* games, athletics or rowing, and field sports enabled pupils at school and students at university to display their unquestionable masculinity to their respective admiring peers. Some excelled in one masculine world. H.M. Mesey-Thompson at Eton, for example, won the hurdles and the mile in 1863, the steeplechase in 1864, was also a top school oarsman and basked in the glory of being an 'all-round' athlete. Some bridged the worlds of the two masculinities. Rowland Hunt, who was at Eton between 1871 and 1877, won the steeplechase, 'with consummate ease' for two consecutive years, and was revered for his versatility, 'a wonderful runner, excellent shot, fearless rider and good fisherman'.[116] In addition, Hunt was one of the best exponents of the Eton Football Game, was keeper (Captain) of the Field Game, won the School Diving and House Racquets trophies and was in the School Shooting Eleven. Furthermore, he was Master of the Beagles in 1876. In due course, he went up to Magdalene, Cambridge. There, he never 'wasted much time in attending lectures, chapel or Hall; he did pass Part I of the 'Little-Go'[117] which satisfied his aspirations for academic honours'.[118] In short, while games, athletics and rowing with their intense inter-college rivalries based substantially, if not completely, on public school habits, clearly predominated at Cambridge during the late nineteenth century, hunting still found staunch support in a few quarters within the university. For some, killing wildlife for sport fitted easily into the fabric of a university experience, which produced 'tastes, inclinations, even vices which were positive and virile'.[119] It was reported that while there were hardly any ladylike men in the University, there was not a single one at Magdalene. The tendency was to the manly rather than to the effeminate.[120] Charles Kingsley, obsessed with manliness, was a passionate apologist for Magdalene manners. University education, he asserted, was not the prerogative of scholars but of *men*, 'bold, energetic, methodic, liberal-minded, magnanimous'.[121] For his part, he looked back fondly on his undergraduate days at

Magdalene as spent largely in 'drink, horses, gambling, cards, prize-fighting, fishing and poaching; the keeping of horses and dogs, the latter inside college itself ...'[122] The merits of such masculine behaviour in Kingsley's typically romantic opinion, of course, lay in the moral message: killing wildlife for sport promoted a love of nature. This in turn produced the ideal naturalist 'gentle, courteous, sympathetic to the poor, brave and enterprising, patient and undaunted, reverent and truthful, selfless and devoted – he would aspire to the ideal of chivalry'.[123] Others, equally famous, were no less committed to college custom. Arthur C. Benson[124] spent a good bit of his time at Magdalene in the company of his gun. Most Saturdays he was out shooting with his two siblings, Fred and Hugh Benson. This trio of sportsmen were described as a 'happy band of brothers'.

Interestingly, despite caste differences between 'Beaglers' and 'Bloods' both groups had become, to varying degrees, bound by the imperatives of 'fair play'. The Trinity Foot Beagles and the Eton College Hunt were created in the mid-nineteenth century, a significant time in the application of utilitarian values in the form of compulsory and regulated team games. This new code of conduct, contrary to the claims of Pierre de Coubertin,[125] was not the instinctive behaviour of upper-class youth, but depended on the acquisition of new attitudes through the medium of sport, towards self-control and self-discipline. Many of the public school 'hooligans' were taught the new virtues of 'fair play' on new school playing fields. The hunting clubs for their part, at Eton and Cambridge in turn shifted from the uncontrolled to controlled killing of wildlife, regulated by a tight sporting code. Of course, there is some truth, even if it is far from the whole truth, in the suggestion that the late nineteenth century concept of 'fair play' was in part a continuation of subscription to the older aristocratic chivalric tradition of honour, decency, style and manners.[126] Consequently, upper-class sporting periodicals of course, such as *Baily's Magazine*, never abandoned the belief that traditional landed families retained a superiority which incorporated a sense of decency and style. It paraded an impressive set of exemplars. John Poyntz Spencer, educated at Harrow and Trinity College, Cambridge in the 1850s, Master of the Pytchley Hounds, for example, inspired *Baily's* to write: 'we believe that sport of every kind is calculated to promote generous and manly impulses, and to strengthen a character for honesty and chivalry which has usually been considered a national peculiarity of Englishmen'.[127] H. Wentworth Fitzwilliam, from a family of churchmen, soldiers and statesmen, country gentlemen and sportsmen, also, in *Baily's,* view, embodied the necessary attributes of traditional manhood, being 'a true and courteous gentleman, quiet in demeanour, a sportsman, but not a sporting man'.[128] His social class credentials were impeccable. Like most of his family before him, he was educated at Eton, then Trinity College, Cambridge. There, he became Master of the Drag-Hounds and hunted regularly with the Fitzwilliam hounds. According to *Baily's,* the Duke of Bedford, clearly of unquestioned pedigree, who was educated at Westminster and Cambridge in the early nineteenth century, was a 'bold and elegant rider, whose leading quality was his sense of justice'.[129]

A belief in the superiority of aristocratic tradition in the eyes of at least some, is clearly revealed in the fact that when between the 1850s and 1860s, sport at Eton was being transformed from unregulated recreation to a regulated system of rowing, cricket and football house competitions,[130] an *Eton College Chronicle* editorial of 1864 suggested that all school athletics should be organised by the newly created *Master of the Beagles* not by the long established Captain of the Boats! Articles on sport within the influential *Chronicle*, incidentally, were usually sequenced as 'Beagles, Fives, Athletic Sports and Rowing'.[131]

Of course, hunting at Eton and Cambridge after the 1860s did not reflect an untrammelled continuation of noble aristocratic demeanour, but an amalgam of newly acquired sporting codes and traditional customs. Hunting was an evolving sport. The attitudes, procedures, language and dress code of both hunts at both places did respond to change and changed. However, association with historic codes of conduct enabled pupils at Eton and Cambridge to adopt an attitude of superiority based on past privilege. They acquired confidence from a legacy of class confidence. When evangelical pressures 'civilised' the public schoolboy, producing a new regard for playing games under new rules, there was a knock-on effect on the hunting field and an appropriate rationalisation. Respect for the quarry now heightened the intrinsic manliness of hunting. And, as a by-product, the application of fair play to the Hunt tended to produce a more compassionate morality. Several members were ousted from the Hunt, for example, during the 1860s because they complained of poor sport[132] by which they meant over-regulated killing. During the early years of the Eton College Hunt, its moral code did not exclude the hunting of 'bagged' or released quarry, either fox or hare, usually obtained from Leadenhall Market. However, the hunting of 'bagged' hares was later used to question the manliness required of this form of hunting.[133] With the development and regulation of the Hunt only wild hares were used for sport. New codes of conduct after the 1860s reflected the notion that wild animals were the proper quarry of a *manly* sport.[134] In this way the enthusiast for field sports joined the enthusiast for team games in the pursuit of a proper period masculinity.

It should not be overlooked, of course, that in pursuit of manliness at least three ideals co-existed, sometimes in harmony and sometimes in disharmony, at Eton – and certainly at King's College, its finishing school[135] for Etonians, at Cambridge. To record this is to introduce a timely and appropriate note of complexity into the Victorian middle and upper middle class making of masculinity. To borrow a useful term from Christopher Hibbert[136] and redefined here for the purposes of this chapter, after 1850 there was the increasingly influential and popular phenomenon of 'Bloodism', the product of athleticism, in conjunction with the celebration of the athlete of the games field as an iconic representation of all that was virtuous in the period public school male. There were cynics and critics of 'Bloodism', of course, but they were heavily outnumbered.

There was also, to borrow a term from Siegfried Sassoon, 'Loderism' which he coined in celebration of his friend Norman Loder[137] (Dennis Milden in *The Memoirs of a Fox-Hunting Man*). At late Victorian Eton Loder 'did little but hunt with the beagles'.[138] After Cambridge, where he did not get a degree, he 'spent most of his life on the hunting field as master of various packs'.[139] And on his death in 1940 he was described as 'the perfect knight of the saddle, a gallant English gentleman'.[140] Loder, 'the very picture of an English sporting gentleman',[141] represented for Sassoon a way of life of the county set that was 'healthy, decent but animal and philistine'.[142]

There was also 'Socratism' preached *and* practised by a small number of masters and their protégé pupils. They were opposed to the tyranny of games, rejected its associated 'manliness and all its works'[143] and in slightly 'furtive subcultures' (they would have needed to be at least on the part of pupils)[144] they 'proclaimed the importance of "love, truth and beauty"'.[145]

Socratism, very much a minority movement, is not the concern here. It has been interestingly discussed elsewhere,[146] but its existence should be noted in order to provide depth and breadth to Victorian masculinity at Eton and Cambridge, and elsewhere.

CONCLUSION

Thomas Arnold at Rugby stressed Christian manliness as a means of improving English gentlemen. Arnold was concerned that 'the sturdy rough and tumble manliness of the games field and the poaching expeditions could easily lend itself to the lawless tyranny of physical strength'.[147] For Arnold, therefore, games were 'subordinate to moral and religio-political goals',[148] whilst field sports, because of their privileged associations and connotations and heartless brutality were to be proscribed. Arnold advocated the shortest route possible from boyhood to manhood by way of a moral maturity achieved by acquiring the compassion of Christ.

Shortly after Arnold's death, other headmasters, in contrast, asserted that muscular manliness was to be admired and encouraged. However, while increasingly this came to be demonstrated on the games field, Eton and Cambridge, in particular, remained true to field sports in the belief that they still made the man. This conservatism is illustrated in part by Beagle Club social and dining evenings, where behaviour often descended into accepted mayhem, in imitation of the robust hunting behaviour of their elders.

Horace Hutchinson wrote of his experiences at Eton in the first half of the nineteenth century that 'the education of future sportsmen begins with the first stone thrown from childish fingers at a confiding sparrow, and is continued with the use of that series of boyish missile weapons which leads up to the adult dignity of the gun'.[149] He concluded that, as boys, 'we never had a moment's doubt as to our ambition: the killing, skinning and stuffing, or the capturing, caging and taming of every wild thing that came our way'.[150] By the second half of the nineteenth century this was only half the story, or less than half the story. The making of élite masculinity had moved for many, but not for all, from the hunting field to the playing field. Two popular public school and university masculinities of 'Bloodism' and 'Loderism' (one more popular, one less popular) now existed side by side, sometimes in co-operation and sometimes in confrontation. One has attracted quite considerable attention; the other should not be overlooked – hence this chapter. *Both* jointly helped create an imperial ethnocentric sense of a superior English masculinity summed up perfectly by one historian of the hunting field:

> Lord Granby was in many respects the type of Englishman formed
> by our school life and our sports; and if the type is commoner now,

as it undoubtedly is, than was the case in the eighteenth century, that is one of the results of the ideals in school life and in sport being to raise all training, mental and bodily, to the level of the higher classes, rather than to bring down the higher to the level of the lower. Every Englishman, as Mr Rudyard Kipling has told us in verse and prose, is an aristocrat when among an inferior race; and from the rare insight Kipling has into the many-sided character of our national life, that great genius has risen to be the laureate of England, and the English as formed by the hunting field, the cricket pitch, and the football ground.[151]

NOTES

1. The term field sports is used here as a generic term for the killing of game under the Game Laws, and other birds and wild life, such as vermin, which were not included in these laws. For a discussion of game laws as social conflict in England see H. Hopkins, *The Long Affray* (London, 1985), and H.L. Knight, 'The Game Laws in the Nineteenth Century, With Reference to Reform' (Ph.D. thesis, University of Missouri, 1945).

2. Witness the current furore over foxhunting in response to Tony Blair's pledge to abolish it (July 1999), which in part is heir to this tradition.

3. A. Clark, 'When We Middle-Aged Fogeys Were Boys', *Baily's Magazine*, 33 (Jan.–June 1879), 147–8.

4. Ibid.

5. Ibid.

6. Felix (pseudonym), 'How to Become a Good Big Game Shot', *Baily's Magazine*, 86 (July–Dec. 1906), 273–4.

7. H.J. Torre, 'Harrow Notebook 1832–1837' (HSA). For a further description of 'toozling' see *Harrow Association Record* (1907–12), p.29. See also J.A. Mangan, *Athleticism in the Victorian and Edwardian Public School: The Emergence and Consolidation of an Educational Ideology* (Cambridge, 1981), pp.18–21, 273. *Athleticism* has been reprinted by Frank Cass with a new introduction by the author and additional introductions by the distinguished cultural historians Jeffrey Richards and Sheldon Rothblatt.

8. Bird-nesting seems to have preoccupied many an 'errant scholar' at certain schools. E.P. Rawnsley of Uppingham noted with some regret bird-nesting had become unfashionable amongst boys by the early twentieth century, in W.R. Rawnsley, *Highways and Byways in Lincolnshire* (1922), pp.86–7. See also 'Schoolboys as they were', *Blackwoods Magazine*, 159 (Jan. 1896), 606–12.

9. Mrs Charles Kingsley (ed.), *Charles Kingsley: Letters and Memories of His Life*, Vol.2 (London, 1877), pp.163–4.

10. A.C. Bradley, *A History of Marlborough College* (1893), pp.106, 126. See also Mangan, *Athleticism*, pp.18–21.

11. A. Burns (ed.), *A Victorian Schoolboy: Tom Brown's Schooldays, from the Letters of Thomas Harris Burns, 1841–1852*, quoted in J. Chandos, *Boys Together: English Public Schools, 1800–1864* (Oxford, 1984), p.150. See also Mangan, *Athleticism*, pp.18–21.

12. C.J. Apperley, *The Life of a Sportsman* (London, 1905), pp.76–7. See also Gerald Lascelles, *Baily's Magazine*, 83 (Jan.–June 1905), 421.

13. Chandos, *Boys Together*, pp.149–50, 341–2.

14. Letter by A. Turner in A.C. Crossley, *A History of the Eton College Hunt* (Eton, 1922), p.10.

15. Sir John D. Astley, *Fifty Years of My Life*, Vol.1 (London, 1894), p.13.

16. R. Kipling, *Land and Sea Tales for Scouts and Guides* (London, 1923), pp.162, 269, 270.

17. T. Card, *Eton Reviewed: A History from 1860 to the Present Day* (London, 1994), p.50.
18. G. Himmelfarb, *Victorian Minds* (London, 1968), p.2802.
19. C.L.R. James, *Beyond a Boundary* (London, 1969), p.164.
20. A.P. Stanley, *The Life of Thomas Arnold* (1844, 1910), p.60; see also J. Gathorn-Hardy, *The Public School Phenomenon* (London, 1977).
21. A. Whitridge, *Dr Arnold of Rugby* (London, 1928), p.133.
22. T. Arnold, *Miscellaneous Works* (London, 1845), letter 6, pp.1967.
23. A.P. Stanley, *The Life and Correspondence of Thomas Arnold* (London, 1901), p.554, and Arnold, *Misc.*, letter 2, p.176.
24. H. Perkin, *Origins of Modern English Society* (London), p.298.
25. L. Gautier, *Chivalry* (London, 1959), pp.9–31. See also, J. Strutt, *The Sports and Pastimes of the People of England* (London, 1801), reprinted (ed. J.C. Cox) (London, 1901), p.4.
26. T.W. Bamford, *Thomas Arnold* (London, 1960), p.159.
27. J. Gathorn-Hardy, *Public School*, pp.72–3.
28. N. Wymer, *Dr Arnold of Rugby* (London, 1953), p.119.
29. F.G. Aflalo, 'The Infinite Variety of Sports', *Baily's Magazine*, 94 (July–Dec. 1910), pp.28–9.
30. Letter from C. Vaughan to L.A. Tollemache, quoted in L.A. Tollemache, *Old and Odd Memories* (London, 1908), pp.126–7.
31. A.W. Merivale, *Family Memorials* (London, 1884), p.330.
32. T. Bamford, 'Public Schools and Social Class, 1800–1850', *British Journal of Sociology*, 12, 3 (1961), 225.
33. F. Dunning and K. Sheard, *Barbarians, Gentlemen and Players* (Oxford, 1979), p.77.
34. See Mangan, *Athleticism*, Chs.3, 4.
35. Ibid.
36. Ibid.
37. Lord Berners, *A Distant Project* (London, 1964), p.23.
38. D. Newsome, *Godliness and Good Learning* (London, 1961), p.197.
39. See E. Grayson, *Corinthian Casuals and Cricketers* (London, 1983).
40. See C. Ellis, *C.B: the Life of Charles Burgess Fry* (London, 1984).
41. See H. Perkin, *The Origins of Modern English Society* (London, 1969), p.269.
42. E.P. Thompson, *The Making of the English Working Class* (London, 1963), p.218.
43. E. L. Jones, 'Industrial Capital and Land Investment: The Arkwrights in Herefordshire', in E.L. Jones and G. Mingay (eds.), *Land, Labour and Population in the Industrial Revolution* (London, 1967), p.51.
44. D. Rapp, *Economic History Review*, 2nd Series 27 (1974), p.380.
45. C. Shrimpton, *The Landed Society of Essex in the Late Eighteenth Century* (London, 1977), p.1.
46. F.M.L. Thompson, *The Rise of Respectable Society, 1830–1900* (London, 1988), p.270.
47. *Sporting Magazine*, 132 (Nov. 1858), 317.
48. Anthony Trollope, *British Sports and Pastimes* (London, 1867), 75.
49. 'The Game Laws', *Saturday Review*, 31, 2 (April 1871), 481.
50. C. Milnes-Gaskell, 'The Country Gentleman', *Nineteenth Century*, 10 (Sept. 1882), 460–3.
51. *The Times*, 10 Oct. 1865, 10.
52. See R. Jeffries, *The Gamekeeper at Home* (London, 1878), p.45. Also R. Jeffries, 'Defence of Sport', *Baily's Magazine*, April–Oct. (1885), 323 and P.A. Graham, *The Revival of English Agriculture* (London, 1899), p.94.
53. Quoted in B. Martin, *The Great Shoots* (London, 1988), p.19.
54. Dunning and Sheard, *Barbarians, Gentlemen and Players*, p.306.
55. See J.R. de Honey, 'The Victorian Public School 1828–1902' (D.Phil. thesis, Oxford, 1969), pp.20–1.
56. Bamford, *Journal*, p.225.
57. Remaines of J. Aubrey, 1688, quoted in H. Salt, *Memories of Bygone Eton* (London, n.d.), pp.241–6.
58. A.C. Crossley, *The History of the Eton College Hare Hunt* (published privately, 1922), p.2.
59. Oppidan Hunt. The term Oppidan referred to 'non-scholars', who were not King's Scholars, usually residing in the town with a landlady (College Archivist).

60. 'The Diaries of Edward Charrington', in Crossley, ch.1.
61. Both positions were highly prestigious and indicated institutional success, popularity and status. Valentine Lawless, later the fourth Lord Cloncurry, was at Eton from 1850 to 1858. He rowed in the VIII in 1857 and 1858 and also played in the Oppidan Wall Game and Field Games teams in 1857. He was elected to Pop (the Eton Society) in 1856. Eyre William Hussey was at Eton from 1853 to 1858. He rowed in the VIII in 1857 and 1858. Thanks are extended to Mr P. Hatfield, College Archivist, Eton College for this information.
62. Dr Charles Old Goodford (1812–1884), Headmaster 1853–1862, Provost 1862–1884.
63. Clarendon Commission, *Report of Her Majesty's Commissioner, Appointed to Enquire into the Reserves and Management of Certain Colleges and Schools and the Studies Perused Therein with an Appendix and Evidence*, 1864.
64. Dr Edward Balston (1817–91). He was educated Eton, then went to King's College, Cambridge, where he was a Fellow from 1839 to 1850. He was an Assistant Master at Eton from 1840–60, Fellow 1860–62, Headmaster 1862–68 and Vicar of Bakewell, Derbyshire 1869–91.
65. A. Clark (The Gentleman in Black, pseudonym), 'School Life: its Sports and Pastimes', *Baily's Magazine*, 2 (Oct.–April 1861), 370–1.
66. J. Carleton, *The Young Sportsman's Manual* (London, 1867), pp.51–2. See also 'Modern Sport', *Baily's Magazine*, 28 (Dec.–June 1875–6), 274–81.
67. *The Eton College Chronicle*, 24, 28 Jan. 1864), 60.
68. *Eton College Hunt Diaries*, Vol.2, 1863–73.
69. G.W. Cornish (ed.), *Extracts from the Letters and Journal of William Cory* (Oxford, 1897), pp.59–60.
70. E.C. Mack, *Public Schools and British Opinion since 1860* (New York, 1941), pp.24–5.
71. Collegers was the term for 'King's Scholars' who resided at the College itself.
72. *Eton College Hunt Diaries*, Vol.2, 1863–73.
73. As will be shown, many Etonians took these skills on to Cambridge. See F. Kempson, *The Trinity College Beagles* (London, 1913).
74. *The Eton College Chronicle*, 32 (May 1863), 4.
75. *The Eton College Chronicle*, 55 (April 1866), 217.
76. *The Field*, 26 Aug. 1865), 131. See also P. Self and H.J. Storing, *The State and the Farmer* (London, 1962), p.37; J.A. Scott-Watson and M.E. Hobbs, *Great Farmers* (London, 1937), p.111.
77. *The Eton College Chronicle*, 55, 26 April 1866, 217.
78. *Eton College Hunt Diaries*, Vol.4 (1888–9), p.21.
79. See Mangan, *Athleticism*, p.106.
80. Crossley, *Hunt*, p.24.
81. L. Ford, *Essays in Secondary Education* (London, 1898), p.289, quoted in Mangan, *Athleticism*, p.68.
82. At this time Spartan qualities were more highly valued than Athenian values in the public schools.
83. Crossley, *Hunt*, p.14. The 'Saying Lesson' involved constant oral repetition of a text or task.
84. Letter by A. Turner in Crossley, *Hunt*, p.8. A.J. Pound was a King's Scholar 1859–1867. Later he went on to Exeter College, Oxford. After working as a lawyer, he became Stipendiary Magistrate in British Guiana, 1867–77. (This information from Mrs P. Hatfield, Archivist, Eton College).
85. See Mangan, *Athleticism*, for a wider treatment of this notion.
86. 'George Osbaldestone', *Baily's Magazine*, 2 (Oct.–April 1860–1), 295.
87. See C.R.L. Fletcher, *Edward Warre* (London, 1922), pp.64–5.
88. Ibid.
89. Quoted in E. Warre, in *Boy's Own Paper*, 17 Sept. 1898), 10.
90. William Edward Currey, MA, Master of Magdalene, 1862–5.
91. W. Rouse-Ball, Assistant Master of Trinity College, Cambridge, 1859–63.
92. 'Diary of the Journey of Philip Julius, through England, 1602', in G. von Bulow and W. Powell (eds.), *Transactions of the Royal Historical Society*, n.s., vi (1892), p.35.
93. H. Gunning, *Reminiscences of the University Town and County of Cambridge from the year 1780* (Cambridge, 1854), pp.40–2.

94. Francis Coventry, *The History of Pompey the Little* (Cambridge, 1978 edition), pp.179–9.
95. See *Sketches of Cantabs* (Cambridge, 1849); A.C. Croome, *Fifty Years of Sport at Schools and Universities* (Oxford, 1913), pp.174–86.
96. See *Sporting Magazine*, 63 (Dec. 1823), 110.
97. E.D. Cumming (ed.), *Squire Osbaldestone: His Autobiography* (London, 1927), p.10 and R. Onslow, *The Squire* (London, 1980).
98. 'Captain John White', *Baily's Magazine*, 4 (Dec.–June 1862), 271.
99. 'Lays of Modern Oxford', Sports and Pastimes at the Universities, *Baily's Magazine*, 53 (Jan.–June), 364–5.
100. Quoted in L. Edwards, *Famous Foxhunters* (London, 1932), p.77.
101. Letter from F.W.M. Cornwallis to F. Kempson in *Trinity Foot Beagles*, p.36. And see, 'Oxford and Cambridge Sports Histories', *Baily's Magazine*, 89 (Jan.–June 1908), 101–11.
102. Cambridge University Archives, Magdalene College, C/SAD/1, no iii, letter from Richard Neville, 5 Dec. 1910.
103. Henry J. Haines, Letter to *Baily's Magazine*, quoted in Kempson, *Trinity Foot Beagles*, p.102.
104. 'J.W. Larnach', *Baily's Magazine*, 75 (Jan.–June 1901), 398–9. Of course, it was not uncommon for even the highly intelligent to leave the ancient universities without a degree. Evelyn Waugh, John Betjeman, Alan Pryce-Jones and Roger Hollis all left Oxford without degrees as late as the 1920s. See W.J. West *The Truth About Hollis* (London, 1989), p.15.
105. R. Hyam, *A History of Magdalene College* (Cambridge, 1992), p.201.
106. W. Everett, *On the Cam: Lectures on the University of Cambridge* (London, 1866), pp.18, 151.
107. Latimer Neville, Rev., 6th Baron Braybrooke (1827–1904). He was educated at Eton and Magdalene. Fellow of Magdalene 1849, Vice Chancellor of Oxford University 1859–1861, Rector of Heydon, Herts, 1851–1902, Rural Dean of Saffron Walden 1879–1897. In 1902 he succeeded to the title of 6th Lord Braybrooke.
108. 'The Appanage of Audley End', *Spectator*, 23 Jan. 1904, 1201.
109. A. Briggs, *Victorian People* (London, 1965), p.152.
110. See W.B. Gallie, *An English Public School* (London, 1949).
111. See Mangan, *Athleticism*, p.142.
112. S. Sproston, *College Magazine*, Cambridge, 3, 4 (1910), 65–9,108–10.
113. A. Edgecumbe, 'Magdalene College, Cambridge: A Retrospect' (unpublished ms, Magdalene College, Old Library), 2.
114. Ibid., p.3.
115. Kempson, *Trinity Foot Beagles*, pp.172–3.
116. Crossley, *Hunt*, Ch.2.
117. Little-go. This was the preliminary examination taken by all undergraduates.
118. Rowland Hunt was a supreme example of the highly regarded all-round athlete. See Kempson, *Trinity Foot Beagles*, pp.104–5 and 'Rowland Hunt', *Baily's Magazine*, 59 (Jan.–June 1893), 145.
119. 'Magdalene in the sixties', *Magdalene College Magazine* (March 1910), 106.
120. Ibid.
121. Letter to Mrs Scott, in Mrs Charles Kingsley, ed. *Charles Kingsley, Letters and Memories* Vol.2 (London, 1877), p.198.
122. O. Chadwick, 'Kingsley at Cambridge', *Historical Journal*, 18 (1975), 305–6.
123. Charles Kingsley, *Glaucus: or the Wonders of the Shore* (London, 1855), p.43.
124. J. Edgcumbe, 'Magdalene College, a Retrospect'. See also, D. Newsome, *On the Edge of Paradise, A.C. Benson the Diarist* (London, 1980), pp.184–5.
125. See J.A. Mangan, 'Coubertin and Cotton: European Realism and Idealism in the Making of Modern Masculinity', Proceedings of the First Conference of the European Society for Sports History (Rome, 1996), *passim*.
126. R. Holt, *Sport and the British: A Modern History* (Oxford, 1993), p.364. For a fuller and more subtle discussion of 'fair play', see J.A. Mangan, 'The Nordic World and Other Worlds', in Henrik Meinander and J.A. Mangan, *The Nordic World: Sport in Society* (London, 1997), pp.180–3.
127. 'John Poyntz Spencer', *Baily's Magazine* (Dec.–June 1862), 273.
128. 'H. Wentworth-Fitzwilliam', *Baily's Magazine*, 489 (1888), 231.

129. 'The Duke of Bedford', *Baily's Magazine*, 1 (1860), 51.
130. Newsome, *Godliness*, pp.224–5.
131. For one example of many, see *Eton Chronicle*, 27 Sept. 1864.
132. See, for example, *The Journal Book* (1867).
133. J. Brinsley-Richards, *Seven Years at Eton (1857–1864)* (London, 1883), pp.90–1.
134. See, for example, Eton College Hunt, 1–4, *Diaries*, 1899–1906, p.83.
135. For a good part of the nineteenth century King's College was the Cambridge College for Etonians, while 'the Ancient Universities' in the words of Noel Annan were 'little more than finishing schools for public schoolboys', see Mangan, *Athleticism*, p.122.
136. Christopher Hibbert, *No Ordinary Place: Radley College and the Public School System, 1847–1997* (London, 1998), p.195.
137. Jean Moorcroft Wilson, *Siegfried Sassoon, The Making of a War Poet* (London, 1995), pp.111–12.
138. Ibid., p.111.
139. Ibid., p.112.
140. Ibid., p.111.
141. Ibid.
142. Ibid., p.112.
143. Clive Dewey, 'Socratic Teachers: Part 1 – The Opposition to the Cult of Athleticism at Eton 1870–1914', *International Journal of the History of Sport*, 12, 1 (April 1995), 51.
144. Ibid.
145. Ibid.
146. Ibid. See also Part II, *IJHS*, 12, 3 (1995), 18–47.
147. Dunning and Sheard, *Barbarians, Gentlemen and Players*, p.78.
148. N. Vance, 'The Ideal of Manliness', in B. Simon and I. Bradley (eds.), *The Victorian Public School* (Dublin, 1975), pp.1–7.
149. H. Hutchinson, 'The Sportsman at School', *Badminton Library*, 1 (Aug.–Dec. 1895), 614.
150. Ibid., 629.
151. T.F. Dale, *The History of the Belvoir Hunt* (London, 1899), p.40.

The Masculine Road through Modernity: Ling Gymnastics and Male Socialisation in Nineteenth-Century Sweden

JENS LJUNGGREN

Nowadays one easily overlooks the historical impact of Ling gymnastics. It was created at the beginning of the nineteenth century by Per Henrik Ling (1776–1839). Throughout the nineteenth century and for nearly half of the twentieth it was the predominant form of physical education in the Swedish school system. Internationally it competed successfully with both English sports and German *Turnen*. It had an important role in spreading and consolidating conceptions of gender and body, not only in Sweden but globally. A major attraction was the fact that in contrast to English sport Ling gymnastics was never competitive. It took the form of exercises and its pedagogic aim was to develop the body harmoniously.[1]

What was the ideological role of Ling gymnastics? How can its popularity and wide impact be understood? In this chapter, it is suggested that Ling gymnastics was an attempt to find solutions to the certain difficulties and problems in nineteenth-century society. These can be summarised in two words: manliness and modernity. They were, as will now be made clear, intimately interwoven.

Modernity is a difficult concept. Many scholars have tried to capture the essence of modern society. With the help of theorists like Ferdinand Tönnies, Emile Durkheim and Max Weber it is possible to list certain characteristic values of traditional and modern society. Traditional society is often pictured as a community that brings people together organically. The basic values are religious, and the people believe in a higher form of spirit. Modern society is, in contrast, flexible. Human relations are often formal. Specialisation reigns in working life. The world view is materialistic and practical conduct in life is utilitarian. The demands of rationality also influence the conception of the human body in a way that furthers bodily restraint and discipline.[2] It can be debated how well this picture mirrors reality. Most important in this context is, however, that these views on the modern and the traditional were important to the people of the nineteenth century.

The main argument of this chapter is that Ling gymnastics evolved as an attempt to resolve some of the masculine problems with modernity. This it did by presenting a kind of masculinity that was a synthesis of traditional and modern. Ling gymnastics was designed to resolve a complex of problems in the first half of the nineteenth century. At the end of the century Ling gymnastics became heavily criticised. This can be explained by the process of modernisation, and changes in the gender order.

MODERNITY AND MASCULINITY

In nineteenth-century Swedish society it was the man who represented modernity. It was first and foremost men who succeeded in linking their character with rationality, physical self-restraint and control of instincts. Women on the other hand were, to a greater extent, associated with nature. Personality traits such as emotional instability, exaggerated sensitivity, lack of rational and logical thinking were part of a general pattern attributed to female temperament and distinctive nature. But modernity as a normative system also had another side, that was considerably more problematic for masculinity. Deeply embedded in society's iron-clad bureaucratic, economic and political system, the citizen of the nineteenth century had difficulty, in his role as a worker and family man, in identifying himself as a warrior and in showing aggression. Moreover, as a wage-earner he was unable to win masculine esteem from being an independent owner of private property. At the end of the century yet another threat emerged – the feminist movement.[3] Ling gymnastics presented itself as a solution to these challenges.

An important source of inspiration for Per Henrik Ling at the beginning of the nineteenth century was the contemporary celebration of the ancient Nordic past, the so-called 'gothianism'. This in itself was not a novelty of the nineteenth century. Already during the seventeenth century gothianism flourished in celebration of Sweden as a great power. The gothianism of the nineteenth century, however, was different. Negative aspects were considerably stronger. Swedish nationalists mourned a Sweden that was no longer the same powerful nation it once had been. This kind of nationalistic lamentation was sometimes connected to a powerful critique of civilisation. Supporters of gothianism argued that the negative consequences of civilisation – such as vanity, luxury, effeminacy, selfishness, superficiality – threatened to destroy the nation and to dissolve its distinctiveness.[4]

A search for a national identity and national culture arose incorporating the use of an obviously sexual coded language, with stereotyped sexual images that were virtually synonymous, not only with national strength, but with Swedish national identity. Masculinity in terms of its status was strengthened when it acquired both national and social meaning. With contemporary celebration of the ancient Nordic past (gothianism), Nordic masculine strength and force, best symbolised by Viking forefathers, was contrasted with southern Europe's somewhat more over-refined and overly civilised effeminacy with its aristocratic opulence and parlour culture. Criticism of vanity, luxury and over-abundance stimulated class criticism. To a great extent, the Viking symbolised the attempt of an emerging middle class to distance itself from the cultural values of the aristocracy and upper class. The middle class considered itself on a par with Rousseau's noble savage: genuine, strong and honest. In contrast to the aristocrat, middle-class man considered himself transparent, without hypocrisy or a false façade. Above all, he was manly, quite unlike the exaggeratedly elegant, semi-effeminate aristocrat.[5]

In terms of this imagery, it was manliness, on the lines of the rugged Viking that was associated with nature, not femininity. Man was thus not only perceived as master of nature, but also as nature. To accommodate this view, nature now was not thought of as something negative, but as something loaded with positive values, such as strength, virility, vitality, honesty, and transparency.

Per Henrik Ling himself longed for the masculine powers of the forefathers he believed were lost in contemporary society. In poetry he saw a force that could reawaken the ancient masculine traits of the Swedish people.[6] In the poem *Gylfe*, which led to his recognition as a poet, he portrayed the current problem of the nation as a question of masculinity. This he did by means of allegory. At the beginning of the story is Gylfe (Sweden), depressed and down-hearted after the loss of his beloved Aura (Finland). (Sweden had recently lost Finland in the wars of 1809). He even weeps. Lost in an unmanly incapacity to act, he is unable to reconquer his 'Woman'. At the end of the poem, the story is

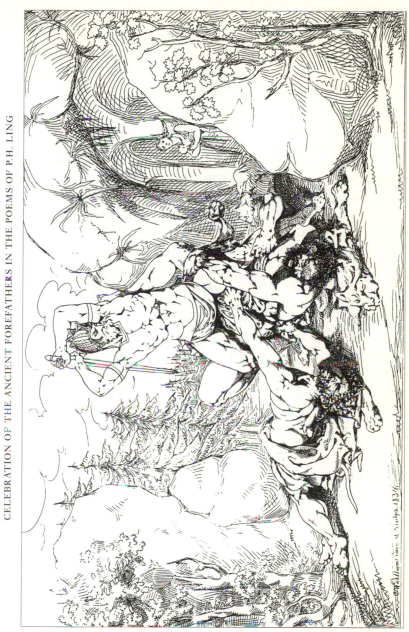

FIGURE 1

CELEBRATION OF THE ANCIENT FOREFATHERS IN THE POEMS OF P.H. LING

told in a more hopeful way. Gylfe and his warriors inspire each other to develop a fresh masculine fighting spirit.[7] (See Figure 1.)

The purpose of gymnastics, according to Ling, was like that of poetry – to regain the forces of the ancient Viking forefathers.[8] However, the Viking was not an unproblematic male prototype in modern bourgeois society. He was, as contemporary observers already perceived, much too savage to bear the responsibility constitutional freedom demanded.[9] This meant that between the concept of natural man and civilised man a difficult contradiction presented itself. The assertion here is that Ling's gymnastics was a way of settling this problem. C.F. GutsMuths, his German colleague and source of inspiration, had asked the following question. How can one recreate the physical strength and noble character of a savage within the framework of bourgeois society, without reverting to savagery? His answer was gymnastics.[10] Ling, too, it is argued here, found in physical education a way of resolving the conflict. Gymnastics would combine the military virtues of forefathers with the qualities of self-restraint and control of the modern citizen. The primitive masculine strength of the Viking forefathers was to be reconstructed in modern society as obedience and discipline. Gymnastics gave Ling the necessary tool to unite the two polarities and create the 'controlled Viking': strong and robust and yet acceptable as a citizen of modern society.[11] The successors of Ling at the Gymnastiska centralinstitutet (GCI),[12] the school for gymnastic teachers that Ling created, were preoccupied with this problem.[13] Ling and his followers formulated ideas that came close to what the historian George L. Mosse has called the 'national stereotype', that is, a symbol for masculinity which, by simultaneously expressing virility and resistance to primal instincts, became at the time in a number of countries an effective model for desirable civic virtues as well as national strength.[14]

Towards the middle of the century the problems of masculinity became associated with the development of the Swedish school system. In the school personal virtues such as industriousness, foresight, high performance and individual responsibility were expected. The restrained bourgeois masculine ideal was fundamental in the elementary schools where the pupils had to learn a rational life-style.[15] But such consolidation of bourgeois masculine traits also highlights a masculine crisis of the nineteenth century. Many saw in this development a threat to various traditional masculine values. There was a lively discussion about intellectual over-indulgence and physical weakness in the secondary school. Gymnastics was believed to be a method of counterbalancing the negative influences. In other words, with more gymnastics, masculinity could be saved.[16]

To summarise, the modern problems of Swedish masculinity were clearly expressed in the discussion about pedagogic gymnastics. The values of rationality that were associated with modernity were one the one hand used to legitimise the superiority of male over female, and on the other the same values could also be perceived as a threat to traditional aspects of masculinity. Gymnastics was presented as a solution to the contradiction by allowing the male to be both powerful, with a touch of historic primitivism, and restrained according to the norms of conduct of modern bourgeois society.

MASCULINITY AND SPIRITUALITY

One aspect has been far too little considered in recent historical research on masculinity. The construction of masculinity and the problems of masculinity in modernity were also connected to that aspect of modern life which Max Weber called 'Entzauberung', or dissolution of spiritual values. Philosophical idealism played an important part in the formulation of masculinity in Ling gymnastics. With regard to this aspect one cannot speak of a manifest problem before the end of the nineteenth century. During the first half of that century the spirituality of male physical education was treated as something which simply must be included in any proper upbringing. In this sense Ling gymnastics constituted a masculine synthesis. During the second half of the century the earlier idealism was challenged, with consequences for the ideals of both masculinity and femininity in Ling gymnastics.

Male socialisation in Ling gymnastics cannot properly be understood if the contemporary currencies of philosophical idealism are overlooked. It is not easy to trace precisely the ideological sources of inspiration of Per Henrik Ling. A most important influence on him, however, was the natural philosophy of F.W.J. Schelling. Even though it is possible to trace other influences, Schelling's natural philosophy is the most important one. Like Schelling, Ling was of the view that existence was constructed as a power play between opposite forces. The two fundamental ones he identified were the spiritual force and the material force. Character and form of all phenomena in the world were decided by the relationship between these two forces. The tension between them manifested itself in what Ling called the three 'basic forms' (*grundformer*): the chemical, the mechanical and the dynamic. The chemical and the mechanical forms expressed material force. The dynamic form represented the 'divine', the 'eternal'. Ling pictured the world in terms of analogies. In the human body the dynamic force corresponded to the brain and the nervous system, the mechanical force to the muscles, and the chemical to the heart, lungs, liver and the circulation of the blood.[17]

This way of thinking in analogies also had important consequences for the place of man in the world. Ling pictured the human being as a microcosm. The purpose of gymnastics was to enhance the balance in every individual, as well as between the individual and the macrocosms of the universe. According to natural philosophy, the essence of the universe was spiritual; and in the context of Ling gymnastics, this also meant that physical education had a spiritual purpose. To reach a balance as a man in the general order of the macrocosm was the same as bringing oneself nearer to a higher form of divinity.[18]

After Ling died, others took over at the GCI. During the nineteenth century it was the most important institution for supporting and spreading Ling gymnastics in Sweden. Ling's most significant successors at the GCI were Gabriel Branting, T.J. Hartelius, Gustaf Nyblaeus and Hjalmar Ling (son of Per Henrik). All were managers at different levels. In addition they were the most influential ideologists of Ling gymnastics at the time. They were all preoccupied with the moral and physical decadence that they thought characterised Sweden: exaggerated love of pleasure, weakness, sickness, self-indulgence. They saw these everywhere. They complained about the unhealthy urban environment where factory work endangered the health and strength of working people, and where the upper classes were threatened by intellectual excess and lack of fresh air.[19]

They thus saw several profound problems in modern society. Nevertheless, they firmly believed that the problems could be dealt with and that better times were soon to come. They were highly ambitious. With the help of physical education, not only would an improvement in people's physical health occur, but the development of the human being as such would be realised. They had a view of human evolution often expressed by contemporary philosophers and intellectuals, namely that in the ancient high cultures the development of man had reached its peak. Thereafter the development had tailed off, but now humanity was at the point of renewal A synthesis of ancient and modern was to be realised in the near future.[20] This belief characterised the advocates of Swedish Ling gymnastics. Benkt Söderberg has shown that Per Henrik Ling was posthumously portrayed as a hero, almost as a Jesus figure.[21] In the historical Ling, his successors, Hartelius, Branting and Nyblaeus, all saw a prophet of the resurrection of ancient cultural values. And they were ready to follow the light.[22]

By the middle of the nineteenth century, natural philosophy was out of fashion at the GCI. Nevertheless it had left its mark on the ideology of Ling gymnastics. The purpose of physical education was still to further man's development by training the body to ensure aesthetic and harmonious fulfilment according to the ideals of the ancient Greeks. The GCI authorities, mentioned above, all used the temple as a metaphor for the body. This is an ancient metaphor to be found in the texts of Plato as well as the Bible.[23] Through gymnastics, the nineteenth-century pedagogues at GCI wanted to form the harmonious body as a worthy temple of the spirit.[24] It is important to note that this ambition was associated with a distaste for specialisation, quantified physical performances and movements that were adapted to practical working life because they endangered the aesthetic and balanced development of the body.[25] It is for this reason that the supporters of Ling gymnastics subsequently became so hostile towards modern sports.

One of the interesting paradoxes of Ling gymnastics is that despite its great efforts to develop a higher spirituality in man, it was also rational. Rationality distinguished the way that gymnastic movements were systematised. The effect of every one of the movements had to be calculated very carefully in order to choose only the most efficient ones. The human body was analytically taken apart. The different parts were treated and exercised one by one. The same was true of the gymnasts. They were to be judged carefully one by one and graded in order of competence.[26] Ling gymnastics was in fact a 'system of discipline' in the terms of the French philosopher, Michel Foucault. In Ling's gymnastic system there was severe control, surveillance, order of precedence, strong attention to detail, scrupulous analytical treatment and so on.[27]

WAR AND PEACE

War and manliness were traditionally closely associated with one another, but with the modernisation of society the conception of war changed. Already in the first half of the eighteenth century the argument had been formulated that inner cultivation of the country ought to have priority over territorial expansion, war and honour. People from the middle class maintained that greater efforts towards furthering the inner economic development of the country was the most efficient way of strengthening the nation. By the mid-nineteenth century Sweden had experienced a long period of peace. Many liberals and representatives of the countryside argued for cutbacks in the defence budget. Some even believed in the possibility of eternal peace and permanent easing of international tension. But at the same time warfare developed in quite another direction. Wars now tended to be total and to involve all a nation's resources.[28]

The question of conscription was hotly debated in Sweden at the time. The problem was to find a means of both satisfying the interests of warfare and the peaceful economic development of the country. By letting schoolboys practise gymnastics and military exercise, influential politicians thought that it was possible to bring the boys up to be men who were at the same time responsible citizens and effective soldiers – a masculine synthesis to be furthered through gymnastics. In 1866 the well-known military leader and politician, J.A. Hazelius, wrote that by using physical education and a system of common conscription it would be possible to bring 'the warrior' closer to the 'heart of the citizen'.[29] The parliamentarian A. Adlersparre, however, argued that Swedes did not want to become an aggressive people who threatened their neighbours, but 'a militaristic people that no hostile power dared to lay hands on'. The answer, it was thought, lay in Ling gymnastics.[30]

Idealistic influences at the GCI further complicated the relation between war, peace and masculinity. The martial element in gymnastics was always present, but there was much more to it than that. As mentioned earlier, Ling strove for an inner harmony in the human being. This inner harmony was paralleled by balance between man and nature. These two aspects of human balance and harmony with nature were different sides of the same coin. Ling also preached peaceful relationships between human beings and nations.[31] There was a message of peace in Ling gymnastics. The manliness to be developed was therefore not only a question of martial values such as courage, endurance and strength, but also of qualities such as love, compassion and friendliness.[32] Once again a new masculine synthesis was sought. The values of masculinity covered both war and peace. The ultimate ambition was Ling gymnastics as a form of moral fusion. This kind of masculine synthesis maintained its grip on the leading pedagogues at the GCI long after the ideology of natural philosophy had disappeared. The peace message of P.H. Ling was no longer explicit, but the harmoniously developed male body did indeed continue to function as a symbol of a masculinity that combined intellect with strength and martial skills with civic virtues.[33]

Ling gymnastics thus presented a concept of masculinity that was in fact a synthesis of the traditional and the modern. The kind of man to be recreated through gymnastics possessed some of the vigorous power and male bonding of the forefathers. In this sense gymnastic manliness had its roots in an era that preceded modern civilisation. Manliness also expressed traditional values in yet another sense. One of the characteristics of Ling's ideal man was his higher form of spirituality. At the same time, however, there were modern citizen values in this form of masculine training: discipline, temperance, self-control, rationality. Ling gymnastics thus promised to anchor manliness in a wide spectrum of values. The ideal man was primitive and civilised, spiritual and rational, intellectually and physically strong, prepared for war but working for peace.

THE PLACE OF WOMEN

Ling gymnastics was also directed towards women. Ling gymnastics also meant taking part in the gender order of the nineteenth century. The early Ling gymnasts at the GCI did not write much about women's gymnastics. They felt that women, too, could benefit from gymnastics, but in a different way to men. Above all women's duties as mothers were underlined. The aim of gymnastics was to allow women to become better at taking care of their sons and to bring them up to be 'real' men. The advocates of physical education saw a threat to masculinity in the home. This environment was dangerous, since parents were considered to be too ignorant to rear their children in a correct and rational manner. There was a constant fear of the emasculating impact of the luxury, comfort and indulgence of the upper class. The mother occasioned particular concern. The ideal mother of the era, warm and loving, as gymnastic enthusiasts perceived the situation, was not an ideal woman. If she was allowed, at her own discretion, to lavish too much care and warmth on her sons, she threatened to smother their natural male instincts.[34]

It was Hjalmar, Ling's son, who developed female gymnastics. In contrast to his colleagues, Hjalmar Ling wanted to develop gymnastics with a theoretical base of materialism, not idealism. Yet his systematisation of gymnastic movements contained several ingredients of the earlier idealism. He still thought of truth and beauty as different sides of the same coin and that the main gymnastic purpose was to form the male body harmoniously.[35]

This meant that the gymnastics of Hjalmar Ling was based on a unisex model, as understood by the American historian Thomas Laqueur.[36] The norm was the harmoniously developed male body. It was towards this standard that the other and, according to Hjalmar, less developed sex had to strive. The qualitative differences between male and female gymnastics were minor. Indeed, he argued that women were better adapted to graceful movements, whilst boys were better suited for wrestling and military exercises. But the differences were most of all formulated in quantitative terms – above all, that women were slower and weaker.[37] Another aspect of the unisex model present in the gymnastics of Hjalmar Ling was the instability of the borderline between the sexes. On occasions, he argued, women could actually surpass their own limits. With the help of moral virtues such as persistence, he thought that women were able to compensate for the inadequacy of physical strength. According to Hjalmar Ling, the strong working–class women as well as the women of ancient Sparta, where boys and girls had done the same kind of gymnastics, gave evidence that a dualistic view of both sexes was insufficient.[38] Apart from some aesthetic movements that were preserved for girls, Hjalmar Ling wanted boys and girls to do the same kind of gymnastic exercises. The difference was that the girls had to give up the most difficult ones. Another significant aspect of the unisex model can be seen in the drawings of Hjalmar Ling (see Figure 2). Here it is quite obvious that the differences between the sexes were more quantitative than qualitative. Women were generally pictured as smaller than men, but not particularly different in form and appearance.[39]

MANLINESS, WAR AND SPORT

By 1870 Ling gymnastics had reached its peak ideologically. It was thereafter confronted with growing criticism, and its particular concept of manliness became somewhat redundant. The kind of symbolic

FIGURE 2
THE UNISEX MODEL IN THE DRAWINGS OF HJALMAR LING

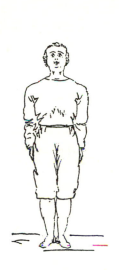
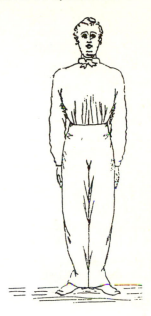

FIGURE 3

EXAMPLES OF THE MOVEMENTS IN LING GYMNASTICS FROM 1860

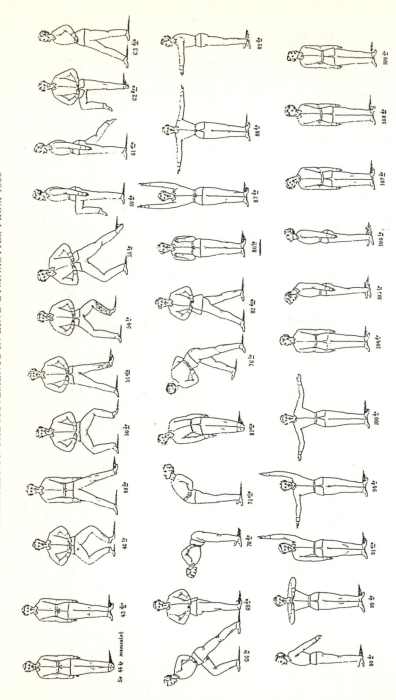

balance between modern and traditional that Ling gymnastics had expressed during the first half of the century became all the more fragile as the process of modernisation continued. As Henrik Meinander has shown, liberals began to propagate pedagogics that furthered individualism and self-assertion. In terms of physical education this meant sport, not gymnastics.[40]

In addition Social Darwinism created serious difficulties for Ling gymnastics. This it did in several ways. Ling gymnastics had once been created from a standpoint of philosophical idealism. Social Darwinism was a secular ideology, and it left no room for a supreme being. The notion of war was also different in the two ideologies. Based on the standpoint of the German philosopher Schelling, Ling viewed war as a necessary evil and a sign of man's inevitable lack of perfection, not a prerequisite for moral development. With Social Darwinism some gymnastic pedagogues began instead to conceive of war as a necessary precondition for moral development, by testing the male body. In this way developments in Sweden followed a path similar to that in England and America.[41] The ideal of manliness became more militaristic, which in turn made competitive sport more desirable. Only in competitive sports, it was believed, could sufficient masculine martial aggression be fostered.

The GCI pedagogues now confronted the issue of Social Darwinism. Truls Johan Hartelius, director of the medical department at GCI, interpreted Darwinism in a Christian, peaceful way that was common in contemporary Sweden. According to this interpretation evolution was not accidental. There was instead a divine hand guiding it. Hartelius also argued that when evolution had fully evolved the interaction between peoples and nations would be peaceful.[42]

Gustaf Nyblaeus, director of the military department of GCI, came to quite a different conclusion. It is clear that he was, like Hartelius, inspired by Christian idealism. But he interpreted the relation between Social Darwinism and Christianity in a different way. He finally arrived at the conclusion that the battles that had been fought in the history of mankind had been won by the most spiritually superior beings and that war could therefore be viewed as an act of Providence to lead the spiritual development of mankind towards higher ground. In the term 'duty', he saw man's ability to develop and perfect himself morally and physically. It was his opinion that physical education with an element of militarism promoted the ethic of duty. By demanding obedience, duty fulfilment and self-sacrifice for a noble cause, it was not only warlike training, but the action of war itself that was morally refining.[43]

In time, he became a rather controversial figure at the GCI. As an alternative to Ling gymnastics' carefully constructed and abstract forms of movement with emphasis on medical and physiological rationality, he introduced the 'natural method'. By this he meant gymnastics without the usual formalism, based instead on natural movements, such as, walking, running and jumping. Opposite to what he called the predominant artificiality, he emphasised terms such as humanity, active movements and practical application.[44]

Nyblaeus had an interesting perspective on war and the content of physical education. The element of 'sportification' should not be exaggerated but obvious pressures now existed to accept competitive sports. Gymnastic pedagogy entailed physiological formal exercise and practical application. He intended that a balance should exist between the two. But if there was any one part that would 'tip the scales' it should be the practical. In a way that challenged the followers of Ling gymnastics, he stated that 'Willpower and strength of character is glory of even greater worth than health and physical strength.' This was promoted best of all by 'well-led physical education and sports'. He praised sport in itself which, even in times of peace, made it possible to win male victories. He thought that the task of athletics was to counteract the self-indulgence that had overtaken the 'better-off classes' during the long period of peace. An obvious closeness between sport and war is illustrated in his phrase that 'the greatest and most extensive sport is war'.[45]

In his position as director of the military division of GCI, Nyblaeus entertained views that were to be developed with even greater emphasis by his successor, Viktor Balck. Without ever denying the excellence of Swedish gymnastics, he took additional steps in the direction of competitive sports. Like Nyblaeus, Balck liberated himself from medical science's warning against competitive athletics by following the English pedagogic model and concentrating on the influence of physical education on moral development and character training, rather than its physiological aspects and effects on body development. Inspired by Social Darwinism, he argued more clearly and extensively than his predecessor, that there was evident kinship between competitive sport and war.[46]

In 1876 Balck posed a question during his speech to the Stockholm Labour Association. 'Is war then a mere thorn that torments mankind, or is it at all possible to think that it perhaps, at some point in time, can bring with it something other than just misery?' Undeniably, a number of atrocities and a great deal of suffering were the traits of war, he argued, but sometimes it was necessary to fight in order to protect one's freedom and independence. However, Balck did not wish to maintain that war was only necessary now and then. War in itself also constituted quite positive characteristics: 'it awakens the people from apathy, it pulls one out from depravity, strengthens the laws of the country and reawakens the fear of God'. In addition, he maintained that suffering borne with manly calm increases one's longing to work and keeps insanity at a distance. Likewise he promoted competitive sport. 'Fighting is competing,' he declared.[47]

Balck not only separated himself from the most conservative followers of Ling gymnastics but also from Nyblaeus with reference to one other important point – the lack of belief in progress. His attitude was strangely defensive, despite his statements about fighting as a source of development. Both Ling and his followers had pictured their gymnastics as a part of a master plan in development. Pierre de Coubertin's ideology of the Olympic Games placed both international peace and continual human progress – *citius, altius, fortius* – on the horizon. Balck had done none of this. It is argued that as an athletics ideologist, he spoke from a strictly conservative standpoint. The thesis here is that, even if Balck firmly believed in the concepts of God and the nation, his idealism was weak and incomplete. A belief in divine progressive development, or mankind's gradual realisation of its intrinsic goal (*telos*) was absent. What he worked for was maintenance of the *status quo*. He wanted to maintain, at all costs, stability in society, but felt the ground tremble under his feet: war, class struggle and man's inner instincts threatened to surface and invert the inherited order. The turn of the century represented, as is well known, not only the belief in progress, but also cultural calamity. In this situation, the sporting ideal of manhood was allotted a compensatory role.

Balck did not equate competitive athletics with setting records nor with continual advancement of human limits of performance, but with its ability to promote patriotism, a sense of duty, the will to defend, reduce social conflicts and, in man himself, to ward off 'internal evil forces'. Athletics became the cure for all evils that threatened man and society: social unrest, sexual temptation, decadent entertainment, and so on. The task of athletics was to harden, a word that was not only used by

Balck but by many others in the world of athletics. If one made the body's skin and muscles hard and tense, and stable as iron, one should be able to cope with all the evil that threatened their existence and the dignity of mankind.[48] It is incidentally not a long step to the Nietzschean Superman – invulnerable, stoical, steel-muscled.[49]

The characteristic to be favoured was more self-control than dynamic performance, on or beyond the athletic field. It is maintained here that greater weight was put on self-reliance than running fast. This tendency is apparent in Balck's explicit definition of the manhood that athletics should favour:

> A man should be tall and slender and straight as a tree, with an arched breast and a strong and sturdy head, held high, wide shoulders, hard muscles and nerves of steel. He should own a warm heart and a strong will; he should be courageous and calm when in danger or in the face of calamity. At the same time, he should be ready to find paths of retreat in an emergency. He should own true courage never to diverge from the call of duty, even in the event of one's own demise. He should endure need as well as strain, pain through hunger and thirst but also cold and rain without complaint. Such men are needed even today. Such men should be moulded through work, struggle and athletics.[50]

The advantage of competitive sport, in comparison with gymnastics, was due to the fact that it alone had the power to prepare the individual for the modern world. The seamy side of modern times could not, as the advocates of Ling's gymnastics and medical practitioners thought, be reformed with moderate, proportionate and harmonious education, but must be fought with force. Only training in competitive athletics could produce enough resistant masculine strength for life's many battles.

Modern sport as well as modern industrial society became a problem for the supporters of Ling gymnastics, causing defensive reactions which brought the idealistic heritage to the surface. The body ideal which was established in Ling gymnastics seemed to be threatened, as was its ethical idealism. There were several similarities between the way that Ling gymnastics criticised modern sport and the way that many intellectuals criticised modern society. In modern sport and in modern society, the human being seemed to lose the urge to strive towards 'Bildung' and idealism; instead he was drawn into short-term egoistic individualism.[51]

SPORT AND GENDER

Gender studies have pointed out that around the end of the nineteenth century in Sweden there was a crisis in masculinity. Traditional norms, values and boundaries seemed to dissolve. Slowly women gained access to education and labour markets at the same time as they organised themselves and demanded the vote and liberation. This created a male identity crisis. The liberation of women was believed to threaten masculine virility, and cause all society to degenerate. As a response to this, the process of gender construction was intensified, and the 'natural' differences between men and women were legitimised in medicine, psychology, and biology of race. The desire to establish once and for all the 'true' essence of the two sexes was very strong.[52]

The development of sport at the time can be interpreted as an answer to this new crisis of masculinity. Ling gymnastics, developed in response to past problems associated with masculinity, had had its day. It was no longer the answer. Some scholars argued that in sport men were able to create room for themselves where they could act without female interference and where 'typical' masculine traits such as physical strength, speed and virility, and manly friendship and tenderness could be displayed. Above all, sport, like science, became an efficient way of demonstrating that men were physically, morally and biologically superior to women. In the sports arena it seemed obvious that men and women were created completely different beings.[53]

Nybleus and Balck argued for the importance of physical education in order to regenerate the lost masculine character in modern society. It was however not explicitly the liberation of women or their entry into public spheres of education, working life or politics that was thought to be threatening to masculinity. They indeed perceived several problems and difficulties in modern society, for example the long peace in Sweden that had weakened the people and working–class affinity with the nation. But neither of them mentioned feminism as a threat to society. Nevertheless, Balck and other directors at the GCI did oppose women's entry into sport.[54]

The balanced masculinity and the gymnastic unisex model of Ling gymnastics had functioned very well to establish a hierarchic relationship between the sexes during the middle of the nineteenth century. At the end of that century, due to a sense of masculine crisis, more distinctive markers were required. In this situation there was a part

FIGURE 4

AESTHETIC GYMNASTICS FOR MEN

FIGURE 5
GYMNASTIC MOVEMENTS DESCRIBED BY P.H. LING

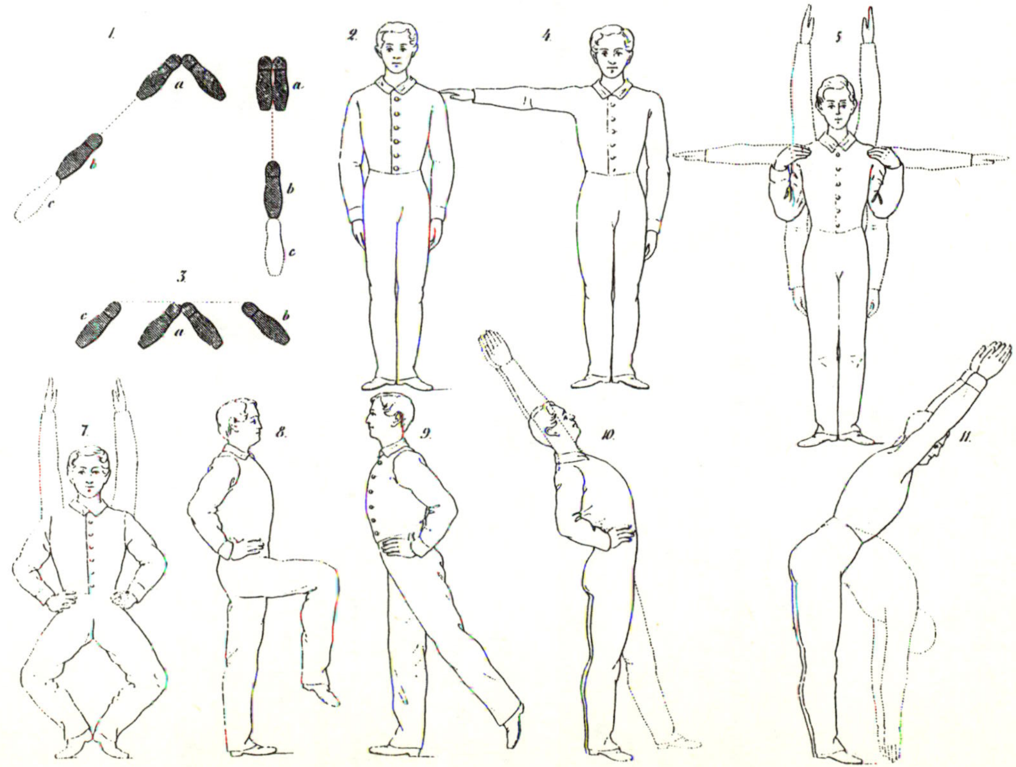

for modern sport to play. Competitive sport opened up to a more
challenging and aggressive kind of masculinity. Despite the fact that
neither Nyblaeus nor Balck explicitly mentioned the need to distance
men from women, their willingness to support a more athletic and
combative ideal of masculinity should be seen in this context.

An interesting effect of the process of modernisation was that
aesthetic gymnastics changed sex. In Ling gymnastics during the first
half of the twentieth century, men were supposed to learn dance-like
gymnastic movements in order to express themselves soulfully (see
Figure 4). In comparison with other branches of Ling gymnastics –
pedagogic, military and medical gymnastics – aesthetic gymnastics
remained in the background and was only mentioned in a few books.
Nevertheless it was thought of as a future activity that men subsequently
would handle with great skill.[55]

According to the idealistic outlook of early Ling gymnastics, beauty
was highly valued as a manifestation of magnificent divine creation.
However, a materialist point of view entered the discussion on physical
education at the turn of the century. Within this mode of thought
resided another challenge to the ideals of Ling gymnastics. Already at
the beginning of the nineteenth century, the German physiologist
Herman von Helmholz had introduced a materialist concept of energy.
This concept of power was formulated in the first law of
thermodynamics, which states that the amount of power in the universe
is always constant. As the American historian Anson Rabinbach has
written in his interesting book, *The Human Motor*, physiologists,
especially in France and Italy, adopted the theory at the end of the
nineteenth century. Etienne-Jules Marey, Georges Demeney and Angelo
Mosso developed equipment to calculate the human use of energy in
different situations.[56] These ideas also reached Sweden, with challenging
consequences for the ideal of manliness in Ling gymnastics. An
important result of this was that the human body was no more looked on
as a temple for the soul, but as a motor. Initially it seemed that the new
theory was supportive of Ling gymnastics. Demeney praised Ling
gymnastics as being highly rational. But subsequently, contradictions
came to the surface. In time, both the aesthetics of the body and ethical
idealism were removed in order to save energy.[57]

At the same time aesthetic gymnastics increasingly developed into an
occupation for women. This tendency was present already in the
theories of Hjalmar Ling. As we have seen, he wanted to create a

materialist basis for physical education. He despised aesthetic gymnastics, but retained it for women![58] Considerations of aesthetics were often conclusive arguments when women's involvement in sport was discussed. For example Balck argued that cricket and football were completely inappropriate for women because of the lack of aestheticism. In contrast he was prepared to allow fencing for women because this was a sport of beauty.[59]

Some female gymnasts also wanted to replace the unisex model of gymnastics. For them, this was a way of escaping the control that male gymnasts exercised over them and to create a gymnastic sphere of their own. Within political life, this kind of separate organising of women was rather common.[60] The Finish teacher of physical education, Eli Björksten, had developed a systematic dual sex model of gymnastics. Beauty, grace and rhythm had to reign within female gymnastics in order to be an expression of the inner soul.[61] However, the soul no longer preoccupied the male.

CONCLUSION

The ideal of manliness in physical education changed considerably during the nineteenth century in Sweden. The pedagogical aim of Ling gymnastics has here been analysed in an attempt to solve some of the paradoxes and problems of manliness in modern society. A spectrum of masculine traits involving both traditional and modern values was assembled in the socialising objectives of Ling gymnastics. An ideal man was to be warlike as well as peaceful, rational as well as spiritual, civilised as well as primitive. All these traits were fused and symbolically expressed in harmonious gymnastics for women as well. But women were never expected to approach perfection to the same extent as men. This unisex model in gymnastics prevailed up to the end of the nineteenth century.

From about 1870 far-reaching changes occurred in physical education. Instead of the human body as a temple of the spirit, it was increasingly conceived as a vehicle to be trimmed and rationalised as efficiently as possible. At the same time Social Darwinism contributed to a more militaristic ideal of manliness. New pedagogical policies that argued for the importance of practicality and personal achievement opened the way for modern sport. The philosophical idealism that had underpinned Ling gymnastics during the first half of the century was no longer fashionable. As a result, the ideal of male bodily beauty faded. The changes did not occur at once, but progressively the masculine body became less and less aestheticised. The development of female gymnastics was almost reversed. Dualism between the sexes was sharpened. Competitive sport became a masculine sphere, while women moved towards aestheticism. These tendencies were to become more obvious early in the twentieth century. The ideals of male socialisation in Ling gymnastics went into retreat. Masculinity through sport replaced masculinity through gymnastics. The twentieth century was to see further revolutionary changes to concepts of masculinity and femininity as they were perceived in and through sport, but that is another story.

NOTES

1. On the history of Ling gymnastics in general see J. Lindroth, *Idrottens väg till folkrörelse: Studier i svensk idrottsrörelse till 1915* (Uppsala, 1974), Ch.2, pp.7–9; H. Sandblad, *Olympia och Valhalla: Idéhistoriska aspekter av den moderna idrottsrörelsens framväxt* (Gothenburg, 1985), *passim*.
2. D Frisby, 'Modernità', in *Encyklopedia delle Scenze Sociali* Vol.5 (Rome, 1996), pp.756–8; H. van der Loo and W. van Reijen, *Modernisierung: Projekt und Paradox* (Munich, 1992), pp.15–18, 93–7, 132–4; B. Turner, *The Body and Society: Explorations in Social Theory* (London, 1996), pp.12, 50; E. Palmblad, *Medicinen som samhällslära* (Gothenburg, 1990), pp.165–76.
3. For example B. Turner, *The Body and Society*, pp.126–8; E.V. Spelman, 'Woman as Body: Ancient and Contemporary Views', in W.J. Morgan and K.V. Meier (eds.), *Philosophic Inquiry in Sport* (1995), pp.73–84; G. Lloyd, *The Man of Reason: 'Male' and 'Female' in Western Philosophy* (London, 1995); K. Johanisson, *Den mörka kontinenten: Kvinnan, medicinen och fin-de-siècle* (Stockholm, 1990); C. Florin and U. Johansson, '*Där de härliga lagrarna gro…*', *Kultur, klass och kön i det svenska läroverket 1850–1914* (Stockholm, 1993), pp.195, 286; M.A. Messer, 'Sports and Male Domination: The Female Athlete as Contested Ideological Terrain', in M.A. Messer and D.F. Sabo (eds.), *Sport, Men and the Gender Order: Critical Feminist Perspectives* (Illinois, 1990), pp.275–83; M.S. Kimmel, 'The Contemporary "Crisis" of Masculinity', in H. Brod (ed.), *The Making of Masculinities: The New Men's Studies* (Boston, 1987), pp.137–49; M.S. Kimmel, *Manhood in America: A Cultural History* (New York, 1996), pp.81–9; Ute Frevert, '"Wo du hingehst…"'— Aufbrüche im Verhältnis der Geschlechter: Rollentauch anno 1908', in *Jahrhundertwende: Der Aufbruch in die Moderne 1880–1930*, Vol. 2 (Hamburg, 1990), pp.100–3; U. Wikander, 'Sekelskiftet 1900: Konstruktion av en nygammal kvinnlighet', in *Det evigt kvinnliga: En historia om förändring* (Stockholm, 1994).
4. H. Schück and K. Warburg, *Illustrerad svensk litteraturhistoria:* Pt 5, *Romantiken* (Stockholm, 1929), pp.344–5.
5. B. Grandien, *Rönndruvans glöd: Nygöticistiskt i tanke, konst och miljö under 1800-talet* (Stockholm, 1978), p.107; Jens Ljunggren, 'Nation-building, Primitivism and Manliness: The Issue of Gymnastics in Sweden Around 1800', *Scandinavian Journal of History*, 21 (1986).
6. C.A. Westerblad, *Ling: Tidshistoriska undersökningar II: Personlig och allmän karaktäristik samt litterär analys* (Stockholm, 1916), pp.16–17; H. Sandblad, *Olympia och Valhalla*, p.47.
7. P.H. Ling, *Samlade arbeten*, Vol.1 (Stockholm, 1866), pp.2–8, 7; H. Schück and K. Warburg, *Romantiken*, p.331.
8. H. Sandblad, *Olympia och Valhalla*, p.47.
9. B. Grandien, *Rönndruvans glöd*, p.49; H. Schück and K. Warburg, *Romantiken*, pp.62–4, 348, 351, 459–60.

10. C.F. GutsMuths, *Gymnastik für die Jugend* (Vienna, Leipzig, 1983, [1792]), pp.74–6.
11. P.H.Ling, 'Något om gymnastik', *Iduna*, 3 January 1814, 79–81; idem, 'Gymnastikens allmänna grunder', in *Gymnastikens allmänna grunder* (facsimile published by Svenska gymnsatikförbundet, 1979). This book contains many of Ling's texts on gymnastics. The Ling references hereafter are to this except where indicated), p.68.
12. The [Royal] Central Gymnastics Institute.
13. T.J. Hartelius, *Gymnastiska iakttagelser* (Stockholm, 1865), pp.6, 15, 29; idem, *Gymnastiken historiskt framställd:* Pt 1, *Gymnastiken hos forntidens folk* (Stockholm, 1872), pp.105, 167; *Tidskrift i gymnastik* (TIG) 1 (1874), p.17; see also L.M. Törngren, *Gymnastik och andra kroppsöfnigar* (Stockholm, 1888), p.21; G. Nyblaeus, *Något om gymnastik och vapenöfning såsom medel för allmän uppfostran* (Stockholm, 1863), p. 24; idem, *Hvad är en folkbeväpning och hvartill kan den gagna?* (Stockholm, 1857), pp.27–8.
14. G.L. Mosse, *The Image of Man: The Creation of Modern Masculinity* (Oxford, New York, 1966).
15. C. Florin and U. Johansson, '*Där de härliga lagrarna gro...*', pp.21, 37–42.
16. B. Janzon, *Manschettyrken, idrott och hälsa: Studier kring idrottrörelsen i Sverige, särskilt Göteborg, intill 1900* (Lindome, 1978), p.22; See debate in the Swedish parliament. Pr 1829: 5, p.374; Bg 1834 bil; p.556; Ad 1834: 3, pp.31–4; Ad 2, 1856–1858, p.209; Ad 1856–58: 2, p.303; Utsk 1856–58: saml. 4, adv 1, no. 148, pp.51–2; Pr 1829, saml. 5, p.374; Bg 1828–29, saml. 3 p.354; Bg 1856 bil no. 145, pp.333–4; see remarks from Örebro; Nyköpings Elementarläroverk; Nya Elementarskolan; Uppsala Domcapitel; Skellefteå Consistorium, Wexiö läroverks kollegium; Läroverkskolegiet i Christianstad; Göteborgs Domcapitel; Kungsbacka skola; Arvika; Härnösands konsistorie; Sundsvall, in *Ecklesiastikdepartementet* 9/1, Konseljakt no. 1 (1863); AK 1869: II, pp.134–5,142; Första kammarens Tillfälliga utskotts No. 1 Utlåtande 1872, No. 5, p.6; SFS 1863:3, pp.2–4; A. Zimmermann and A.F. Stjernstedt, *Samling af författningar mm rörande elementarläroverken och pedagogierna* (1877), pp.103–6,104; see also Jan Lindroth, *Gymnastik med lek och idrott*, pp.33–42.
17. P.H. Ling, 'Gymnastikens allmänna grunder', pp.12–14, 21–4.
18. Ibid., pp.36–9.
19. L.G. Branting, Speech 1852; Speech 1855; Speech 1856, in *Gymnastiska Centralinstitutets samling av enskilda arkiv* (RA), Vol.6. All the Branting speeches below can be found in this volume. Idem, Speech 1841, p.4, Speech 1846; Speech 1857, p.2; Speech 1858; T.J. Hartelius, *Bref innehållande reflexioner öfver gymnastiken och Gymnastiska Central-Institutet* (Stockholm, 1863), pp.49, 51–3; G. Nyblaeus, *Något om gymnastik och vapenöfning*, pp.4–7; T.J. Hartelius, *NDA*, 27, 1 (1861); idem, *Bref från utlandet* (Stockholm, 1860), p.27; G. Nyblaeus, *Något om gymnastik och vapenöfning*, pp.4–7,19; Hjalmar Ling on degeneration, *Om pedagogiska föreningens discussion öfver skol-gymnastiken vid årssammanträdet den 21 maj 1856* (Stockholm, 1858), pp.3–4, 6, 13, *Bihang*, 2, 4–5.
20. C. Taylor, *Hegel och det moderna samhället* (Gothenburg, 1988), pp.16–17 (*Hegel and Modern Society* (Cambridge, 1979)).
21. B. Söderberg, 'P.H. Ling – Heron, vetenskapsmännen och gudsbelätet: Något om Lingbilden under 1800- och tidigt 1900-tal', *Idrott, historia och samhälle* (1995), 111–34.
22. T.J. Hartelius, *Bref från utlandet*, p.9; cf. G. Nyblaeus, 'Ling och gymnastiken: Tal vid uppställandet av Lings bröstbild å gymnastiksalen i Lund d. 12 Maj 1853', in *Vers och prosa* (Stockholm, 1890), pp.133–6; In the Branting see 'Tal af Branting hållet den 31 Mars 1836 då Lings bröstbild aftäcktes vid K. Gymn. Centralinstitutet', *TIG* (1884), 490–2; L.G. Branting, Speech 1846, p.7; Speech 1848, pp.3–4, 4–5.
23. T. Weimarck, *Akademi och anatomi* (Stockholm, 1996), pp.21–2.
24. G. Nyblaeus, 'Vid folkskolemötet i Augusti 1864', pp.146–7; 'Ling och gymnastiken', pp.129–30, idem, 'En blick på utsidan av den danska kulturen', in G. Nyblaeus, *Vers och prosa* (Stockholm, 1890), p.225.
25. P.H. Ling, 'Gymnastikens allmänna grunder', p.38, 98, 114, 117–11; idem, 'Elementarläroverket', p.273, in *Vers och prosa*; T.J. Hartelius, *Gymnastiken historiskt framställd*, pp.189–193; see also L.G. Branting, Speech 1852, p.2, Speech 1847; also B. Söderberg, 'P.H. Ling – Heron', p.126.
26. G. Nyblaeus, 'Ling och gymnastiken', pp.131–2; idem, 'En blick på utsidan', p.219; T.J. Hartelius, *Bref innehållande reflexioner*, pp.49–50.8; idem,'Gymnastik för Krigsmän och skolor',

p.239; idem, 'Aforismer', pp.340–2.

27.	Ling, 'Gymnastikens allmänna grunder', pp.55–6, 72–3, 117–18, 157, 250; idem, 'Gymnastik för Krigsmän och Skolor', pp.210–16, 239, 245–52, 312; idem, 'Soldat-undervisning i gymnastik och bajonettfäktning' (1838), pp.163, 167; idem, 'Förslag till gymnastikens nytta…', p.216; idem, 'Aforismer', pp.343–53; manuscript by Ling of 1805 in C.A. Westerblad, *Ling. Tidshistoriska undersökningar IV: 2* (Malmö, 1946), pp.5–7; Michel Foucault, *Övervakning och straff* (Lund, 1987), [*Surveiller et punir* (1974)].

28.	A. Nordencrantz, *Tankar om krig i gemen och Sweriges krig i synnerhet samt hwaruti Sweriges rätta och sannskyldiga intresse består* (Stockholm, 1767); M. Roberts, *Sverige under frihetstiden 1719–1722* (Stockholm, 1995), p.79; A. Jansson, *Försvarsfrågan i svensk politik från 1809 till krimkriget* (Uppsala, 1935), pp.713–14; A.W. Johansson, *Europas krig: Militärt tänkande, strategi och politik från Napoleontiden till andra världskrigets slut* (Stockholm, 1988), pp.8, 22, 40–6.

29.	J.A. Hazelius, *Om stående härar och folklig beväpning* ([Stockholm] 1827), pp.40–48; *Underdånigt betänkande angående Landförsvaret afgivet den 12 maj 1866 av der til i nåder förordnade kommitérande II* (Stockholm, 1866), pp.3–8; cf. G. Nyblaeus, *Om militarism och patriotism: Några ord i försvarsfrågan* (Stockholm, 1875), pp.10–11; Debate in parliament Bg 1844–45, bil 21, p.21–23; Bg 1859–60; motion no. 13; FK 1869: I, p.528; See also in *Eklesiastikdepartementet* 9/1, Konseljakt no. 1, 1863: 'Landförsvars Dep protokollsutdrag med öfverlämnande af förslag till den allmänna medborgerliga krigsbildningens ordnande', ink 30 Juli 1862; 'Remissutlåtande från Direktionen för nya elementerskolan', ink 24/2 1861; för förhållandet kunskap moral G. Brantings remisssvar ink 6/9 1861.

30.	Debate in parliament, motion AK 1896: no. 4, p.25.

31.	P.H. Ling, 'Aforismer', p. 341; 'Gymnastikens allmänna grunder', pp.62–3, 126.

32.	Ling, 'Gymnastikens allmänna grunder', pp.54, 126.

33.	T.J. Hartelius, *Gymnastiska iakttagelser*, pp.5–7,15,29; idem, *Gymnastiken historiskt framställd*, pp.105, 167; *TIG*, 1 (1874), 17; G. Nyblaeus, *Något om gymnastik och vapenöfning*, p.24; idem, *Hvad är en folkbeväpning och hvartill den kan gagna?* (Stockholm, 1857), pp.27–8.

34.	A.B. Santesson, *Gymnastik för unga qvinnor och skolflickor* (Stockholm, 1866); in *Svenska gymnastikföreningens tidskrift* (1865), pp.127–31 (1866), pp.81–3. On strength and aggressiveness for the entire population with physical education for women see G. Nyblaeus, *Vers och prosa*, p.157; On women as allies see also G.A. Adelsparre, *Öre-skrifter i gymnastiska ämnen, för gymnastikföreningar, 1a: avdelningen* (1858), p.11; I. von Vegesack, *Några ord om den fysiska uppfostran, samt skolgymnastikens ordnande med afseende derpå* (1861), pp.11–15; A. Georgii, *Rational Gymnastics: Reviewed in their Relation to the Health and Education of the Young of both Sexes* (1873), p.11; see also C. Dickson, 'Om Qvinnans fysiska uppfostran', in *K Vetenskaps- och Vitterhetssamhällets handlingar. Ny tidsfjöld* 6 (Gothenburg, 1859).

35.	Hjalmar Ling, *Tillägg vid användningen af de tabeller hvilka varit begagnade för Gymnastiska centralinstitutets pedagogiska lärokurs*, 2nd edn (1871); p.17; idem, *Förkortad öfversikt af allmän rörelselära*, pp.10, 57; idem, *De första begreppen af rörelseläran*, pp.343–5, 347, 349, 364–5; cf. C.A. Westerblad, *Hjalmar Ling: hans levnad och hans betydelse* (Malmö, 1839), pp.164–5, 216.

36.	T. Laqueur, *Making Sex: Body and Gender from Greeks to Freud* (1984).

37.	Hjalmar Ling, *Tillägg till tabeller* (1869), pp.46–50; (1902), pp.88–105.

38.	Ibid. (1869), pp.48–9.

39.	Idem, *Tillägg till tabellerna* (1902), pp.89,126; (1869), pp.47, 59; *Kungl. Gymnastiska centralinstitutets historia 1813–1913: Med anledning av institutets hundraårsdag utgiven av dess lärarekollegium* (Stockholm, 1913), p.254.

40.	H. Meinander, *Towards a Bourgeois Manhood: Boys' Physical Education in the Nordic Secondary Schools 1880–1940* (Helsinki, 1994).

41.	J.A. Mangan, *Athleticism in the Victorian and Edwardian Public School: The Emergence and Consolidation of an Educational Ideology* (London, 1986).

42.	*TIG*, 1 (1874), 5–10 (1875), 150; T.J. Hartelius, *TIG*, 1 (1874), 5–6; idem, *Om arbetarebostäder, föredrag hållna i Stockholms arbetareförening* (Stockholm, 1874); T. Gustafsson, 'En harmonisk och hierarkisk ordning: Synen på utveckling i 1800-talets svenska biologi', *Lychnos* (1994), 87–111.

43.	Gustaf Nyblaeus, 'Menskligt, medborgerligt, militäriskt', in *Vers och prosa*, pp. 248–252; idem, 'Några ord om fäktövrignar', GCI's arkiv enskilda delen *Nyblaeus* Vol.60 (RA); idem, *Krigs och krigsväsende för lärde och olärde* (Stockholm, 1874), pp.9–15; idem, *I beväringsfrågan* (Lund, 1859); idem, *Om allmänna värnplikten* (Stockholm, 1875).

44. G. Nyblaeus, *Ytterligare i försvarsfrågan: 2 Hvad innebär allmänn värnpligt?* (Stockholm, 1878), pp.28–34; idem, *100 Gymnastiska aforismer* (Stockholm, 1889), pp.12–18.
45. G. Nyblaeus, *100 Gymnastiska aforismer*, p.6.
46. H. Sandblad, *Olympia och Valhalla*, pp.344–5.
47. 'Allmän värnpligtig. Ang förslag till ny härordning.' Lecture to the Trade Union, Stockholm, 20 February 1876. *Balcks arkiv*, Vol.2, RA; cf H. Sandblad, *Olympia och Valhalla*, pp.337, 346–9.
48. 'Manuskript 1', *Balcks arkiv*, Vol.2, p.18 (RA); on strengthening see Hans Bonde, *Mandighet og Sport* (Odense, 1991), p.89.
49. See J.A. Mangan (ed.), *Shaping the Superman: Fascist Body as Political Icon – Aryan Fascism* (London, 1999), *passim*.
50. 'Manuskript 2', *Balcks arkiv*, Vol.2, p.2 (RA).
51. J. Ljunggren, *Kroppens bildning: Linggymnastikens manlighetsprojekt 1970-1914* (Stockholm, 1999), Ch.8.
52. U. Wikander, 'Sekelskiftet 1900: Konstruktion av en nygammal kvinnlighet'.
53. M.A. Messer, 'Sports and Male Domination', pp.275–83; Hans Bonde, *Mandighet og Sport*; K.E. McCrone, *Playing the Game: Sport and the Physical Emancipation of English Women 1870-1914* (Kentucky, 1988).
54. *TIG* (1899), 779–857, 857; L.M. Törngren, *Gymnastik och andra kroppsöfningar* (Stockholm, 1888), pp.11–12.
55. T.J. Hartelius, *Linje och estetisk gymnastik med figurer* (Stockholm, 1863); G. Nyblaeus, *Plastiska kroppsöfningar. Grunddrag i estetisk gymnastik* (Stockholm, 1882).
56. A. Rabinbach, *The Human Motor: Energy, Fatigue, and the Origins of Modernity* (Los Angeles, 1990).
57. J. Ljunggren, *Kroppens bildning*, Ch.9.
59. Hjalmar Ling, *Tillägg* (1869), p.6; idem, *Förkortad öfversikt af allmän rörelselära*, p.103; idem, *Tillägg* (1880), p.66.
59. *TIG* (1899), 779–857, 857; L.M. Törngren, *Gymnastik och andra kroppsövningar*, pp.11–12.
60. K. Östberg, *Efter rösträtten: Kvinnors utrymme efter det demokratiska genombrottet* (Stockholm, 1997).
61. E. Olofsson, *Har kvinnorna en sportslig chans?: Den svenska idrottsrörelsen under 1900-talet* (Umeå, 1989), pp.90–1, 93–4.

Athleticism in the Service of the Proletariat: Preparation for the English Elementary School and the Extension of Middle-Class Manliness

J.A. MANGAN and COLM HICKEY

In 1888, with the publication of the Report of the Cross Commission,[1] it was clear that the teacher training colleges of England and Wales had been subjected to a thorough examination and had been found wanting. One significant omission from their educational provision was the absence of any conversion to the playing of team games. In the London colleges, the concern of this chapter, the emerging ideology of athleticism[2] had been neglected or ignored, either deliberately as in the case of Westminster in response to widespread Wesleyan opposition to games playing, or financially as in the cases of Borough Road and St Mary's, neither of whom had the space for these games. Even where games playing was established as in the Anglican colleges, it was on an *ad hoc* basis and did not reflect the acceptance of this increasingly influential educational ideology in the public schools and ancient universities. Within a generation, however, athleticism was to dominate college life. For the first time in the academic community, the reasons why, and ways in which this ideological transformation took place, will now be considered. This chapter, in general, will focus on the process of diffusion and, in particular, on the way in which rituals were used to underpin the diffusion process.

What this process amounted to, at one level, was the extension of a model of middle-class masculinity to the late Victorian and Edwardian teacher training college which served the working-class elementary school. As mentioned above, this extension has not been considered before, and moreover this aspect of socialisation into masculinity *as such* has also been overlooked. It adds another layer to various layers of European inculcation into 'proper' period masculinity. Of course, it is difficult, if not impossible, to measure its full impact although it is clear that it had some impact. It is not difficult, however, to record the attempt to promote an image of masculinity in elementary education which owed much to the image of masculinity energetically promulgated in the middle-class secondary school systems of England, Britain and the Empire.[3]

If European masculinity is to be understood in its full complexity, and the making of European masculinity is to be considered in all its manifestations, then it is certainly time *teacher training colleges and their equivalents* throughout Europe, came into the reckoning. These institutions from the second half of the nineteenth century onwards, through the teachers they trained, had an influence on the gender expectations, attitudes and behaviour of working-class children, if for no other reason than the fact that these children were a captive audience for much of their childhood. A European comparative study of teacher training as an agency of inculcation into masculinity would be a valuable contribution to gender studies.

It was suggested somewhat tardily in the late 1980s that the sociologist and historian of sport could usefully adopt an interdisciplinary approach since it offers the possibility of a comprehensive analytical framework. 'Sociologists frequently complain that historians lack a conceptual framework for their research, whilst historians tend to feel that social theorists require them to compress the diversity of the past into artificially rigid categories and dispense with empirical verification of their theories. In truth both disciplines need each other.'[4]

This advice came rather late in the day. It was a well-meaning if belated recommendation. This interdisciplinary approach, had already been implemented, of course, some considerable time earlier. The 'new historian', utilising concepts from the social sciences, had been about for quite some time in the history of sport, as well as elsewhere in historical studies. Arguably, J.A. Mangan's *Athleticism* led the way as early as 1981. Mangan, trained in social anthropology, sociology and social history, utilised an integrated conceptual framework that allowed an explanation of key ritualistic manifestations of the Victorian and Edwardian public school system.[5] The distinguished cultural historian, Sheldon Rothblatt, has written of Mangan's integrated approach in *Athleticism in the Victorian and Edwardian Public School*, 'A central question of all exceptional historical work now is how to conceive and describe the ways in which new values and new arrangements for living and bringing meaning into life enter into and inform everyday social and institutional arrangements. This Mangan achieved superbly, combining an eye for the apt, even colourful, moment *with conceptual understandings drawn from sociology (the sociological process) and anthropology (the use of ritual and symbol). No one had quite done this before or done it so consistently* [emphasis added].... The result was a breakthrough in depicting the development of the public schools and their histories down to our time.'[6] Academic perceptiveness, it could be argued, is far more useful as early implementation than eventual realisation. It is also the outcome of the awareness and recognition of source material. Perhaps it should not be over looked therefore that Mangan had published as early as 1971 papers on sociology, sport and ritual which included references to issues involving historical continuity and ritualism. His analysis of the rituals of the public school system, it is suggested, will now permit an explanation of significant aspects of ritual in the late nineteenth and early twentieth-century teacher training system.[7]

Athleticism in the second half of the nineteenth century influenced all middle–class educational institutions.[8] Donald Leinster Mackay has traced athleticism's development in the preparatory schools[9] while Mangan, especially, has discussed its impact in the public schools, grammar schools and the universities of Oxford and Cambridge.[10] By the late 1880s it had become, at the very least, an influential educational movement. When the teacher training colleges were scrutinised by the Cross Commission and it was found that their curriculum did not match up to mainstream middle–class educational philosophies, a new set of institutional educational priorities inspired by the movement were demanded, and implemented by new 'Oxbridge' educated principals who now introduced athleticism into the colleges.

Athleticism was spread among the colleges by downward 'diffusion'. The term is defined by Everett M. Rogers as 'the process by which an innovation is communicated through certain channels over time to members of a social system'.[11] He identifies six main elements of diffusion: innovation, compatibility, complexity, visibility, communication, and a social system.

As made clear above, by the 1880s athleticism was already becoming an established educational ideology in the middle–class schools and the ancient universities. At this time it was new, however, to the colleges. Rogers asserts that, 'it matters little ... whether or not an idea is objectively new as measured by the lapse of time since its discovery or invention … If an idea seems new to the individual and he uses it then it is an innovation', and so it was in the colleges.[12] Somewhat self-evidently, an innovation, claims Rogers, will be more readily adopted by a group if it is felt to be advantageous and if the innovation is shown to be compatible with the existing values, past experiences and needs of the group. He adds, perhaps equally obviously, that if an innovation is not too complex then there is a much greater chance of successful adoption and that the benevolent visibility of an innovation is important for its widespread adoption. In short, the easier it is for individuals to see the beneficial results of an innovation, the more likely they are to adopt it. Rogers further claims that the essence of any successful diffusion process is the enthusiastic emulation of the ideas of those who have persuaded their neophytes of the value of these ideas. Truistically, successful communication is also a significant factor in the diffusion process: most individuals depend greatly upon a positive evaluation of an innovation clearly conveyed to them by individuals who have previously adopted it.

Finally, an important element in any successful diffusion is the presence of a social system. It allows the promotion of innovation. Within the social system individuals have an important role to play. Rogers identifies two distinct types: 'change agents' and 'opinion leaders'. Change agents introduce change formally within institutions. The men appointed as college principals in the wake of the Cross Commission were undoubtedly change agents *par excellence*. They implemented the values and practices of athleticism in the colleges, not least by the provision of facilities. Opinion leaders influence others within the system in an informal way. They are more cosmopolitan, enjoy higher social status and are more innovative than others with the result that 'they are at the centre of interpersonal communication networks'.[13] Their leadership is earned and maintained by personal competence, social accessibility and institutional conformity. The last decade of the nineteenth century and the first decade of the twentieth century saw a cadre of young, well educated, athletically minded Oxbridge men appointed to posts as junior tutors within the colleges, who ensured, consolidated and accelerated the assimilation of athleticism. They were clearly opinion leaders.

As agents of change, the principals of the London Colleges in the role of influential proselytisers such as P.A. Barnett, H.L. Withers, A. Burrell and F.J. Hendy at Borough Road; G.A. Gent and L.A. Hudson at St

Mark's, Canon Cromwell and E. Daniel at St John's, H. B. Workman at Westminster and the Irish triumvirate of W. Byrne, A. Moynihan and E. Sheehy at St Mary's, all sought to advance athleticism within the colleges, but they required the support of opinion leaders. Confident, articulate staff who had been educated in schools and universities where athleticism already prevailed and who could persuade by word *and* deed were necessary. The principals, therefore, purposefully sought and appointed young mostly Oxbridge graduates who exemplified an enthusiasm for the ideology. Earlier in the public school system, this policy of recruiting similar enthusiasts had been adopted, of course, by G.E.L. Cotton at Marlborough for exactly the same purposes.

A particularly good college example is Leigh Smith who was appointed to the staff of Westminster College[14] as a history lecturer in 1905 some two years after the appointment of Herbert Workman who had become principal on the death of J.H. Rigg in 1903. Smith was educated at Kingswood School, Bath, which was mainly for the sons of Wesleyan ministers, and which had as its headmaster, Workman's brother. In 1898 Smith entered Durham University, the 'Oxbridge' of the north, as a classical scholar. In 1901 he obtained a first class honours degree in classics and philosophy. This was followed by a fellowship from 1903–4. He then joined the staff at Harrogate College for a year. Then followed a brief period as a tutor at Hatfield Hall, Durham. At Westminster, Smith's official role was to lecture in classics and English history and to be one of four house tutors. However, his impact was to be significant in other ways! As the college historian, F.C. Pritchard, has observed, 'There was … nothing of the academician about him. He had shown his athletic prowess at school; he had represented his university also at cricket and rugby football; he had represented both Durham County and Lancashire at cricket.'[15]

The college had a lamentable record in competitive sport, and Pritchard is quite explicit about Workman's purpose in appointing Smith: 'the new principal resolved that the college should be pre-eminent in other directions besides academic study. That was the real reason why Dr Workman was determined to obtain the services of Leigh Smith, a man of 'boundless and contagious enthusiasm'.[16] Westminster, of all the London colleges, had the worst facilities for games, but under Smith's inspirational leadership, as will now be made clear, the students eventually made the most of their limited surroundings. They took to athletics and to the streets, running energetically about the area. Smith had his work cut out. An inter-year athletic sports meeting had been instituted by Workman in February 1906 inspired by the recent presentation of a London Inter-College Challenge Shield by G.B. Clough, a former student (1875–77). Smith organised training programmes for the students in preparation for the Shield competition that the college had entered for the first time two years earlier with disastrous results. It had finished bottom and Workman had ruefully noted in his log book, 'the participation of Westminster College in these competitive sports between the London training colleges for the first time was accompanied with some difficulty in getting the men to join'.[17]

Workman and Smith therefore systematically devised a programme of athletic events designed to ensure that Westminster's record in the Inter-College Shield would improve. Rather than waiting until the summer term to pick a scratch side the students were placed on a year-long athletic treadmill. An athletics meeting was held for the junior students in the autumn term. This meeting resulted in a junior team being selected for the annual seniors versus juniors meeting in the Easter term. The result determined the inter-college team. As Pritchard noted:

> Athletics became in fact what it has been ever since: an all-the-year round interest and not one limited to a mere few weeks. Individuals were encouraged to enter for events in various sports meetings in different parts of London, and experience began to make itself felt as a valuable ally of keenness. Leigh Smith persuaded the Principal (who needed little persuasion) that the holding of the inter-Year Sports at a recognised athletic centre would have a good psychological effect, and they were held at Stamford Bridge...[18]

This new competitive programme was augmented, as mentioned earlier, by regular training sessions inevitably supervised by Smith. They were not without their urban dangers. 'Training runs were organised, mainly taking place in the evenings, through the streets past the walls of the Gas, Light and Coke Company's domain; [and] in other directions, round Vincent Square which did at least provide fewer hazards in the shape of hansom cabs, though excited dogs have always been a problem!' And, records the college historian approvingly, 'it was in all this determined effort Leigh Smith himself who showed in practical fashion what is the keynote of all success: Keenness'.[19]

Workman and Smith thus did all they could to motivate the students. It is not entirely surprising, therefore, that articles urging the students to keep fit appeared with increasing frequency in the college magazine, *The Westminsterian*. Rhetoric reinforced running! As one contributor observed sanctimoniously:

> To keep in training is not a hard matter, if the rule of simplicity and moderation in all things be kept well in view. Some people think that to get themselves into training they must make themselves miserable and deny themselves everything they have been used to, and everything they like. There is no greater delusion. Peace of mind is of as great importance as soundness of mind and limb ... if a man gets plenty of sleep, is careful not to smoke too much, eats and drinks just enough good wholesome food to satisfy him, takes two or three short brisk runs each week and plays football once or twice a week he is bound to be in good trim...[20]

In 1908 Westminster *won* the coveted Inter-College Shield. It was, it appears, a worthy corporate effort! The winning team, it was reported in *The Westminsterian*, 'was truly representative of the efforts of the *entire* (emphasis added) College, for not only had the Principal sanctioned increased expenditure, but the kitchen staff had co-operated in the provision of a special diet'.[21]

Unquestionably the most extraordinary illustration of Leigh Smith's serendipitous influence on the students came in the First World War. Lieutenant William Thomas Forshaw of the Manchester Regiment, a student of Westminster between 1908 and 1910, won the Victoria Cross fighting against the Turks. Forshaw held his trench for 41 hours continually throwing bombs at the enemy for the entire period. After the war Forshaw, in a visit to the college and 'in a modest speech told his hearers that it was to Leigh Smith that he owed most, for the correct method of dealing with bombs was to go for the bomb and throw it out; that on the occasion he was holding the trench he remembered Leigh Smith's teaching in rugger: go for the ball! He had gone for the bomb each time one appeared and thrown it out, and in that very act he said, he recalled the practice in putting the shot at Westminster and felt that it was indeed standing him in good stead.'[22] Forshaw's tongue was certainly as smooth as his arm action.

Leigh Smith is clearly both the post-Cross Commission epitome of period middle class masculinity, and the ideal period opinion leader, while Workman clearly fulfilled the part of institutional change agent.

They were an impressive ideological 'double act'. Leigh Smith, for his part, effortlessly fitted into Workman's new post-Cross Commission vision for the college. His public school, university and athletic background ensured that he was a period *persona grata* in the new ideological climate. Unsurprisingly, when he left Westminster in 1914 to take up a post inspecting secondary schools in what was then Ceylon, the governing body was moved to note in its minutes that

> In parting with Mr Leigh Smith the Governing Body desires to put on record its sense of the great service that Mr Smith rendered to the College during the nine years that he fulfilled the post of Tutor in Classics. Not merely in the lecture room but in the life of the students Mr Smith held a place that cannot easily be filled. By his unfailing courtesy, tact and spirit of helpfulness, he won the affection and respect of all. The Governing Body, while congratulating Mr. Smith on his promotion recognises the loss which the College has suffered by his removal.[23]

On the face of it, even this encomium was something of an understatement! Leigh Smith is an outstanding example of one of the successful means by which athleticism was assimilated into an Edwardian London teacher training college. He participated, he motivated, he organised, he coached – all with considerable success. In his years at the college it won the coveted Inter-College Shield four times. He proved to be the perfect opinion leader; he was also a presentable muscular Christian in the Kingsleyian mould: robust, decent, conscientious. In a word, manly. It is reasonable to suggest that at Westminster he was an influential and inspirational mover in the genesis of a new educational ideal, as well as the personification of period moral masculinity.[24]

Other examples of the transforming opinion leader are easily located. Cecil Rolo Peyton Andrews was educated at Merchant Taylors' School[25] from 1879 to 1888. He was awarded a scholarship to St John's College, Oxford, from where he graduated with a first class in classical moderations and a second class in literae humaniores. On leaving Oxford in 1893 he served the obligatory muscular and other educational apprenticeships. He was first a master at Highgate School.[26] A year later he became Master of the sixth form at Forest School.[27] In 1896 he was appointed to the staff of St John's College, Battersea.[28] An appreciative article about him appeared in the college magazine three years later.

'Mr. Andrews' honours are not confined to the Examination Room. As a boy at Merchant Taylors' he won his colours in the school boat and the 'Fives' Team. He rowed at Oxford for three years in his College Eight and was tried for 'Trials'. Since joining Battersea he has acted as Hon. Treasurer of the Sports Committee and has taken an active interest in the athletic life of the College which he has represented both in tennis and 'Fives'.[29] Here then is yet another ideological inseminator spreading his influence and bringing his college into the educational, *and gender*, mainstream of the period as demanded by the Cross Commission.

Another St John's tutor, H.S. Foster, was appointed as lecturer in classics and history in 1904. He had been educated at Marborough[30] from where he had gained an open exhibition to Merton College, Oxford. At Marlborough he had been an accomplished athlete gaining his colours at rugby and winning the 880 yards in the Public Schools' Championship in record time. At Merton he was Captain of Rugby and President of the Athletics Club. At St John's, the editor of the college magazine observed approvingly soon after his arrival, 'He has already turned out for the College fifteen and we hope to have his advice and guidance in preparation for the Inter-College Sports on May 7th.'[31]

And yet another with impeccable mainstream middle-class manly credentials was Clement Henry Swann. He attended Perse Grammar School, Cambridge, and Christ's College, Cambridge, in 1902–5 and became a member of staff at St Mark's College[32] in the same year. Some time later he wrote an article on cross-country running for the college magazine. It is informative. It began with a quotation from Robert Browning:

> Oh our manhood's prime vigour! No spirit feels waste,
> Not a muscle is stopped in its playing nor sinew unbraced.
> Oh, the wild joys of living! the leaping from rock up to rock,
> The strong rending of boughs from fir tree, the cool silver shock
> Of the plunge in a pool's living water.[33]

The article continued in the same vein. It was a didactic piece of Edwardian prose celebrating confident *manliness*. 'You have endured a course of training, more or less rigorous, and this is to be the final test of the discipline you have made yourself subject to … you are determined to do your best, and what is more, feel a calm confidence in the certain knowledge of a latent power thus to extend yourself, owing to your fit condition.'[34]

G.F. Bartle has offered an almost convincing explanation for the appointment of these young Oxbridge games-playing tutors. Residential teacher training colleges, he has argued uncontroversially, had come in for a great deal of criticism at this time from many educational commentators and observers. One criticism centred on low academic standards. In consequence, the Education Department's regulations now permitted students to take university in place of Teachers' Certificate examinations. This new concession led to a rapid growth in the number of students seeking matriculation, intermediate and even degree qualifications while at college. To provide for the academic demands of these courses, the college committee gradually extended the policy it had adopted in the case of the principal and senior tutor and engaged young Oxford and Cambridge graduates on short-term contracts as junior tutors alongside the ex-students it had employed during the previous twenty years.[35] Bartle sees this change of policy as highly significant arguing that for example it,

> hastened the transformation of Borough Road[36] at Isleworth from a prototype of the Victorian residential training college into an institution not unlike a Victorian public school, with a new emphasis on examination successes, a prefectorial system and a strong emphasis on games and physical fitness ... Junior staff were selected almost as much for their athletic prowess as for their academic qualifications and all staff apart from Vice-Principal Barkby, were expected to participate personally in games.[37]

Bartle is walking on quicksand in his claims for a late Victorian public school emphasis on examination success but on all the other points he is on firm ground.[38]

What is clear of Borough Road is that to accommodate the new 'strong emphasis on games', new staff and new premises were urgently sought. The result was both a new site and a new principal, P.A. Barnett, whose arrival was described by a contemporary as the start of a new era.

> The College received a new life and a new milieu. The spirit of the elementary school and the grammar school was replaced by the richer and freer spirit of the university; the drab streets of Southwark were exchanged for the open fields of Isleworth. The new Principal looked a mere boy, but in the skill with which he affected the grand trek, and in the wisdom with which he reformed

the system of education at the College, lifting it to a higher level and fitting it better to the tastes and talents of the students – in all this he proved himself a man, and a man of insight and courage.[39]

In the provision of 'open fields' he certainly showed himself 'a man'. Oxbridge staff at the new Borough Road include L.B.T. Chaffey, Christ Church Cathedral School, Oxford, and Christ's College, Cambridge, where in 1894 he represented his college at cricket, tennis and football as well as playing for the university XI at football, A.V. Houghton, Hertford College, Oxford, who presented the college with a Goodwill shield for cross-country running in 1895, and an interesting odd man out, Frank Harry Busbridge Dale. His father was an electrician and the family lived at 38 Connington Road, Shepherds Bush. He was a Foundation Scholar at St Paul's School in 1885, and won an Exhibition to Balliol College, Oxford, in 1889. He had a brilliant academic career at Oxford: Craven Scholar 1891, first class classics moderations 1892, fellow of Merton College 1894, Derby Scholar 1895, MA in 1897. In 1888 he joined the staff at Borough Road. And odd man out though he was – lower middle-class academic *par excellence* – he was a man for all athletic seasons. He had an immediate impact on the college. An editorial in the *B's Hum* (the college magazine) of February 1897 commented 'All Bs are proud of the fact that such a brilliant classical scholar is on the staff of the B.R.C. His work throws him into … intercourse with the Inter-Arts men and he has gained much popularity among them because of the vigorous way in which he is carrying them through their studies.' More to the period point perhaps, the editorial continued, 'He takes a prominent interest in sports and may frequently be seen in the fives courts. Mr Dale is too, an enthusiastic supporter of the football teams, even accompanying the teams when playing away.'[40]

As an influential period opinion leader, keen to make his mark, involvement in games was essential to Dale's masculine image, his professional popularity *and* his career. It is clear that Dale was not an outstanding athlete. There is no evidence in the Balliol College archives of his involvement in college or university teams, but he was nonetheless a period games enthusiast. His encouragement of the college sports teams, it may be quite reasonably suggested, had beneficial long-term educational consequences for himself, the training colleges and the elementary schools. His subsequent career after leaving Borough Road in 1900 prompts this suggestion as he left to become an HM Inspector of

Schools, a post he held until 1906 when he became a HM Inspector of Training Colleges. A period as Divisional Schools Inspector followed and, in 1913, he became Chief Inspector for Elementary Schools in England and Wales. Here then was a man of influence in elementary education who subscribed to sport as an integral part of the gender education of working class boys and who was in a position to ensure his views were taken into account. After 1906, it might be noted in passing, team games *as well as* drill, became part and parcel of formal elementary schooling![41]

An equally important figure in the spread of athleticism into the colleges arrived on the scene in 1900 with the appointment of Allan Ramsey Smith as house tutor at Borough Road. Smith had been educated at Loretto School,[42] a highly influential school in the heyday of athleticism,[43] under the headship of Hely Hutchinson Almond. He had a brilliantly successful career at the school representing it at fives, hockey and rugby and captained the XV. He was also a prefect and editor of the school magazine *The Lorettonian* before, predictably, becoming head boy. From Loretto he went to Trinity College, Oxford, where he was secretary of the athletics club as well as captain of the university XV in the varsity matches of 1897 and 1898, and from 1895 to 1900 he was a Scottish rugby international, captaining the side in 1900. He graduated from Oxford in 1898 with a 3rd class in classical moderations and a secnd class in literae humaniores, and then spent two years travelling around the world (his father was a wealthy cotton broker in Liverpool) before taking up his post at Borough Road.

Smith's stay at Borough was just over a year, but during that time he made an impressive impact on college life. He played for the 1st XV and was a dominant figure, who contributed substantially to the ethos first introduced by Barnett. After leaving Borough Road in 1901 he was for two years a Junior Inspector of Schools and then, from 1903 to 1908, Inspector of Schools in Liverpool. The governors of Loretto School then appointed him headmaster. They declared that they were satisfied they had 'chosen a man strongly imbued with the teachings of the late Dr Almond, and ... whose training and experience pre-eminently fit him for the Headmastership of Loretto'.[44] Later Frank Stewart, author of a history of the school, almost superfluously, commented that 'Smith was a devotee of Almond and in full sympathy with his educational theories including a determination to train the body as well as the mind'.[45]

It is instructive to consider Smith more closely to obtain a full measure of his commitment to Almondian principles. This commitment was so complete that he would certainly have carried it with him into the English elementary schools which he inspected and advised. It certainly inspired his work with working-class boys outside school hours.

At Loretto Smith faithfully followed in Almond's footsteps, espousing what Almond had described as Lorettonianism.[46] He was a muscular Christian of non-doctrinal inclination concerned with the health of body and soul. His collected school sermons,[47] published the year after he died in 1927, reveal a man who saw life as a series of struggles against temptations and vices of all kinds that could only be rejected through a combination of moral and muscular fitness. He once counselled his Lorettonian boys: 'If you would strengthen your faith, be not ashamed to show admiration for what you know to be right, for moral courage always brings faith with it.' He went on to link physical and moral courage.

We have many opportunities here for showing courage in the face of difficulties, and you are generally quick to appreciate it when it is shown upon the cricket or football field. But this is not always the most difficult kind of courage. If you would strengthen your faith – the shield wherewith ye shall be able to quench all the fiery darts of the wicked – you must learn to appreciate and practise the courage which will not win applause, but which will be greeted with ridicule or resentment.[48]

Sermons that he preached during his headship covered such varied topics as 'The Great Call, Patriotism, Arming for Life's Battles and True Greatness'. All, however, contained the moral imperative that one should walk in the footsteps of Christ, be prepared for possible criticism, and by drawing strength from Christ's life, rise above it: 'Teach yourself now, as the choosing and chosen followers of Christ, to find in His example a greatness of spirit. Be courageous for His sake where you will gain nothing here.'[49]

It is important for the purposes of this chapter, to appreciate that Smith was a committed supporter of Almond's Lorettonianism for all social classes. He sought a classless acceptance of his views. As Stewart, has observed:

> Smith, among his many qualities was a great humanitarian. His main interest was in people, and especially in boys. But his interest was not limited to the class of boys which fortune had put into his

care. When a young man, working as an Inspector of Schools in the Liverpool area, he felt a desire and responsibility to spread the principles of Lorettonianism further afield in some practical way. The large mass of the population, he declared, and especially the poor classes, were absolutely ignorant or regardless of the laws of health, and an organised effort should be made to spread the knowledge of these laws. So, in 1908, he and some other Lorettonians in Liverpool had started a Boys' Club there which was run in conjunction with St James' Parish Church and was called the St James' Lorettonian Club.[50]

After the First World War, anxious to spread the Almondian principles of health further, Smith approached the Headmaster of Fettes and together they founded a boy's club in Edinburgh known as the Fettesian–Lorettonian Club which was run on the same lines.[51] Like Dale, he unquestionably exerted an influence on the elementary school and the elementary schoolboy and attempted to shape him in his own 'manly' image.

The evidence then, is clear: public school and university-educated games-playing enthusiasts were deliberately sought by the Principals of Borough Road, St Mark's, St John's and Westminster. The recruitment of these men represented at least an attempt to establish a symbiotic relationship between the world of relative privilege – public school and Oxbridge, and the world of relative poverty – elementary school and pupil–teacherdom. The teacher training college was a conduit along which middle-class experiences, ideals and values were transmitted. The Oxbridge-educated tutor could bring things to the colleges that they badly lacked – social status, bourgeois idealism, a middle class muscular morality and a games-playing commitment, whilst the colleges could give the young graduates embarking on an educational career the one thing that they had no knowledge of, experience of elementary education. Many of the junior tutors used the college as a stepping stone to educational administration, 'and after a brief stay went on to better paid posts and more distinguished careers elsewhere'.[52] In transit they brought with them contemporary educational ideas, ideals and activities and ensured their acceptance.

How successful were these Oxbridge tutors in promoting athleticism, and a manly, muscular Christianity in the colleges? How quickly did these ideals spread? How fully were they accepted by staff and students?

Answering these questions *in part* will involve an examination of the ways in which ritual was used to advance acceptance. It will also provide an illustration of how an inter-disciplinary approach on the part of cultural historians can throw light on historical change.

The introduction of athleticism into teacher training college life was reinforced by patterns of behaviour that were highly ritualised in nature. Before discussing and analysing the ritualistic life of the students and demonstrating the ways in which ritualism helped promote athleticism's diffusion, it may be helpful to consider the general importance of ritual and symbol to individuals and communities.

As J.A. Mangan has observed, 'To define ritual is not a simple task. Social scientists have many definitions and diverse opinions.'[53] He favours the definition of T. Paterson: 'Rituals are formalised behaviour patterns, methods of communication, verbal and non-verbal, necessary for the establishment of relations among members of a group or between groups.'[54] In his discussion of ritual Mangan sees it as having five main purposes: it serves as a mechanism for the transmission of cultural values through the systematic repetition of actions; it strengthens the accepted value system by the development of a mass reflex action; it acts as a focusing mechanism by creating a frame for experience which assists concentration and minimises distractions; it helps memory by making vivid what was dim and recalling what was forgotten; finally, it controls experience and shapes social reality 'in the sense that by producing powerful emotive responses to relationships it makes these relationships lasting'.[55] In these ways ritual helps develop, promote and reinforce feelings which determine roles and role playing in society. This fundamental view of ritual, it is argued here, has both relevance and significance to an analysis of the late Victorian and Edwardian London teacher training colleges and their espousal of athleticism as means of inculcating period moral manliness.

B. Bernstein, H.L. Elvin and R.S. Peters for their part, in a complementary consideration, believe that ritual 'generally refers to a relatively rigid pattern of acts specific to a situation which construct a framework of meaning over and beyond specific situational meanings'. For Bernstein, Elvin and Peters 'the symbolic function of ritual is to relate the individual through ritualistic acts to a social order, to heighten respect for that order, to reverify that order within the individual and, in particular, to deepen acceptance of the procedures used to maintain continuity, order and boundary and which control ambivalence towards the social order'.[56] Bernstein and his colleagues also maintain that schools (and by extension here training colleges) operate at two levels, transmitting both an instrumental and expressive culture. The instrumental culture relates to the specific curriculum, whereas the expressive culture is concerned with consensus.[57] This expressive culture utilises consensual and differentiation rituals. Consensual rituals bind a community together. 'They recreate the past in the present and project it into the future ...relate the school's values and norms to those held by, or alleged to be held by, certain dominant groups in the non school society ... give the school its specific identity as a distinct and separate institution,'[58] and they 'consist of assemblies and ceremonies of various kinds together with the consensual lineaments of dress, the imagery of signs, totems, scrolls and plaques for revivifying of special historical contests and other symbolic features'.[59] Differentiation rituals, on the other hand, 'are concerned to mark off groups within the school from each other, usually in terms of age, sex, relation or social function ... [They] deepen local attachment behaviour to, and detachment behaviour from specific groups; they also deepen respect behaviour to those in various positions of authority, and create order in time.'[60] In this latter way, these differentiating rituals can, and do, bond communities and individuals through the creation of stable, ordered, hierarchical frameworks within which to operate.

Mangan has further identified three of the most common types of school ritual activity: rites of passage, rites of deference and rites of intensification. Rites of passage 'assist individuals or groups [to] effect a successful change of status by providing formal and public recognition of the change'; rites of deference stress a pattern of 'subordinate superordinate relationships so as to create social order through regularised social relationships', and rites of intensification 'are a means of strengthening group cohesion primarily in times of stress, but not necessarily so. They also function as regular on-going cohesive processes.'[61]

Mangan, together with Berstein and his colleagues in their respective discussion of ritual in schools, it is suggested, offer useful conceptual tools with which to explore the role of ritual in the London teacher training colleges in their effort to implement both the precepts and practices of athleticism. The last years of the Victorian age and the beginning of the Edwardian age witnessed a burgeoning of ritualised behaviour in the colleges linked to sporting activities and associated dress codes and hierarchical relationships, that served, directly and indirectly, to bind the members together and to promote order and stability.

For reasons that will become apparent later, to reiterate, it should be made absolutely apparent that differentiating rituals are commonly used to establish institutional 'pecking orders' in the interest of community cohesion and control, and this was the case in the colleges. This is made abundantly clear from the following comment by P.B. Ballard, writing of his time as a student at Borough Road during 1883–85. He observed that between

> the Seniors, or second-year men, and the Juniors, or first-year men, was a great gulf fixed. It was the Seniors who fixed it, and they who preserved it. A Junior who met a Senior in the street had to raise his hat, but the Senior was not obliged to return the salute. A clear lack of respect was punished by slippering. The culprit's bedroom was raided at dead of night, and he received an assault upon his person which left him smarting – and thinking.[62]

This was not all. It was 'during the first week of the year that the Seniors made their privileged position most palpably felt. They had a set of hoaxes, some traditional, some spontaneous, which they sprang on the new-comers.'[63] There was, for example, the traditional football hoax. In an early football match between the Seniors and Juniors, the Seniors deliberately fielded a weakened team thus allowing the Juniors to win. Then, with the replay, observed Ballard, 'came the real match, which involved a penalty for the losers (such as providing jam all round for tea), and this time the Juniors were beaten to a frazzle!'[64]

Similar rituals were to be found in all the London colleges although the precise nature of the ritual differed from college to college. They were, however, by no means unique to the metropolitan colleges. A particularly good example is provided by St Paul's, Cheltenham.[65] On their first morning at St Paul's the juniors were woken at 6.30 and told to dress for drill. The drill sergeant was a senior student who took them on a countryside march and slipped away unnoticed leaving them completely lost, and on their second night 'the juniors were subjected to a visit from the "Jury", twelve men chosen from the Senior Year to undertake the management and education of the Juniors. The Jury grotesquely attired, holding candles and whistling a mournful tune marched through the Junior corridors, halted and shouted "Juniors must not be familiar with their Seniors. Juniors beware. This is not a joke!'"[66] Juniors were subsequently christened with nicknames, including demeaning names such as 'Nancy' and 'Soapy'. 'The christening involved the anointing of students with various obnoxious substances.' Furthermore, throughout the year 'the Juniors had to perform various minor acts of abasement, such as snapping their fingers when entering a room. They could be punished for failure to do this or for generalised crimes such as "cheek". Punishment consisted of "cold baths, gauntlets of knotted towels and the like."'[67] The pecking order was thoroughly established.

Similar ritualised behaviour occurred at St Luke's College, Exeter, a Church of England college founded in 1839. F. Fuller, the college historian, has described the first day of the college year. When the new students arrived they were met by a number of leading senior students. The same Drill hoax as at St Paul's followed. The seniors would form 'the whole junior year into a drill squad and march them to Exeter Drill Hall, leaving the poor Juniors to work out their own salvation'.[68] This was to ensure, of course, that they quickly appreciated that there was 'a great distinction between the Senior and Junior years'. Furthermore, the newcomers soon learnt, painfully if necessary, that 'Seniors ... had to be addressed by the Juniors with almost awe and reverence'.[69]

From these descriptions of the ways in which new students were received into the various colleges, it is clear that the colleges had elaborate, well-prepared and well-rehearsed rituals which served to ensure the humiliation of juniors. These activities were far more than student high jinks. They had a more profound significance and it is now time to emphasise their fundamental purpose. The actions of the senior students are assertive rites of differentiation and deference, relating 'the individual through ritualistic acts to a social order, to heighten respect for that order... and in particular, to deepen acceptance of the procedures used to maintain continuity, order and boundary'.[70] From the first moment of their arrival these 'freshmen' were made sharply aware of institutional precedent. Juniors were subordinate to seniors, seniors to their elected officers (the 'Jury' at St Paul's and 'the Poets' at Borough Road) who in turn were subordinate to the junior tutors, who were subordinate to the house tutors and so on, in a reflection of the considerable importance attached to hierarchy in Victorian and Edwardian education and society.

Charles More, rather curiously, in his analytically myopic history of St Paul's Training College, Cheltenham, is critical of the transparently obvious comment that such rites 'can be defined as ways of stressing a structured pattern of subordinate/superordinate relationships ... which create social order through regularised social relationships',[71] and thus by extension, of the views, of both Mangan and Bernstein and his colleagues, not to mention the views of the most distinguished of social anthropologists.[72] Since More does not appear to have consulted the work of anthropologists of the calibre of Victor Turner and Mary Douglas, he remains easily confident in his ignorance. More argues that while rites of deference might or might not have a functional role, 'their functionality for an institution depends on whether structured patterns of subordinate/superordinate relationships are the aim of the institution'. The fact that many institutions at the time got on perfectly well without such rites, claims More, bravely without a scrap of supporting evidence, 'shows that they are not functional to social order as such'. Therefore, he concludes that 'given that there was no particular reason in a training college why senior students should lord it over juniors, it seems likely that the St Paul's rites of deference were needless to say actively dysfunctional'.[73] There are, of course, several obvious institutional reasons why seniors should 'lord it' over juniors. They have been mentioned above. They will be discussed further shortly.

More adds somewhat brashly that, whatever *post hoc* reasons anthropologists, in his injudicious words, 'dream up', at St Paul's, deferential rituals had no positive institutional reason for existing![74] More's idiosyncratic argument that not only St Paul's but *many* institutions, crucially unnamed and unlocated by him, got on well without rituals functional to social order, is interesting. Clearly it would be illuminating to obtain an accurate list of Victorian and Edwardian educational institutions *indifferent* to structured patterns of subordinate/superordinate relationships! A new field of scholarship would open up.

More's analysis then leaves a great deal to be desired. His reading is unacceptably limited and his empirical evidence casually omitted. Mangan, in contrast, has the basic virtue in his analysis of the public school of providing ample evidence of the functional *and* dysfunctional purposes of ritual.[75] In his analysis of the teacher training college, unfortunately, the same cannot be said for More. His unsubstantiated assertion that as many institutions got on perfectly well without such rites reveals that they are not functional to social order as such, should not go unchallenged. It is a glib assertion. Evidence from the London colleges alone contradicts his casual and complacent view. There is clear evidence that rites of deference were an integral part of the college ritualisation process. These rites served positive purposes. For this reason, and others, they were endorsed by the college authorities. Among other things, they taught students to *know their place* – a valuable lesson for later schoolroom discipline, a point More overlooks completely. A further salient point that More overlooks is the crucial role that the public school and ancient university personnel had as 'change agents' and 'opinion leaders' in an age much given to the security and stability provided by hierarchical structures. The public schools and ancient universities were replete with deferential rituals. What these institutions also had was cachet. For this reason alone if no other, they were to be imitated by the colleges. There are more compelling purposes served by ritual. They will be considered later.

By the time More wrote dismissively of rites of deference, Mangan, of course, had devoted an important segment of what has become accepted as a seminal work, to the processes of ritual, symbol and myth in the *public school*. He had not extrapolated to the training colleges. He might usefully have done so. His analysis fits them tightly. Any blindness of vision is More's.

There is a further dimension to any consideration of ritual in the colleges. One significant way in which ritualisation for order, security and stability was promoted was by what has been elegantly called the invention of tradition, 'a set of practices, normally governed by overtly or tacitly accepted rules and of a ritual or symbolic nature, which seek to inculcate certain values and norms of behaviour by repetition, which automatically implies continuity with the past'.[76] Three overlapping types of invented tradition have been suggested: 'those establishing or symbolising social cohesion or the membership of groups real or artificial communities; those establishing or legitimising institutions, status or relations of authority; and those whose main purpose was socialisation, the inculcation of beliefs, value systems and conventions and conventions of behaviour'.[77] This list is important for understanding the ways in which the various forms of ritual affected behaviour in the colleges. The invented deferential rites that new students had to endure for example, were clearly meant, among other things, to legitimise an institutional system of student authority. An authority established in this way by students over students resulted in a student hierarchy which ensured order and discipline within the student body, and thus by extension within the college itself! Such a system, of course, was perfected, initially, in the public schools.[78] One perfectly understandable purpose was that it reduced the burden of control carried by the senior college authorities and made life more tolerable for them!

In the assertion of student authority, the 'Poets' at Borough Road appear to have had a role similar to the public school 'bloods' (successful athletes). Every year 12 of the most prestigious athletic seniors were elected and given the name 'Poets' after the corner of the dormitory that they occupied.[79] Bartle states that one of their functions was 'to maintain college enthusiasm at football and cricket matches, where they acted as cheerleaders' – a practice common in public schools of the time! More particularly, says Bartle, their role was to keep the juniors in their place – a practice equally common in the public schools of the time.[80] The 'Poets' were augmented by college prefects 'who applied college rules and supervised private study and who seem, on the whole, to have collaborated with the 'Poets' in enforcing subordination'.[81] Juniors from their first evening in the college:

> ... were regimented in Nazi-style by Prefects, given orders with shouts, threatening, and epithets, and instructions on their behaviour when in the presence of Prefects, Poets, Seniors in general. They were forced to button their coats, to wear certain ties, to be practically dumb and certainly without a laugh at the meal table... forbidden to leave till 'their Seniors' had finished. In the Common Room they sat clear of the easy chairs, in their cubicles they listened in silence to chants, threats and fearsome stories of former Juniors who had transgressed the law ... they were excluded from privileges and sometimes from teams. And not till they got to know each other and found safety in numbers did they dream of finding their feet, let alone swim against the tide.[82]

The power of the Poets was considerable. Juniors who tried to stand up to them would find themselves 'seized at the dead of night by the Poets and slippered in a particular cubicle along "Poet's Corner" which was used for the purpose'.[83] As Mangan has written of similar punishment rituals in the public schools 'Through a single punishment ritual they defined social position, emphasised the location of power and moulded group behaviour.'[84] Apart from physical beatings the Poets could also order acts of public humiliation for junior students such as sweeping the leaves off the football pitch for displaying insufficient enthusiasm at a college football match. E.J.W. Killick, at Borough Road from 1912 to 1914, has written that the juniors were made 'to sing for the amusement of the Seniors after Saturday tea, which was the occasion for the vociferous rendering of the College song, finishing up with the "war cry"'.[85] Bartle has observed significantly that 'No interference with this practice seems to have come from the House Tutors who had themselves been Prefects and Poets in earlier college generations and probably believed that awkward Juniors deserved putting in their place.'[86] Furthermore, the Poets were clearly sanctioned and supported by the principal. One of his favoured students, Herbert Milnes, was a prominent Poet. In this role he upheld college policy to the satisfaction of Burrell. 'In the B.R.C. Parliament of 1894 he entered with a fancy waistcoat expanded to the utmost, kid gloves, walking-stick, button-hole, tall hat, and even an eye-glass ... His answers to all political questions referring to Fives Courts, Rushers, and Brown Bread Returns were considered very happy and all opponents were silenced.'[87] Burrell's admiration for Milnes' orthodoxy was such that when Allan R. Smith, the Loretto and Oxford educated house tutor left for a position with the Inspectorate, 'the Committee on Burrell's strong recommendation, immediately appointed Milnes as House Tutor'.[88] Thus deference rituals should not be carelessly dismissed. As the eminent social anthropologist Mary Douglas has reminded us:

> if we accept that the social relations of men provide the prototype for logical relations between things, then, whenever this prototype falls into a common pattern there should be something common to be discerned in the system of symbols it uses... The first logical categories were social categories; the first classes of things were classes of men... It was because men were grouped and thought of themselves in the forms of groups that in their ideas they grouped other things. The centre of the first scheme of nature is not the individual; it is society.[89]

Douglas further refers to the 'rule of distance' in which 'the more the social situation exerts pressure on persons involved in it, the more the demand for conformity tends to be expressed by a demand for physical control'.[90] The sometimes trivial, sometimes terrifying, but always purposeful rites of deference, physical and otherwise, of the Poets and others are crucial to an understanding of the ordered group arrangements of the London colleges.

The views of Victor Turner are also illuminating on this topic. He provides thoughtful explanations of the purpose and value of deference rituals as mechanisms of social order. Turner has written informatively of hierarchy, humility, status elevation and status reversal. In his consideration of rituals of status reversal, he writes of 'the liminality frequently found in cyclical and calendrical ritual usually of a collective kind in which, at certain culturally defined points in the seasonal cycle, groups or categories of persons who habitually occupy low status positions in the social structure are positively enjoined to exercise ritual authority over their superiors; and they, in their turn, must accept with good will their ritual degradation'.[91] The jam hoax at Borough Road is an excellent example of this. By deliberately allowing the junior students to win a preliminary football match, the senior students appeared ridiculous and second best. However, they reasserted their power by subsequently defeating the juniors some weeks later, to the juniors cost in more ways than one. In this way the seniors and their superior status was driven home and reinforced and internal order established and secured. More may find Turner's anthropological analysis unconvincing, 'dreamed up' to use his expression, but it is certainly more convincing and intellectually rigorous than his own explanation of a 'gradual historical process' of emerging stability, security and order due exclusively to rites of intensification, which incidentally, he neither defines, explains, or traces.

In summary, ritualisation in various forms was an integral part of the students' lives, ordering, stabilising and structuring their relationships. It reveals a lack of investigation, contextualisation, comprehension and sensitivity to suggest otherwise. In the college, rites of deference maintained discipline, established order, provided a stable hierarchical security, ensured desirable and desired positions of power and offered the opportunity for the acquisition and display of high status – all functional elements in college, and later, life.

Of course, rites of intensification *were* also powerful phenomena in college life. One was the annual athletics meeting of the colleges held at Stamford Bridge. First inaugurated in 1898 by the Principals of Borough Road, St John's and St Mary's, it soon became *the* major sporting event for all the colleges. This athletic meeting was a pre-eminent rite of intensification. As Mangan has written, such rituals 'bound together the whole group as a moral community'.[92] In this regard, for the public schools, he suggests, the annual Eton versus Harrow match at Lord's was 'a focusing mechanism, mnemonic agent and value filter *par excellence*'.[93] For the colleges the athletic meeting at Stamford Bridge served the same purposes. It is difficult to overstate its importance. T. Adkins, the author of *St John's College History*, and himself a former student of the college, provides clear evidence both of the seriousness with which the students viewed this competition and other athletic activities, and of the new muscular masculine world they now inhabited: '...the Sinjun of today is a vigorous and enthusiastic athlete keeping himself in training for sports of all kinds and scoring successes all round ... we see energetic younger brethren hard at it sprinting, leaping, putting the weight and preparing themselves in all sorts of ways to go anywhere and do anything'.[94]

By the end of the first decade of the twentieth century athleticism was firmly entrenched in the London colleges. Its diffusion from private school and privileged university to teacher training college was more or less complete. Diffusion had been promoted, reinforced and consolidated in part by a student lifestyle that was marked by a new and highly ritualised masculine behaviour. Rituals had played a part in establishing in the young students, a masculine, muscular Christian view of the world. It was a view ensured essentially by certain criticisms made by the Cross Commission, by the appointment of middle-class principals sympathetic to these criticisms and to the public school and university games cult that in part produced them, by the recruitment of appropriate young staff from the same background with the same convictions – that there were moral values to be learnt on games fields, that in part 'manliness' was to be achieved there, that in part masculinity was to be learnt there, that in part by way of these things a 'proper' masculinity was to be transmitted via the elementary school to the working-class boy to his advantage, for his betterment and for the harmonious well-being of society.

Athleticism, of course, was a complex educational ideology. It became both a popular and fashionable college ideology for more than educational reasons. It was popular because it offered a distraction, as in the public school, from what was otherwise a sterile and restricted training college classroom curriculum. It was fashionable also because it allowed the college the chance to emulate the upper and middle classes. In a period when the status of the elementary schoolteacher was held in low esteem, the opportunity to mix with, ape and compete against socially more advantaged opponents, was attractive. In a valedictory farewell in the *B's Hum* to A.V. Houghton, a graduate of Hertford College, Oxford, who was a tutor at Borough Road from 1895 to 1898, the writer wrote appreciatively:

> Of his powers in the cricket and football fields we cannot speak too highly, and it must be remembered that it was largely through the instrumentality of Mr. Houghton that our teams have been able to meet (and even vanquish) such redoubtable opponents as Old Etonians or the strong cricket team which Mr. Lacey brought down last year.[95]

The teacher training colleges fully recognised that they needed to improve their social image if they were to flourish, win favour, earn greater respect. So it was due to mixed motives that athleticism arrived, flourished in and spread from the teacher training college. Whatever the reasons behind the diffusion, assimilation and reproduction of athleticism, however, it was responsible for gradually promoting a new masculinity, a masculinity of the games field, in the elementary schools and among the elementary schoolboys of England, Britain and the Empire.[96] This responsibility within the colleges is considered here for the first time. In a consideration of the making of masculinity in Europe, it is argued here in addition that the significance of this chapter goes further. It establishes a precedent. The relationship between gender construction, identification and expectation and the teacher training college and the consequent influence on the working class boy in the elementary school system merits further and fuller consideration *throughout* Europe.

NOTES

1. Education featured strongly as an issue in the general election of 1885, which was won by the Conservatives under Lord Salisbury. The Catholic Archbishop, Cardinal Manning, had led a campaign to protect the status of denominational schools and had written to Salisbury seeking his support. When in power Salisbury established a Royal Commission to 'inquire into the working of the Elementary Education Acts, England and Wales'. The chairman was his Home Secretary, R.A. Viscount Cross (1823–1914). The Commission sat for three years before producing a final, but divided Report in 1888. See R.A. Cross, *A Family History* (Eccle Riggs, 1900) *and A Political History* (Eccle Riggs, 1903). Interestingly, in neither memoir does Cross refer to his role on the Commission.
2. For what is generally recognised as the authoritative study of athleticism as an educational ideology, see J.A. Mangan, *Athleticism in the Victorian and Edwardian Public School: The Emergence and Consolidation of an Educational Ideology* (Cambridge, 1981). *Athleticism* will be reprinted by Frank Cass (London) in 2000.
3. See J.A. Mangan, *The Games Ethic and Imperialism* (London, 1998).
4. R. Holt, *Sport and the British: A Modern History* (Oxford, 1989), p.357.

5. See Mangan, *Athleticism*. For a consideration of ritual and symbol in the public school system incorporating an inter-disciplinary approach see especially ch.7.
6. Sheldon Rothblatt, Introduction to the Cass edition of *Athleticism in the Victorian and Edwardian Public School* (London, forthcoming).
7. In fact, J.A. Mangan utilised concepts from the social sciences in a very much earlier study of sport in society. See J.A Mangan (ed.), *Physical Education and Sport: Sociological and Cultural Perspectives* (Oxford, 1975), pp.87–102. Indeed, an earlier paper published in *Research Papers in Physical Education, Carnegie College of Physical Education*, 2, 1 (Jan. 1971), 2–7, dealt with ritual.
8. For evidence of the ideology at 'Oxbridge', see for example, 'Lamentable Barbarians and Pitiful Sheep: Rhetoric of Protest and Pleasure in Late Victorian and Edwardian "Oxbridge"', *Victorian Studies*, 34, 4 (Summer 1991), 473–90.
9. See Donald Leinster-Mackay, *The Rise of the English Prep School* (London, 1984).
10. See J.A. Mangan, 'Grammar Schools and the Games Ethic in the Victorian and Edwardian Eras', *Albion*, 15, 14 (1984), 313, and see notes 2,7 above.
11. Everett M. Rogers, *Diffusion of Innovations* (London, 1983), p.5.
12. Ibid., p.11.
13. Ibid.
14. Westminster College was established in 1851. The impetus for its construction came from the Wesleyan Education Committee who believed that a Training College was vital if Methodism was to spread throughout Britain. A number of sites were examined in London with Westminster being chosen as it was an area containing a large and poor population. The College was built to accommodate 100 students, male and female, with a satellite practising school of 1,333 pupils. See F.C. Pritchard, *A History of Westminster College 1851–1951* (London, 1951).
15. Pritchard, *A History*, p.104.
16. Ibid., p.108.
17. Principal's Log, 7 May 1904, Westminster College Archives A/3/C/1.
18. Pritchard, *A History*, p.109. Stamford Bridge was built for two brothers, James and William Waddle of the London Athletic Cub by R. and G. Neale of Wandsworth for £2,899 in 1876. The ground was first used on Saturday, 28 April 1877. The ground hosted many Amateur Athletic Association Championships. It became the home of Chelsea Football Club in 1905. For full history, see Colin Benson, *The Bridge: The History of Stamford Bridge* (London, 1987).
19. Pritchard, *A History*, pp.108–9.
20. *The Westminsterian* (Oct. 1906), 11.
21. Pritchard, *A History*, pp.109–10.
22. Ibid., p.111.
23. Minutes of Governing Body of Westminster College, 12 Oct. 1914, p.46.
24. See Mangan, *The Games Ethic*, p.173 for a description of Bishop John Coleridge Patteson, a role model for men like Leigh Smith.
25. Cecil Rolo Peyton Andrews (1870–1951) attended Merchant Taylors' School from 1879 to 1888 and St John's College Oxford (1889–93). After a short spell teaching in Highgate School and Forest School in London he became a lecturer at St John's Training College in Battersea. He emigrated to Western Australia and became Principal of a Teacher Training College from 1901 to 1903. He was made head of the Education department of the University of Western Australia in 1903 and a member of the Senate in 1912. He became Pro Vice-Chancellor and retired in 1929. For a history of Merchant Taylors' see F.W.M. Draper, *Four Centuries of Merchant Taylors' Schools* (London, 1962).
26. Andrews was appointed to Highgate school in Sept 1893, and stayed less than a year leaving in March 1984. See T. Hinde, *Highgate School: A History* (London, 1993).
27. Forest School was founded as a Proprietary School in 1834 and catered for about 200 boys at the time of Andrews' appointment in 1894. For a full history see Guy Deaton, *Schola Sylvestris* (the School, 1972) and G. Wright, *Forest School 1834–1894* (the School, 1994).
28. St John's College was originally founded as a private venture in 1840 by Edward Tufnell and Dr James Kay-Shuttleworth who was the Secretary for the Committee for Council on Education which had been set up in 1839. The College was built according to the principles of the Established Church. By 1842 the cost of maintaining the College was beyond the resources

of the two men and the College passed into the hands of the National Society. For a complete history see T. Adkins, *The History of St. John's College Battersea. The Story of a Noble Experiment* (London, 1906).

29. *St. John's Magazine*, 11, 2 (Dec. 1899), 19.
30. Marlborough, of course, played a major role in the evolution of the ideology of Athleticism, see Mangan, *Athleticism, passim.*
31. *St John's Magazine*, 11, 3 (Feb. 1904), 54.
32. St. Mark's College Chelsea was founded by the National Society in 1841. The Society had the official aim of 'promoting the education of the poor in the principles of the Established Church throughout England and Wales'. The first Principal was Derwent Coleridge (1800–83) who was the son of the poet Samuel Taylor Coleridge. The College was located in Chelsea and from the earliest times tried to have a more liberal and relaxed environment than was ever the case at either Borough Road or Westminster. See G.W. Gent, *Memorials of St. Mark's College* (London, 1891).
33. C.H. Swann, 'Cross Country Running', *St. Mark's College Magazine*, 6, Michaelmas Term (1905), 91–3.
34. Ibid., p.91.
35. G.F. Bartle 'Staffing Policy at a Victorian Training College', *Victorian Education*, Occasional Publication no.2 (1976), 16–23.
36. Borough Road College was originally founded by Joseph Lancaster in 1798. The College was run on non-denominational lines (Lancaster was a Quaker) and administered by the British and Foreign School Society. By 1888 it was one of the best and most famous teacher training colleges in the country. For a complete account see G. F. Bartle, *A History of Borough Road College* (Kettering, 1976).
37. Bartle, 'Staffing Policy...', p.20.
38. See Christopher Hibbert, *No Ordinary Place: Radley College and the Public School System 1847–1997* (London 1998).
39. P.B. Ballard, *Things I Cannot Forget* (London, 1933), p.47.
40. *B's Hum*, 8, 67 (Feb. 1897), 1.
41. See J.A. Mangan and Colm Hickey, 'English Elementary Education Revisited and Revised: Drill and Athleticism in Tandem', *European Sports History Review*, Vol.1 (1999), 63–91.
42. Frank Stewart, Loretto *One-Fifty: The Story of Loretto School from 1827 to 1977* (Edinburgh, 1981), p.159.
43. See Mangan, *Athleticism, passim.*
44. Stewart, *Loretto*, p.159.
45. Ibid., p.164.
46. Lorettonianism was 'an elaborate and systematic programme of health education covering food, clothes, physical exercise, sleep, fresh air and cold baths', Mangan, *Athleticism*, p.54.
47. A.R. Smith, *Loretto School Sermons* (Oxford, 1929), p.5.
48. Ibid.
49. Ibid., p.28.
50. Stewart, *Loretto One-Fifty*, pp.196–8.
51. For a complete history of the club, see Ian Hay, *The Cliff Dwellers.*
52. Bartle 'Staffing Policy...', p.21.
53. Mangan, *Athleticism*, p.142.
54. T. Paterson, 'Emotive Rituals in Industrial Organisms', *Philosophical Transactions of the Royal Society of London*, 257, Series B (1966), 437.
55. Mangan, *Athleticism*, p.42.
56. B. Bernstein, H.L. Elvin and R.S. Peters 'Ritual in Education', *Philosophical Transactions of the Royal Society*, 251, Series B (1966), 429.
57. Ibid.
58. Ibid.
59. Ibid., p 430.
60. Ibid.
61. Mangan, 'Physical Education as a Ritual Process...', p.88.
62. Ballard, *Things*, p.44.

63. Ibid., p.44.
64. Ibid., p.46.
65. C. More, *The Training of Teachers, 1847–1947. A History of the Church Colleges at Cheltenham* (London, 1992).
66. Ibid., p156.
67. Ibid., p.157.
68. F. Fuller, *The History of St. Luke's College*, 4 Volumes, Vol. II, 1886–1933 (Exeter, 1970), p.324.
69. Ibid., p. 323.
70. B. Bernstein *et al.*, 'Ritual in Education...', p.437.
71. Mangan, 'Physical Education as a Ritual Process...', p.88.
72. There is no reference to these distinguished authorities in More's bibliography.
73. More, *The Training of Teachers*, p.158.
74. Ibid.
75. See Mangan, *Athleticism*, Ch.7.
76. E. Hobsbawm, 'Introduction: Inventing Traditions', in E. Hobsbawm and T. Ranger (eds.), *The Invention of Tradition* (Cambridge, 1983), p.1.
77. Ibid., p.9.
78. See Mangan, *Athleticism, passim.*
79. For a discussion of the public school 'blood', see Mangan, *Athleticism*, pp.171–7.
80. Bartle, *A History*, p.78.
81. Ibid.
82. 'Retrospect by Yeldor', *B's Hum* (1939), 61.
83. Bartle, *A History*, p.78.
84. Mangan, *Athleticism*, p.141.
85. Bartle, *A History*, p.91.
86. Ibid., p.78.
87. A. Burrell, *Bert Milnes: A Brief Memoir* (Letchworth, 1922), p.14.
88. Ibid., p.16.
89. Mary Douglas, *Natural Symbols: Explorations in Cosmology* (London, 1973), pp.11–12.
90. Ibid., p.12.
91. Victor Turner, *The Ritual Process* (London, 1969), p.167.
92. Mangan, *Athleticism*, p.143.
93. Ibid.
94. T. Adkins, *The History of St John's College Battersea*, p.240.
95. *B's Hum*, 9, 74 (Jan. 1898), 2.
96. See J.A. Mangan and Colm Hickey, 'A Pioneer of the Proletariat: Herbert Milnes and the Games Cult in New Zealand', in J.A. Mangan and J. Nauright (eds.), *The Australasian World: Sport in Society* (London, forthcoming).

Gymnastics as a Masculinity Rite: Ollerup Danish Gymnastics between the Wars

HANS BONDE

Niels Bukh is an example of the twentieth-century sports coach as a role model who instills norms of masculine behaviour in boys who have been brought up in female-dominated institutional and family settings.[1] Today the character-forming potential of sport and its role in ensuring 'manliness' and the tough masculine virtues have been outlawed in the Nordic world, in part as a result of the progress of feminism. In contrast, in the decades after the turn of the last century due to the growing importance of work outside the home, men were separated from the upbringing of their own and other people's boys. The family as an educational setting was increasingly left in the hands of women, and a true mother cult developed.[2] The father's role in male socialisation did not wholly disappear. It remained in the world of sport. Sport became a laboratory for making masculinity, where men could create and cultivate a body, motor skills, and competitiveness for modern society.

Sport has been central to Men's Studies no doubt due to the fact that sport both symbolises and publicises desirable masculine qualities in a competitive modern world. These studies have too often been characterised by a naïve, unilateral patriarchalism. *Jocks, Sports and Male Identity* exemplifies this tendency. Several chapter headings are explicit in their one-sidedness: 'Sports and Sexism', 'Violence, Sports and Masculinity', and 'Women, Sex-Role Stereotyping and Sports'.[3] Another example of unbalanced analysis is Varda Burstyn's *The Rites of Men: Manhood, Politics and the Culture of Sport*.[4] Arguably North American sport can be rougher and more stereotypically masculine than sport in Scandinavia, but such extreme feminist approaches wholly fail to explain why so many young American men take up a variety of sports, and fail to explain the increasing attraction of aggressive competitive sports among women! Other more balanced research, however, possesses nuance, subtlety and balance. This is to be found in *The International Journal of the History of Sport*, and particularly in *Manliness and Morality: Middle-class Masculinity in Britain and America, 1800–1940*.[5] In Scandinavia masculinity and gymnastics have caught the attention of gender analysts.[6] This chapter reflects this interest.

Danish gymnastics between the two World Wars is a neglected subject of research on youth as well as of general historical research. This neglect is the result of intellectual myopia in academics – sport and the body were sources of actions not analysis. It was not until the 1980s that the study of sport became definitely accepted as a university discipline in Denmark, in keeping with the development of the alternative movement culture and a new receptiveness among academics to a wider range of socio-historical subjects. Today 'the body' has become a buzz-word in academic circles, which can be included in all sorts of book titles or lectures, without necessarily adding much to our understanding of its role in culture and society.

Niels Bukh was an internationally acclaimed Danish gymnastics teacher. By the late 1930s Bukh became probably the best-known living Dane at home and abroad. By this time he was both well known and well travelled. From 1912 on he participated in all the Olympic Games – except Los Angeles in 1932 and London in 1948 – and was a regular attender at the world fairs. In the 1920s he had promoted Denmark by travelling every summer to various European countries, and in 1923 and 1926 he visited the United States. In the 1930s he extended his travels to the two 'new' continents with visits to South America in 1938 and to South Africa in 1939.

Danish gymnastics between the wars is the subject of this chapter. Gymnastics became a powerful youth movement, especially in rural areas. The pioneer in developing this movement was Niels Bukh, who in 1920 founded Denmark's first gymnastic folk high school, the Ollerup Gymnastic Folk High School (Gymnastikhøjskolen i Ollerup).[7] The Danish højskole, known in English as a 'folk' high school or college, is an educational institution where the young especially can spend some months together to expand their horizons through instruction in general subjects without receiving grades and without any other purpose than that of self-development. Niels Bukh began with the folk high school idea, but made gymnastics the focus of his school.

Niels Bukh was the best known Danish physical education specialist in Denmark and overseas during the 1930s. As mentioned above, he may well have been the Dane who was best known internationally during this period. During the course of the 1920s Niels Bukh toured the world with his gymnastics. But it was not until 1931, in connection with his so-called 'round the world tour', which included the Soviet Union, Japan, Korea, USA and Canada, that his fame was permanently secured.

This chapter considers Ollerup gymnastics as a rite of passage, linking boyhood with adulthood. The presentation of gender norms in a dramatic form, starting with the body itself, was characteristic of Ollerup gymnastics. Why should a 'highly developed' and 'civilised' society feel the need to express these gender norms in such a physically dramatic form? This chapter seeks to find the answer.[8]

YOUTH WORSHIP AND YOUTH REVOLT

In 1922 Niels Bukh published the book *Primitiv Gymnastik eller Grundgymnastik* (Primitive Gymnastics), which can be regarded as his gymnastic manifesto. The book was reprinted many times and translated into several languages, including English, German and Japanese. Niels Bukh's book and practice represented a break with traditional gymnastics in rural areas, which was characterised by the so-called Swedish or Ling gymnastics, which from the 1880s had been widespread in folk high schools and community halls in rural areas.[9] Bukh used Ling gymnastics as a basis, but moved its focus away from the traditional static and rigid postures by stressing rhythm, movement and suppleness. It should be emphasised, however, that even before Bukh, the Danish version of Ling gymnastics had, as far as males were concerned, included leaping. Bukh maintained that Ling gymnastics had not achieved its goal of improving the physical condition of youngsters, and was physiologically ineffective. Bukh's gymnastics comprised 'primitive gymnastics', intended to make the body more supple, and 'sport gymnastics', which stressed the beauty of movement.

Some of the older Ling instructors were strongly opposed to the brisk tempo of Bukh gymnastics and his semi–nude male gymnasts, who appeared in their 'little, black' boxer shorts. Another point of contention was the lack of priority Bukh gave to erect bearing and to the many commands required in Ling gymnastics.

The Bukh gymnasts' 'youth revolt' was a great success, for all over the country young gymnasts eagerly adopted his new gymnastic methods. Bukh was thus a rebel, both with regard to the advocacy of nakedness and the provocatively brisk tempo. He also, of course, challenged contemporary sexual morals by frequent physical contact between males. Nevertheless, the semi–clad primitive gymnastics, with its variety of movements, was not publicly exhibited until the 1930s. The hard, flexed bodies, symbolic of self–control, guaranteed that the sensual message would remain muted.[10] Thus Ollerup gymnastics, from its early phase of 1914 onwards, was anything but traditionally oriented. On the contrary, it unleashed what was to many people a loathsome and heretical 'youth revolt', directed against the prevailing Ling-oriented gymnastics. As Bukh's gymnastics gained increasing popularity after his world tour in 1931, Bukh established himself as the outstanding father figure of Danish gymnastics. The rebellion ended in conformity. It became a ritual.

The book *Primitive Gymnastics* was characterised by a profound respect for youth, which was to be 'cultivated' through gymnastics. Bukh often described youth as if he were a farmer contemplating his fields. Youth was the ground which, if it received the proper cultivation, would become fertile and produce good yields. Bukh, like the other folk high school directors, addressed his former pupils each year in the *Year Book of the Gymnastikhøjskolen*. A monolithic conception of youth is a constant feature of these addresses. Youth appears as a collective mass with a single voice, and Bukh felt himself to be closely involved with this voice.

Bukh did not consider his gymnastics explicitly as a rite of passage, but on the other hand he understood the main purpose of both the school and gymnastics to be to impart to youngsters solid cultural values. Youth was to be reformed and improved through gymnastics.

These youngsters, who were to be developed through gymnastics, were predominantly from the rural middle class. Agricultural labourers' children never attended Ollerup in the same numbers as farmers' children. The student registers during the school years of 1930–31 to 1934–35 reveal that farmers' sons predominated. Some 42 per cent of the pupils' fathers were farmers, whilst only 4.8 per cent had agricultural labourers as fathers, despite occasional grants from the local authorities. In general, agricultural labourers had neither the desire nor the opportunity to take their children out of productive work for anything like the 'superfluous' gymnastic folk high school.

THE CULT CHARACTERISTICS OF GYMNASTICS[11]

Niels Bukh called his fundamental gymnastics 'primitive gymnastics'. The description was anything but accidental. Although he ran the risk of the expression 'primitive' being interpreted in a negative sense by a contemporary society in the heyday of colonialism, all the same he chose it as the title for his gymnastics and his basic work. People in other countries, however, were not always as excited by the word 'primitive'. His book was published in Great Britain, for instance, under the title *Primary Gymnastics*. Perhaps the distinction between the primitive and the civilised was of greater importance in the world capital of colonialism than in Denmark. Bukh's insistence on 'the primitive', along with his determination that young, male gymnasts should appear naked from the waist upward and his energetic and sweat-producing gymnastics, provides the first indication that there was more involved in the Gymnastic Folk High School than could simply be called 'rational gymnastics'. Bukh saw his gymnastics as a defence against the process of civilisation which had reduced human physical capacity. For him, nature was an 'absolute reference' which, after having been suppressed, could be regained through primitive gymnastics. He included girls in his scheme of things although he was predominantly concerned with the male and male physique. In 1929 he proclaimed his opposition to what he referred to as the 'so-called Modern Women's Gymnastics'. As an alternative he offered rational gymnastics, 'which with its well-grounded and purposeful work can best develop the stiff, powerless and awkward body of civilised people into a natural and attractive form.'[12] He maintained that the defence against the decline of civilised people was to be found in 'the sure feeling of Danish youth for things genuine and natural and their strong resistance to anything that was artificial and stilted'.

Interviews conducted with some 30 former pupils of the Ollerup Gymnastic Folk High School have given me the impression that the Folk High School provided many individuals with an experience to be remembered for the rest of their lives. In addition, its enormous alumni association with a present membership of some 6,000 points clearly towards a culture which has left its mark on its participants. Sharing the company of other youths, being able to leave behind often gruelling daily labour, the experience of having the world unfold before them through lectures on cultural subjects of wide variety, travelling and meeting people from other countries, all of this formed the conditions for a lasting experience. In principle, it would have been possible to undergo this experience in all the folk high schools. What was distinctive about Ollerup School, however, was that it was a very physical fraternity with an exchange of energies and the experience of the proximity of other steaming bodies fused in a common choreography. The educational experience lived on in the body and not just in the mind, as did the worship of Norse mythology, national legends and Grundtvig's hymns[13] which were part of the wider folk high school tradition. It should nevertheless be emphasised that other folk high schools also had gymnastics on their timetable, but not to the same extent as Ollerup. Furthermore, the widespread tradition of singing in all the folk high schools also had a unifying effect through the common physical activity that group singing provides.

The impact of the gymnastics display, and the cult characteristics of the gymnastics at Ollerup are well described by a cultural outsider, the Japanese Y. Mihashi, who in 1928 witnessed an exhibition of Ollerup gymnastics in Roskilde.[14]

> People become completely carried away, the sun shines and is reflected by the muscular, sweating bodies, who look like statues come alive, with an unbelievable living rhythm ... the unity of the orders given with the animated responses of the gymnasts is difficult to describe in words. The time passed so quickly that more than an hour of instruction seemed like a mere moment and suddenly one heard voices raised in song and, bearing the Danish flag before them, the gymnasts circled twice, and were happiness itself, like victorious warriors (shoshi), and the applause of tens of thousands of spectators knew no limits. We were all in ecstasy (kofun no rutsubo).[15]

The public reception of Ollerup gymnastics, both in Denmark and abroad, was often characterised by deep silence and concentration. In modern football, spectators are responsible for the boiling uproar of the witches' cauldron that is the stadium and the impulse to create noise by shouting, blowing horns or letting off fire crackers is actually indulged. The contrast could not be greater. It can be difficult, therefore, to appreciate the awe-inspired emotions of the gymnastics public of the time. Bukh himself at times used to silence the audience before the ritual exhibition began.

Time after time Bukh's gymnasts were presented abroad as Apollos,[16] who stood as living testimony to the potential of Danish youth. The myth was constructed on the assumption that practically any boy (or girl) could be plucked straight out of agricultural labour and in six months' time be performing exhibition gymnastics at international level. This presumption was not correct and now and again Bukh's gymnasts were taken to task for their lack professionalism. The truth of the matter was, that as a rule the gymnasts had trained in gymnastics throughout their childhood and a number of them had trained at school term after term for several hours a day.

The mythical resonance of Mihashi's description of the Bukh 'Apollos', and indeed the entire youth cult surrounding the Ollerup Gymnastic Folk High School calls for an explanation over and above that of the purely physiological functional. There was, moreover, an intense emotionalism that could arise, at least momentarily, in the audience and gymnasts. In this capacity Bukh gymnastics managed to transport itself from a tiny gymnasium in a small village in the south of Funen to entrance audiences around the world. It is not sufficient to say that Ollerup gymnastics provided an aesthetic physical expression of the basic characteristics of the agricultural way of life, or to say that its leaps expressed a modern male need to worship speed and dynamism. Indeed, the very fact that Ollerup gymnastics influenced people across the globe provides a full explanation for cult-like elements in the worship of Bukh's gymnastics.

It is necessary to call upon the sociology of religion and social anthropology to gain a deep understanding of the meaning of Ollerup gymnastics. Ollerup gymnastics was a rite of passage, leading youth into the world of adults.

OLLERUP GYMNASTICS AS A RITE OF PASSAGE

A classic researcher into the importance of rites of passage is the anthropologist Arnold Van Gennep, who in 1909 published his principal work, *Les Rites de Passage*. Van Gennep's theory is that major junctures in the lives of humans, such as birth, marriage and death, can involve many conflicts, much fear and great disruptions, both for the individual concerned and for society as a whole. In order that the transition from one phase of life to another may proceed in as secure a manner as possible for society, many cultures have introduced transitional rites which mark the individual's passage to a new status.

Van Gennep regards initiation as primarily a transition from the worldly to the holy sphere, a socio–religious interpretation that is too limited for an analysis of modern sport and gymnastics. Nonetheless, Van Gennep's general criteria for a rite of passage can be put to good use in the case of secular rituals as well. Van Gennep writes that rites of passage consist of three sharply differentiated phases: separation, transformation and incorporation. He calls the transformation phase 'liminal'. The Latin word *limen* means a (door) threshold and the basis for Van Gennep's use of this word is his emphasis on the sharp boundary between the inner and the outer world. Stepping beyond it into the 'transformation space' must give the performer a clear feeling that the person concerned now moves in an area governed by quite special rules and with an entirely different significance. Of course this does not mean that everyday situations cannot occur, but that these take on an altered form.

The radical character of the rite of passage results in a change of identity for the actors: the person emerging from the ritual is not the same as the person who entered it. This change of identity often becomes apparent in the liminal phase, during which the participants leave their earlier identity behind them completely. They may be assigned new names, their clothing changed, or their bodies perhaps given new symbols as an indication that they themselves are undergoing a transformation.

If we look at a typical student's stay at Ollerup Gymnastic Folk High School we can see it conforms to a surprising extent to Van Gennep's definition of a rite of passage from the child's or youth's transition to the adult world. Even the relatively few months' stay at the school meant a physical and geographical change. The architectural framework – the Gymnastic Folk High School – was an impressive indication of the new space where the transformation would take place. For an average farm lad from the country, entering the folk high school with its, for that time, enormous size, was a culture shock. From the road from Svendborg the first thing the student saw was an enormous stadium on the right-hand side, decorated with numerous antique statues. At the main entrance he climbed up many steps and went through a colossal and handsomely carved wooden door into the holy halls. As one of the interviewees put it, the ceilings of the folk high school were high and its prospects wide in comparison with a small, low–ceilinged farmhouse. The many paintings of scenes from Norse mythology on the walls of the large rooms added even more to the impression of being in a place with unusually exalted standards.

The initial fear of doing something wrong and being expelled accentuated the feeling of having entered a place with a completely new set of values. There was almost an impression that a dominant culture of the physical prevailed and the security of everyday identity with its accustomed standards was peeled away. The explicit threat of being sent home for even the most minor transgression contributed to this personal reorientation. In addition, the pupils were, in fact, 're-baptised'. They were frequently given endearing nicknames, such as 'ha'pence' or 'tuppence', by Bukh. The most common nickname was that of one's village. The new name was sewn on to the top edge of the boy's 'small, black' boxer shorts. With regard to outer transformations, the school clothing itself was, for Bukh's boys, noticeably different from their everyday clothes. The nakedness of the torso in primitive gymnastics, for example, emphasised the body as the central aspect of the ritual. In addition to this the use of an identical light blue uniform served to strengthen the sense of corporate identity. Individual variation in clothing was not tolerated.

That an individual should actually emerge from the liminal phase a changed person is evident in Bukh's forceful imagery. The shape of the youths was to be altered, so they would be like clay in the hands of 'the potter' (gymnastics instructor). True to custom, Bukh sought his metaphors chiefly in agricultural reality.

> The material awaits the educator's hand like the unploughed heath the farmer, and how does he begin? He does not demand at once the most refined garden plants, but first uses his plough and harrow to break up the hard, compressed crust; he loosens and shifts the earth and brings it under cultivation, while expecting that it will yield the greatest possible return for the seed he sows – or think of the artist, who takes some clay in his hand! He does not attempt at once to deal in small details, but kneads, moistens, and tosses the entire material until it becomes workable and yielding in his hands, and only then does he begin to shape it and demand that the material give expression for what is inside of him.[17]

Interestingly enough, another of the major ritual-oriented anthropologists, the American, Victor Turner, uses just such a clay metaphor to describe the corporate consciousness which the organisers of the ritual seek to give participants. 'They have to be shown that in themselves they are clay or dust, mere matter, whose form is impressed upon them by society.'[18]

Turner describes this ritual into corporateness as 'communitas', namely, all participants in the ceremony are equal. All external distinctions disappear upon their entrance into the liminal space. Broadly interpreted, this also applied to the pupils at the Ollerup Gymnastic Folk High School. Bukh made a special point of breaking down the class consciousness of the sons of estate owners who were sent to the school during the 1930s. He would not permit them to demand special treatment and he would speak unusually harshly to them in gymnastic classes. On the ideological level, virtually all the informants felt that gymnastic differences separated individuals much more than did social backgrounds.

Rites of passage for boys from child/youth to adult in many societies have often involved painful and extreme situations, involving tests of 'manhood'. Difficult physical challenge may possibly open up the individual, with the result that the experience itself becomes a crucial one, to be preserved deep within the individual's personality. The concentrated atmosphere which results from 'playing' with limits naturally makes the individual receptive to change.

The person emerging from this difficult experience is not the same as the one who entered into it. If the experience is a negative one, it may no doubt leave a trauma, a mental scar, behind it. A positive experience, on the other hand, can contribute to a basic outlook that is clear and meaningful. The individual has his relationship as part of the group confirmed by completing the test and the feeling of understanding physically, through his own body, what it means to be an adult, is reinforced.

Physical training at the Ollerup Gymnastic Folk High School was fairly strenuous. Men's tumbling exercises especially, done without any means of spring propulsion and involving landing on surfaces which were not especially soft, demanded real physical prowess. An incorrect landing could result in spinal damage. Success brought esteem. Even in the informal moments of out-of-class comradeship, being physically strong and able to perform feats of balancing promised the esteem of one's male peers. On occasion, the young male gymnasts stood on their hands on a wheelbarrow used for 'rough work' and did backward flips to impress others. Many former pupils reported that at the start of their training they had to climb stairs backwards, so sore were their muscles from exercising. The aim of primitive gymnastics, actually to change a stiff body into an agile one, was accomplished by simply pressing it forcefully into the preferred position. The pressure could be so great that the pupil was forced to push back in return.[19] Pupils' bodies were transformed by primitive gymnastics. They grew stronger and far more agile, at least in performing certain movements. They became capable of movements which they could not have done previously. In short, the individual who emerged from the liminal space was not the same as the one who had entered it.

According to Van Gennep, the liminal space is often characterised by taboos and asceticism. Everyday possibilities and routines are renounced, which serves to underline the special nature of liminality. At the same time, abstention becomes a test of the participant's suitability and strength of will to complete the test. At the Ollerup Gymnastic Folk High School smoking, drinking alcohol and sexual indulgence were strictly prohibited. The punishment could be instant expulsion.

GENDER RITUALS

Whereas Van Gennep regarded the initiation primarily as an enactment of the transformation of identity from the worldly to the spiritual, in his book, *Initiation Ceremonies*, the American anthropologist Frank W. Young sees it as a rite of transition, which emphasises the development of sexual identity. The transition from being a child to being an adult man (or woman) concentrates on training in the rational and emotion values of adult life. Both the intellectual and physical instruction at Ollerup Gymnastic Folk High School served as training in the values of the rural petit bourgeoisie. Punctuality, restraint, self-discipline and industry were among the main values which were praised and given physical form through the gymnastics, while at the same time classroom subjects were intended to provide a general education and broaden the horizons of the modern adult individual. The relatively few months spent at the Folk high school clearly provided a concentrated physical and mental education.

In order to put together a definition which could encompass both modern and traditional rituals, the following criteria are proposed for rites of passage from childhood/youth to adulthood, based on the conceptions of Van Gennep[20] and S. Fiske[21] of the transition ritual. The greater portion of these criteria must be met before one can speak of a rite of passage from childhood/youth to adult life:

1. respect for the values of adult life shall be introduced in a dramatic[22] and concentrated manner, usually different for young men and women;

2. the focus is on physical activity or events;

3. taboos or restrictions regarding sexuality and the intake of foodstuffs and stimulants are normally involved;

4. the individual emerging from the process is not the same as the one who entered it;

5. where boys are involved, the ritual is generally staged by men;

6. typical isolation from the opposite sex;

7. identical clothing or appearance;

8. transition to a realm superior to or apart from everyday life;

9. on the male side: tests of manhood.

It should be emphasised that points 4, 7 and 9 generally apply to rites of passage.

If we examine Ollerup gymnastics in the light of these nine criteria the following picture emerges. That it fulfils criteria 1–4, as well as 9, has already been argued. With regard to point 5, gymnastic instruction was mainly given particularly to male students by Bukh and his male gymnastic instructors. On point 6, the two sexes were kept separate at Ollerup Gymnastic Folk High School. Regarding point 7, the use of identical outfits for gymnastics was the rule at the Folk High School and the training of the body was not adapted to the individual but based on a common ideal. On point 8, the school was isolated near a rural village on Funen and the pupils resided there for the entire period with the exception of certain holidays.

FEMALE AND MALE GYMNASTICS

Research on modern movement cultures as rites of passage has focused mostly on the masculine rituals. Although at least half the pupils at the

Ollerup Gymnastic Folk High School were female, the following section will follow this practice in keeping with the theme of this volume.[23]

Niels Bukh's appreciation of masculinity and masculine beauty was not the least obvious in his gymnastics. His male gymnasts in their 'little, black' boxer shorts were tactile to an extent that was unheard of in their time, and carried each other about, sat on one another and held each other's hands. They could do this because the gymnastic framework itself was undeniably masculine: large, muscular males carrying out energetic, linear movements. The masculine element was so limited that Niels Bukh openly admitted having been inspired by the female gymnastic teachers Elli Bjørkstein of Finland and Elin Falk of Sweden.

However, the élite male gymnasts, the 'toughies', enjoyed a distinctive masculine high status. Only they received the intensive training required to bring them up to international standards for floor gymnastics. Even the name 'toughie' indicated a close-knit, highly traditional, male community. It personified the masculine ideal's duality of audacity and craftsmanship.

On the whole, Niels Bukh's gymnastics became a national symbol of masculine power. Ollerup gymnastics, to the Danish public, became synonymous with a masculine, physical universe.

MASCULINE AND FEMININE CODES

This masculinity was made perfectly clear by Bukh. The basic values were imprinted by means of contrast. Regarding the effects of gymnastics on the development of girls into adult women, Bukh said:

> For girls, gymnastics should, once the period of gangly and awkward growth has concluded, produce a fit and healthy femininity, that will mature in a natural manner through the years of youth. The body and its bearing become erect, so that the young woman's bearing and personality not only appear to be, but actually are, beautiful, strong and healthy. Until then the work of gymnastics is not complete.

Regarding the development of boys into adult men, Bukh in his book *Primitive Gymnastics* made the following comments:

> The young boy shall be developed from the transitional stage, where his mood and actions are often characterised by a vague

dreaminess and insecure searching, to a strong and well-rounded man, with the capability and will to fight and thus win his independence – and to this end the gymnastics which he is offered shall make a proper and effective contribution.

The problem, however, is how to interpret the 'language' of gymnastics. If gymnastics contributed anything over and above itself, were Niels Bukh and his gymnasts at all conscious of this? Bukh was a man of action, who usually did not speak of the spirit, character or expression. Nonetheless, there are various indications that from a fairly early stage he was very conscious of what his gymnastic positions and movements were meant to express. In this regard the handsomely photographed, designed and well-written book, *Gymnastik im Bild* (Gymnastics in pictures) of 1926,[24] is something of a gold mine. Here Bukh shows through his gymnasts a long series of the basic positions of Ollerup gymnastics and interprets them as expressions of character. In Bukh's own words: 'The picture captions make no attempt to explain the images completely, but are intended instead only to support them in the attempt to reveal in what direction and to what purpose gymnastic efforts in Denmark wish to direct youngsters.'[25]

On the one hand, the women were to be conditioned, through intensive gymnastic activity – together with instruction in their own special subjects such as handicrafts – to become warm, kind, devoted, helpful, cheerful, grateful, fit, aware, natural, mild and hard-working. They, like the men, were also to practise general virtues such as self-control, purity of mind and thought, the ability to follow orders without losing their own identity and the capacity to take part in communal activities and grow with each new task. On the other hand, the men were to be inculcated with a sense of brotherhood, strength of character, security, physical control and strong will. The male ritual thus involves an emphasis on developing an independent, more autonomous and strong profile. Symbolically this was in addition to the dynamics and driving force of male gymnastics, which was expressed especially in the leaps. Both sexes were taught to value the sense of community in hard physical work as one of the central goals in life, together with respect for obedience. On the whole, these distinct gender differences expressed through gymnastics codes agreed well with the ideals of the Danish farming class, but did not preclude the participation of children of other classes.

MODERN AND TRADITIONAL RITES OF PASSAGE

There are undeniably substantial differences between a 'primitive' and a modern rite of passage. One of the most significant is that the traditional ritual marking the transition from child to adult requires all members of the society to undergo the initiation. Despite the fact that tens of thousands of youngsters may have undergone a modern ritual such as Ollerup gymnastics, and thus many more than participate in a typical tribal ritual, the fact that they comprised only a small minority in comparison to the total numbers of rural youth cannot be refuted. Ollerup gymnastics itself cannot be viewed in isolation, but rather as the culmination of a long process of gymnastic training. By far the greatest number of pupils attending Ollerup Gymnastic Folk High School had been involved in gymnastics from a very young age, and thus participated in earlier 'initiations'. A stay at Ollerup Gymnastic Folk High School was thus a privilege for 'élite initiates', who were given the chance to educate themselves as local leaders, who could continue the instruction in community halls (the cultural centres for the rural population) and colleges. But even if we regard gymnastics in the country as a whole as a rite of passage, not everyone underwent gymnastics training. Ollerup gymnastics can thus not merely be classified as a rite of passage of the same sort as traditional initiation ceremonies. And if not, what then?

Victor Turner, both in 1969[26] and 1983, has discussed the difference between modern and traditional rituals. According to him the difference is found especially in the principle of voluntarism, which is found in most modern (sub)cultures, but not, for example, in an initiation from boy to man in a tribal culture. If we focus on this there is a pronounced difference between a modern boy's perhaps alternating choice of sports as compared with a tribal boy's involuntary participation in (when seen from our modern point of view) a barbaric circumcision ceremony, where he shows his manhood by not grimacing at the pain. The individual expansion through choice of activities, which the modern young person enjoys, gives him or her freedom but also the danger of rootlessness and loneliness, if his or her bonding to a youth group is not successful. The occurrence of modern rites of passage, however, contributes to some extent to lessening the feeling of anonymity and to giving young people a feeling of purpose, security and group contact.

Frank W. Young has shown that in a traditional society which becomes integrated into the process of urbanisation tendencies arise leading to the dissolution of the rites of passage. For Young the ritual's primary goal is to confirm the solidarity among members of the same gender. Especially where males are concerned maintaining the social unit's male solidarity can be a problem, when the men leave for the city for lengthy periods and when the tribal culture becomes integrated into larger, complex and class-stratified societies.[27] Ollerup gymnastics can be seen as a modern attempt to ritualise male and female, although that is of course not the emphasis here, solidarity within a more limited (farming) class context. Young maintains that the gender-specific character of the ritual reflects the different labours of the two sexes. During the period between the wars there was a marked division of labour between the two sexes in Danish rural society and Ollerup gymnastics also ritualised gender differences. It is hardly a coincidence that politically and economically the solidly united farming class is the only Danish social class that can boast a ritualisation of its cohesion generally in the folk high school phenomenon and specifically the gymnastic folk high school.

In order to point out at one and the same time the differences and maintain the common elements of modern and traditional rituals, Victor Turner distinguishes between 'liminal' activities, which are common compulsory[28] rituals in tribal cultures, and 'liminoid' activities, which are relatively voluntary, more or less collectively organised activities in modern societies. The suffix 'oid' means 'like'. In other words, here is a phenomenon which is similar to but not actually a rite of passage. This distinction, however, does not appear to be especially illuminating. If modern rituals resemble traditional ones, we still lack an explanation as to what they actually are. It would be more productive to say that *rites of passage* may occur in both tribal and modern cultures. But an *initiation* (enrolment)[29] is typical of tribal cultures and is characterised by being obligatory and by the participation of all members (at least of one sex). Ollerup gymnastics can thus be seen as a rite of passage, but not as an enrolment. And it is, note, only one of numerous possible ritualisations of the transition into the ranks of adults in modern culture. Confirmation is a more traditional example.

The age profile presents a further obstacle for the application of the ritual analysis. If we take the period 1930–35 it transpires that, according to the statistical processing of the student registers, the largest number of youths (17.5%) were aged 19 years, the second largest (16.1%) were 20, followed by 18-year-olds (14.2%) and 21-year-olds (12.3%). In brief, the average age was close to 20 years. Rites of passage in so-called primitive cultures normally occur much earlier in the lives of youths, generally in their early teens. How is this to be explained? In the first place, modern civilisation – including agriculture in the period between the wars – is characterised by the emergence of a true youth culture. This arose partly out of a need for qualified and well-educated workers who had attended school for a lengthy period and had acquired more general qualifications, starting with learning to read and write. That the transition, therefore, is not necessarily from childhood to adulthood, but to an increasing degree from adolescence to adulthood. This should also be viewed in connection with the fact that a relatively lengthy period could elapse before male and female agricultural workers could marry and set up house, if they managed to do so at all. In principle they could only establish themselves finally on their fathers' farms, when either the husband's or wife's father retired. The years of youth especially denote, in modern society, an uneasy, searching and often crisis-ridden period, during which the youth attempts to stand on his own two feet. Ollerup gymnastics can be regarded as a final and very tightly structured foretaste of what adulthood was for a young person searching for his identity.

CONCLUSION

Bukh's gymnastics can be seen as a ritual initiation of a rural élite especially for the male. His primitive gymnastics were physically demanding and both the leaps of the men and many of the suppleness exercises were far from harmless and required considerable courage. Apart from such psychological 'tests of manhood', the pupils underwent a physical reconstruction and were assigned new names. All these features gave the pupils a feeling of being in a whole new space with its own strange laws and made them susceptible to transformation under a strong hand, which contributed to the personality cult of their 'Papa' as they called him.

The period following the Second World War saw the gradual decline of the position of the farmer as the major economic class in Denmark. Ollerup gymnastics suffered a corresponding decline. The focus was more and more on relaxation, rather than on the tensed Ollerup body.

For a large part of the Danish public, Ollerup gymnastics smacked of body language from a vanished era, with masculine, militant, perhaps even fascist strains. This was paralleled by the growing popularity of competitive and motion sports and men deserted traditional male gymnastics to an increasing extent in favour of sports emphasising creative individual capability and the possibility of expression in ways that could be weighed and measured. Gymnastics is still extensively practised in Denmark, but now simply more for exercise in both urban and rural communities, and often with a markedly higher age profile than before. Gymnastics still helps create a sense of communal identity, but has lost the character of a collective youth ritual. As a rite of passage, especially for the children of the farming class, Ollerup gymnastics has never regained the position that it held during the period between the wars, despite the fact that the folk high school still operates today.

The comparison of a circumcision ceremony performed on a seven-year-old boy to a period at the Ollerup Gymnastic Folk High School may appear to be more than a little far-fetched. More far-fetched, in reality, is the identification of tribal rituals and extreme tests of manhood like circumcision, as typical of the homogeneity of the cultural customs of the 'primitives'. In the first place, far from all tribal societies have definite rites of passage from child to adult. Furthermore, circumcision puts in an appearance only very rarely.[30] In addition, there is enormous variation in traditional rites of passage. One of the main points made by Van Gennep in his classical work on rituals was in fact an attempt to counteract the widespread conception of rites of passage as 'puberty rites'. In his opinion these rites were not narrowly concerned with puberty in the physical sense, which in the first place varies considerably from one individual to another, and in the second place – especially where boys are concerned – for which it can be difficult to specify a single point in time. Van Gennep spoke therefore of 'social puberty', as the point in time defined by the culture as the transitional age between child and adult, an extremely variable passage of time.[31] Even the rite of passage itself may last from a single day to over a year. The enrolment's starting point in time can vary from one participant to another by several years. Enrolment can vary for different economic groups within the same culture (hunters, craftsmen and so on).

What does the ritual analysis mean for research on youth? The analysis of a youth culture as a rite of passage opens up possibilities of discerning processes which would otherwise have remained hidden, but it also brings the danger of reductionism. There can be a temptation to disregard all the rebelliousness of youth culture, as this is in opposition to the tradition-confirming character of the ritual. Ritual analysis also runs the risk of losing sight of the dynamic and even chaotic aspects of a youth culture, because its thesis rests on a certain degree of constancy in the values transmitted. And, finally, ritual analysis can easily end in overemphasising the hierarchical relationship between adult and youth.

Nevertheless, ritual analysis may be regarded, it is suggested here, as a key to unlock certain features of Ollerup gymnastics, due to the enormous respect for authority of this movement culture, constancy in its gymnastic expression and its traditional, eventually even reactionary, content. It must be underlined, however, that Ollerup gymnastics, from the time it was established around 1920 and onwards, did involve a rebellion and revolt against prevalent standards regarding decent clothing and respectable forms of movement. What has been described here is a movement from 'youth revolt' to youth ritual.

The question is whether the development from revolt to ritual is a principle which holds true more generally of developments in youth culture. The commercialisation of hip-hop is probably a small indication of this. The introduction of modern competitive sports in the Danish urban environment around the turn of the century could perhaps be seen in this light[32] as well as the wave of oriental martial arts which washed over large areas of the western world from the 1970s onward.[33]

NOTES

1. The time frame is chosen to cover most of the period from the founding of Niels Bukh's gymnastic folk high school (1920) until his death (1950). This chapter is based on 'Gymnastics as a Rite of Passage, Danish Gymnastics, 1912–50', *Nordic Journal of Youth Research*, 2, 4 (1994), 17–36. The essay is part of my work on a biography of the political, ideological and national impact of Niels Bukh on Danish society which is to be published in Danish.
2. Cf. A. Løkke, 'Foraeldrebilleder – Skitser til moderskabets og faderskabets historie', *Social Kritik*, 25–26 (1993), 6–22.
3. R. Sabo and R. Runfola, *Jocks, Sports, and Male Identity* (Englewood Cliffs, NJ, 1980). For a general overview see E. August, *Men's Studies: A selected and annotated interdisciplinary bibliography* (Littleton, 1985).
4. Varda Burstyn, *The Rites of Men: Manhood, Politics and the Culture of Sport* (Toronto, 1999).
5. J.A. Mangan and J. Walvin (eds.), *Manliness and Morality: Middle-Class Masculinity in Britain and America, 1800–1940* (Manchester, 1987).
6. Cf. H. Bonde, *Mandighed og sport* (Odense, 1991); H. Meinander, *Toward a Bourgeois Manhood* (Helsinki, 1994) and J. Ljunggren, *Kroppens bildning* (Stockholm, 1999).
7. This was followed by the Snoghøj Gymnastic Folk High School (1925), the Gerlev Folk High School of Physical Education (1938), The Jutland School of Physical Education in Vejle (1943) and the Viborg Gymnastic Folk High School (1951). The latter three schools were all founded by former pupils of the Ollerup Folk High School.

8. As examples of attempts to analyse the ritual aspects of sport see R. Holt, *Sport and Society in Modern France* (London, 1981) and J. MacAloon, *This Great Symbol* (Chicago, 1981).

9. Niels Bukh's gymnastics was, however, not so original that its roots in Swedish gymnastics were not clearly visible. To begin with, Niels Bukh himself merely referred to his gymnastics as a new 'working method', but after his worldwide success, he began to speak directly of 'Danish gymnastics'. The 1934 edition of his basic book was thus very consciously titled *Dansk Gymnastik (primitiv)* (Danish Gymnastics (primitive)) and in 1936 the title was *Dansk primitiv gymnastik* (Danish primitive gymnastics).

10. See Bonde, *Mandighed*, pp.90–96 for a discussion of the connection between muscular tautness and self-control, inspired by Wilhelm Reich.

11. Ove Korsgaard was the first Danish scholar to analyse sport as an initiation rite and as 'the ritual of industrialised society'. See O. Korsgaard, *Kampen om kroppen* (Copenhagen, 1987).

12. *Aarsskrift, Gymnastikhøjskolen* (Year Book of the Gymnastics Folk High School) (1929), 84.

13. The clergyman N.F.S. Grundtvig (1783–1872) was the great spiritual and poetical inspiration for the awakening of the Danish farming class of which the college movement was part. His hymns and songs played no small role in strengthening the feeling of cultural unity among the rural population.

14. Mihashi's rapture should be taken with a grain of salt, however, as he was deeply involved in introducing Bukh's gymnastics into Japan and in organising Niels Bukh's team tour in Japan in 1931. The quote also expresses the master/apprentice tradition in Japanese pedagogy, where pupils who feel they have found a master to instruct them become, when compared with modern western assessment, uncritically enraptured.

15. Mihashi, *En dag med opvisning* (unpublished, translated by the interpreter Eiki Ishizaki for the author of this article) (Tokyo, 1930).

16. Examples can be found in American newspapers during their American tour in 1923.

17. N. Bukh, *Primitiv Gymnastik eller Grundgymnastik* (Ollerup, 1922), p.6.

18. V. Turner, 'Liminal to Liminoid in Play, Flow and Ritual', in C. Harris *et al.*, *Play, Games and Sports in Cultural Contexts* (Champaign, IL, 1983), pp.136–66.

19. Author's interview with Bukh gymnast H. Meldgaard, 1993.

20. A. van Gennep, *The Rites of Passage* (Chicago, 1960).

21. See S. Fiske, 'Pigskin Review: An American Initiation', in M.M. Hart (ed.), *Sport in the Sociocultural Process* (Dubuque, IO, 1972), pp.241–59.

22. Young says of the ritual's dramatic effects that 'Stimuli that vary greatly in intensity but are restricted in complexity make good carriers of dramatic communication'. The above-named movement tags are examples of this. The word 'dramatic' may not be interpreted as referring to the dramatic arts but should be understood to mean 'full of intense activity and high excitement', F.W. Young, *Initiation Ceremonies* (New York, 1965), p.152.

24. *Gymnastik im Bild* (Gymnastics in pictures) (Oldenburg, 1926).

25. Bukh's text was translated by Anna Sievers, a former pupil of his from Hamburg.

26. V. Turner, *The Ritual Process* (Chicago, 1969).

27. Young, *Initiation*, p.130.

28. The expression 'compulsory' is perhaps an unfortunate choice, as it presupposes the opposite, the 'freedom' to refuse, which is a question that simply does not arise with an initiation. In such a ritual the question is not whether an individual shall participate, which is inconceivable in the actual meaning of the word, but how he or she will complete the test. Initiation is the only way to become an adult male or female. Occasional individuals who do not pass the test, or for some other reason drop out are typically regarded as deviants or eccentrics.

29. My preference for the term initiation rather than enrolment is due to the fact that 'enrolment' in Danish ('indvielse') has connotations of secret societies and isolated, even extreme ceremonies. Initiation, to my mind, is a wider term, which in English broadly encompasses ritualisation of transition periods in all societies.

30. Young, *Initiation*.

31. Van Gennep, *Rites of Passage*, pp.65ff.

32. H. Bonde, *Mandighed*, pp.166–79.

33. H. Bonde, 'Ritualets Genkomst, Orientalsk Kampkunst og Vestlig Ungdom', *Social Kritik*, 13–14 (1991), 77–91.

Pre-Totalitarian, Totalitarian and Post-Totalitarian Masculinity: The Projection of the Male Image in Sports Policy in Bulgaria

VASSIL GIRGINOV

Heroes and Heroines,
Your good cause is close to all our hearts and we follow its development with keen interest. The Unak organisation is important to the cultural and educational development of our people. Healthy, physically and spiritually fit citizens learn civil virtues such as patriotism and national solidarity which are valuable guarantees of a nation's future.

I am confident that during this solemn gathering the cheerful, idealistic youth of Bulgaria will exemplify the dignity of Bulgaria, to us and to the guests among whom are worthy teachers and workers in the hero's movement.

I believe profoundly, heroes, that you, who are filled with the spirit of heroism and cherish national traditions, will maintain the good name of Unak and work devotedly for its greater prosperity.

I declare the Seventh Unak Council open and wish you well. Long live Bulgaria!

Opening address by Tsar Boris III to the VII Council of Union Unak (Hero) in 1931

...Physical culture and sport should also be seen as a powerful means of enhancing working people's capacity for work and longevity, of preparing them for the defence of the country, as well as of creating perfect and beautiful people.

Speech by T. Zhivkov at a meeting of Politburo and activists on the cultural front, 15 April 1963

Can we, for instance, feel easy, when 30% of school-age children have spinal distortions? A good number of conscripts are not accepted for military service due to poor health or physical underdevelopment. The number of employees who become ill with a simple cold is significant. All of this is the result of the poor physical fitness. What kind of builders of Socialism and Communism would people be with their health undermined? What defenders of the country would they be? What generations would they create?

> *T. Zhivkov, speech to the 10th Congress of the Youth Communist*
> *League, 28 April 1963*

Great Industry, The Will to Win and Exceptional Sporting prowess. To m.m.s* Maria Gigova twice Overall World Champion in Rhythmic Gymnastics
Comrade Gigova,
I congratulate you whole-heartedly for achieving the title Overall World Champion in Rhythmic Gymnastics for 1971.
We are proud of the victory – a reward for your enormous industry, talent and fighting spirit, for your love of sport.
Your exceptional sporting skill, so magnificently demonstrated in the World Championship, is yet another manifestation of the Bulgarian Communist woman's tenacity and will to win, high socialist morale and love of country.
To you, your team mates, coaches and leaders I wish good health and further success for the reputation of our dear fatherland – the People's Republic of Bulgaria.
15 November 1971
Sofia

> *T. Zhivkov's personal letter to Maria Gigova, 1971*

Let us congratulate not only those who won gold medals but those who were close to them, for their great self-denial, for the great effort they have made ... for promising a new Bulgarian miracle at the forthcoming Olympic Games in Sydney 2000.

> *Address by President Stoyanov at a meeting with athletes and coaches*
> *from the national wrestling and weightlifting teams, 1999*

I am not going to hide from you that a Ministry of Sport is dear to my heart. And I will tell you why. A Minister of Sport would have a higher official status, which would enable him to meet representatives of other countries on an equal footing.

President Stoyanov at a meeting with Bulgarian sport officials, 1999

INTRODUCTION

The six quotations above are indicative of the political language used by three contrasting politicians. The words were spoken by three heads of state of Bulgaria – Tsar Boris III (1918–43), Todor Zhivkov (1956–89) and Peter Stoyanov (1997–) – from three different historical periods. These comments, however, are not only of interest because they inform us about the dominant political discourse, nor for any comparative value. Rather, they are arguably symptomatic of a kind of sports policy rooted in typical masculine norms, expectations and practices. The aims of this chapter are therefore to examine the ideas, conceptual apparatus and language of Bulgarian sports policy; to analyse the capacity of masculinity to produce a sports policy discourse and related practical policies in different circumstances; and to track down the residual and emerging forms of masculinity in sports policy.

THE STUDY OF MASCULINITY:
IMPLICATIONS FOR SPORTS POLICY ANALYSIS

The theme of masculinity in sociology, and sport sociology in particular, has been explored from a number of perspectives. K. Clatterbaugh[1] gives six perspectives – the conservative, pro-feminist, men's rights, spiritual, socialist, and group-specific – which have dominated contemporary discussions of men and masculinity. Each gives a different assessment of society and the roles of men and women. In his analysis of masculinity, J. Cagnon[2] used one of its basic traits, physical strength, to depict the difference between male and female competition. He claimed that, although undermined by changes in the way of life, strength, as differentiator between men and women, continued to be retained. More specifically, he noted that sport and sexual interaction with women were the two major domains in which the physical expression of masculinity can still be acted out.

A plethora of writers in the 1970s, 1980s and 1990s have tried to explain why and how sport has perpetuated the inequalities between men and women encountered in the wider social-cultural world. Published studies reveal various intertwined attributes of sport pertinent to masculinity, the historical formation of which has been analysed by J.A. Mangan and J. Walvin.[3] One of the recurring roles of sport identified by Cagnon[4] is that it provides a sense of solidarity both for those practising and spectating. Another characteristic of sport that has received close inspection by M. MacNeill[5] and M. Costa and S. Guthrine[6] has been its ability to offer a forum for the representation of masculinity in the form of 'aggression, violence, sexual harassment and ideology', but also to be a form of perpetuating gender and social stereotypes (C. Williams *et al.*,[7] J. Hargreaves).[8] C. Green and L. Chalip,[9] S. Greendorfer,[10] I. Lawrie and R. Brown,[11] and D. Scully and J. Clarke[12] have described various patterns of socialisation in sport, and noted the role of the father as a key socialising agent for both sexes. It has also been argued that sport in early adolescence is characterised by an intensification of gender-related expectations, with subsequent constraints placed upon participation patterns, which are more intense for boys than girls.[13] Numerous studies from different countries (see T. Kamphorst and K. Roberts,[14] and G. Cushman *et al.*[15] for a multicultural perspective) have found compelling evidence that men participate more in leisure and sports activities than do women. Most studies on participation have inevitably tended to challenge the existing sports models, and pointed out that women should be given greater opportunities for participation and choice of sports.

Males, as A. White and C. Brackenridge[16] and A. Doherty[17] have maintained, despite an increasing number of women in managerial positions, still dominate the field of sports management, where females do not have a great say in policy matters, because they are either under-represented or seen as tokens. Similar conclusions are advanced by T. Kay in a comprehensive review of research on women in sport[18] in Western and North American countries, where she found that women were under-represented at administrative, controlling and decision-making levels.

It is beyond the scope of this essay to become involved in an exhaustive discussion on masculinity in sport, but from the above mentioned literature four implications can be suggested which provide a useful framework for examining the conceptual basis of sports policy.

First, it seems indisputable that there is no homogeneous *concept of masculinity*. As G. Whannel[19] has persuasively argued, 'masculinity must be understood in relation to femininity; we need to think in terms not just of masculinity but of masculinities; recognize that masculinities change over time, and consequently there are, always, dominant and emergent masculinities'. Clearly, gender differences have always been socially constructed, and the notion of masculinity has undergone a gradual evolution from that. It was once believed to have been at the pinnacle of the natural hierarchy. Now it is in the position of being equal to femininity. What is more, this is now a stipulation which is part of most modern national legislations including Bulgaria's. Sport is not exempt from this process and it is tempting to quote the emblematic views of the founder of the modern Olympic Games, Pierre de Coubertin, on women's sport which he saw as against the 'law of nature'. 'The greatest show on earth' today, the Olympics, were promoted at the end of the nineteenth century by de Coubertin as '... the solemn and periodic exaltation of male athleticism (with) internationalism as the base, loyalty as the means, art for its setting, and female applause as its reward'.[20] As some 40 per cent of athletes taking part in the Sydney 2000 Olympics will be women, this view clearly appears to be an anachronism.

The second implication concerns the *notion of the body* which is closely bound up with Christianity's insistence on the superiority of the spirit over the body. J. Rutherford[21] has argued that 'a history of masculinity is the struggle to tame and subdue the emotional and sexual self and to recognise the ascendant and superior nature of reason and thought. The dominant meanings of masculinity in our culture are about producing our bodies as instruments to our wills.' Sport is a major means of using the human body for such purposes and one through which masculinity is manifested.

Third, the changing images of masculinity demonstrate that it is not only a *social construction*, but a subjectivity, organised within structures of control and authority. The emphasis here is on structures, relations and positions in the policy-making process, another field for expression of the macho-myth, which N. Mandell[22] has asserted is characterised by 'an exaggeration of male heterosexuality and a refusal to accept women as equals. Thus, who constructs and articulates the values in sport, and how, self-evidently, will be decisive for shaping sports policy.

Fourth, it has been suggested also that masculinity, despite its dominance in social relations and policy-making, gave birth to *social movements* and political actions promoting various agendas for change. Borrowing from Gordon (1979), R. Deem[23] has argued that 'feminism and feminist theory are not just abstract analyses of the subordination of women by men, but contain a political commitment to changing women's position in the world'. M. Talbot's[24] account supports this idea when she claims that one of the major challenges for sport organisations is to work together towards gender equity in sport. This call for action which was echoed by the highest political and sporting forums clearly threatens to erode interests and structures and, in particular, challenges positions of authority within sport. Therefore, the role of various feminist groups in national sports movements will serve as a measure for the restructuring of power and authority in sport in general.

As the work of various commentators has demonstrated, the basic traits of masculinity not only stimulate academic endeavour but underpin several important attributes of sport, which lend themselves perfectly to the political and call for regulation and intervention. No matter how reluctant one might be to subscribe to the feminist slogan 'the personal is the political' it would be hard to dismiss the political nature of these issues.

DEFINING SPORTS POLICY

For the purposes of this analysis, sports policy will be interpreted as *a framework of principles, objectives and planned (unplanned) actions (inactions) developed by a credible local, national or international agency aiming to achieve common ends concerning specific communities within given range of resources, time and space.* This definition involves four classifications which, together with E. Laumann and D. Knoke's[25] approach to public policy, will inform the analysis and define its framework:

1. Whether local or national, sports policy is a *social construct* designed to serve people's particular interests, and involves making conscious decisions on the part of authorised institutions (appointed by the state or the members) about the distribution of always limited resources, and promoting relevant practices over given territories, it must be considered not only as a set of rationally pre-planned actions, but as *ad hoc* reactions and inactions as well. Therefore, attention has to be paid to *policy content* focusing on the origins, intentions and operation of sport policies during the three periods; to sport *policy process* involving the actions taken by the state (primarily

the government) and non-public actors at each stage; and to *policy advocacy* using the analysis to make an argument in favour of a particular policy.

2. B. Hogwood and L. Gunn[26] have suggested that '*for a policy to be regarded as a "public policy" it must to some degree have been generated or at least processed within the framework of governmental procedures, influences and organisations*'. Sports policy represents a particular political *domain* confirmed by the involvement of the state in Bulgaria in physical education and sports governance as early as 1897. It will be seen that, self-evidently, a group of governmental and non-governmental 'actors' involved in sport influence policy and events. In particular, those heavily involved in sport strongly influence policy. They have their own political agenda which must be taken into account by others.

3. The *membership* of the sports policy domain is also a collective social construct representing the outcomes of continuous struggles and negotiations between core and non-essential corporate actors such as unions, federations, associations, committees and clubs who try to promote their strategies and have the greater say in the policy-making process. A perfect example of defining the sports membership domain from the early 1960s onwards was the classification of all sports into three categories – major (group A) and minor (group B) Olympic and others (group C), for the purpose of granting aid according to the sport's contribution to the country's Olympic success. This classification also perpetuated the dominant position of male sports in the domain, such as boxing, weightlifting and wrestling where most Olympic success was to be had.

4. *Structural relations* in the sports policy domain concern the robust, recurrent patterns of interactions linking the core and non-essential actors to each other and to the larger public policy domain. Typical examples include membership of boards, general assemblies, and commissions.

These four key implications of masculinity for sports policy and its definition provide the framework for relating them to policy. The idea that there are different masculinities which change over time suggests over use that the study of the course and discourse of masculinity in sports policy should be placed in particular historical moments. The introductory documents presented earlier set the scene for three specific periods to be discussed in turn. These are labelled pre-totalitarian, totalitarian and post-totalitarian, and the heads of Bulgaria's state, Tsar Boris III, T. Zhivkov and P. Stoyanov represent each of them, respectively. As with masculinity, the notion of totalitarianism will be seen as a tendency and not an absolute. It is instructive for this analysis because the totalitarian attitude towards the human body, and the body–mind dichotomy, inescapably rejects the Christian ideal of the supremacy of the spiritual. Various definitions of totalitarianism in literature emphasise the supremacy of the political dimension in the society–politics relationship. Accounting for this variety, M. Rush[27] offers a short definition of totalitarianism which illustrates its nature: 'a social system involving the political control of and intervention in all aspects of public and private life'. He further suggests that 'applied as a tendency rather than an absolute, totalitarianism is a more useful analytical tool'. From this definition, it is clear that a male-dominated social system can easily promote masculine policy and practices, and marginalise women's interests, of course, and vice versa.

The totalitarian tendency in Bulgarian sports policy making has been set out in detail elsewhere.[28, 29] Throughout the three periods, this tendency has displayed great consistency in the following characteristics:

- conceptually (formulating the general interest, aims, and course of action) – domination of state apparatuses as opposed to society driven visions of sport;

- constitutionally – shaping and controlling the sports domain by omni-present state actors (political parties or government agencies);

- organisationally – clear supremacy of state, or state-controlled bodies, and promoting a 'top-to-bottom' approach to policy-making;

- resourcefully – finance allocations and key appointments in the sports domain strictly under state discretion.

Variations in the interpretation of masculinity suggest that the content of sports policy, that is, its rationale and justification, will also shift.

The second implication of masculinity – the interpretation of the notion of the human body – provides a clear account of sports policy advocacy promoting masculine values and practices. The third implication of masculinity, which sees it as a social construct organised within structures of control and authority, reflects the membership in the sports policy domain, and the formulation of policies. Finally, masculinity as an agent of change concerns the structural relations in the sports domain, and the opportunities and capacities of various feminist and other groups to advocate change.

The rest of this chapter will examine the evidence for the course and discourse of sports policy during the pre-totalitarian, totalitarian and post-totalitarian periods, in the form of policy content, advocacy, membership and relations. 'Discourse' will be used in a specific sense, and will be defined as an imposition of knowledge (concepts and ideas) by structures and individuals about men–women relations, in the form of specific policy, while 'course' will be seen as set of practical policies based on this policy. R. Williams'[30] notion of 'residual', that is practices that tie the present to the past, and 'emerging', those that tie the present to the future, will be employed to trace possible patterns of masculinity in sports policy.

SPORTS POLICY AS A MASCULINE CONSTRUCTION:
ON ITS DISCOURSE AND COURSE OF ACTION

Body Politics: Masculinity in the Pre-Totalitarian Sports Policy

The first document sets the scene for the pre-totalitarian period of sports policy making. The late 1920s and early 1930s were characterised by attempts to restore bourgeois-parliamentary democracy in Bulgaria, which suffered massive blows as the result of two coups and three consecutive wars – the Balkan Wars from 1912 to 1913, and the Great War from 1915. In addition, in 1923, there was a military-Fascist coup followed by a mass anti-Fascist uprising, when thousands of people were exterminated. The end result of these events was great human and material suffering, humiliation and uncertainty.

The head of the Bulgarian state – Tsar Boris III – himself a German subject, was a typical representative of an authoritarian style of governance, which was firmly asserted after the military coup in 1935, established his personal regime. This meant a ban on all political parties, and the Tsar was in charge of appointing and controlling governments, domestic, foreign and military affairs. Between 1935 and 1944, under Boris III's leadership, Bulgaria became Germany's closest ally, and became heavily politically, economically and culturally dependent on the Nazi regime.

The union Unak (Hero), established in 1895 was the first umbrella voluntary sports organisation responsible for co-ordinating the national sports movement and the provision of staff training. However, it never succeeded in its co-ordinating role because of the overemphasis on gymnastics, and disregard of other sports. In his address to the union, the Tsar made reference to two key civil virtues, which underpinned the state policy at the time, and indeed later. The first was the notion of the country (the fatherland, not the motherland in prevailing discourse) which was explicitly intertwined with the production of bodily fit and obedient citizens who were ready to serve it. The second idea, that of public solidarity, when interpreted within an authoritarian and totalitarian context, implied communitarianism. The key to understanding this concept is the notion of the general interest as defined by those in power, which calls for a total subordination of individuals, groups and organisations to the communitarian will.

The origin of this policy, and the use of sport to serve its purposes, can be traced to two main sources: Bulgaria's own past, which has always been tied up with the national ideal for unification of the country and recovery of former glory, and which entails constant sacrifices, struggles and exploits, and the German ideological import, through the misinterpretation of Nietzsche, the guiding philosopher of the Third Reich, who identified leadership with the 'heroic man', and introduced the concept of human domination in the form of the superman (Übermensch). The popular discourse in sports policy was dominated by these two themes, which is evident both from the document ('brisk hero's spirit, and cherishing national traditions' is a direct reference to them), and from the objectives of corporal education and sport. The difference between corporal and physical education, incidentally, is not merely a terminological one. Corporal education was placed at the heart of the educational system, and was considered as a precondition for any education. Moreover, it was assigned a long-term objective: 'the creation of a handsome, healthy and desirable body type'.[31] This, of course, was a masculine type of man, capable of any bodily achievements, at the centre of which was his athletic body emanating power and the drive to conquer, highlighting virility, aggression and strength.

The ideological and cultural cult of the male body was naturally transferred into a political athlete. The Bulgarian epitome of the complete athlete capable of any physical achievements was the epic heroic folklore figure of Krali (Winged) Marko. This 'muscleman' knew no boundaries as he challenged God himself, and after fights relaxed with a faithful lover and contemplated the stars. Here, the secondary role given to women coincides with what Pierre de Coubertin envisaged they should be doing – applauding victorious men.

Bulgaria's defeats and suffering in the wars together with political instability were used to construct an argument advocating a sports policy based on typical masculine traits – strength, military training and skills. This was achieved by transferring the notion of the body as representative of a political athlete to the body as representative of the Politicum.

The claim that the wars asserted the belief that the body is the prime feature of man[32] was subsequently used as justification for disallowing sport to develop as a leisure endeavour for all groups of society, its shaping as a state institution and its use for utilitarian purposes. The example of American and British soldiers' military capability was used to substantiate the argument for introducing an enhanced physical training of the youth. This was implemented through the promotion of 'athletic' manhood in school corporal education, which was seen as contributor to the 'education of the whole person through the body, that is, through physical activities, health efforts, and related educational methods'.[33] A similar rationale was used for the introduction in 1938 of a Soviet military-fitness campaign 'Ready for Labour and Defence' under the name of 'Bulgarian Sport Badge'. The model of the German *Hitler Jugend* and the Italian *Balila* organisations for military training and control of the youth served as models in 1941 for their Bulgarian counterpart *Brannik* (Defender) compulsory state organisation.

The process of transforming the notion of the political athlete to the body as representative of the Politicum was reflected clearly in the new policy orientation of the union Unak, which was initially a proponent of a holistic approach, combining both physical and intellectual education of the person. With the advance of authoritarian and Fascist tendencies in society, however, this vision was substituted by the doctrine of Apollonsim (Bulgaria's equivalent of 'Athleticism', after the ancient Greek god of male beauty, Apollo), symbolised by the strong male body and its use for utilitarian purposes.

Masculinity in sports policy is evident from the social construction of domain membership and policy formulation. Bulgaria's turbulent political and social development pushed the army to the forefront. It made several crucial appearances, but by and large remained a reactionary institution detesting the values of bourgeois democracy. Most modern sports were introduced in Bulgaria by army officers, and subsequently, due to the lack of public facilities, were practiced on army premises and developed by army personnel. Historical circumstances determined the membership of sports and their governing structures in the policy domain. Mainly sports contributing to military training, such as shooting, fencing, cycling, equestrianism and gymnastics developed. These were organised by men and for men, and women's clubs were very rare The establishment of a women's youth club in 1897 in Burgas was a real sensation.[34]

Masculinity in shaping sports policy domain was reinforced by the class division of sport into bourgeois (fascist) and workers (communist). Both, the government and the Communist Party perceived sport as a political battleground and used it to promote similar messages. They revolved around the idea of the triumphant (fascist) male athlete struggle for power, or the suffering (communist) male hero. Subsequently, developing a healthy body and unlimited energy needed for the struggles against state enemies (the communists), or the capitalists (fascists) respectively, was made a central theme in sport policy.

TABLE 1

BULGARIAN PARTICIPATION IN THE OLYMPIC GAMES IN THE
PRE-TOTALITARIAN PERIOD

1896	1900	1904	1908	1912	1920	1924	1928	1932	1936
Gymnastics						Athletics	Fencing		Athletics
						Equestrian	Equestrian		Equestrian
						Football			Fencing
						Cycling			Cycling
									Shooting
									Gymnastics
									Skiing

Table 1 shows Bulgarian participation in the Olympic Games in the pre-totalitarian period. All nine sports were practised predominantly and controlled exclusively by men (army personnel) and no woman took part in the Olympics. From its inception in 1923, the Bulgarian Olympic Committee (BOC) was clearly a male domain as no female representative sat on its General Assembly. One woman was accepted as a representative of the skating club in 1930, and none of the BOC member organisations' chairpersons was a woman. The composition of the membership of the major umbrella sports organisation Unak in 1936 is another illuminating example of the period male supremacy. Of 101 Unak societies leaders, 73 were army (acting or reserve) officers, 14 teachers, seven city mayors, one businessman, one priest, one bank agent and four others, and there was no woman member.[35]

As stated above, sports policy formulation was dominated by masculine images and language. The union Unak and its members were seen as bearers of a historical tradition, according to which they were fighting, suffering and dying for kinship, freedom and the truth. The union's ultimate goal was 'to provide Bulgaria with physically and morally sound citizens, capable of protecting the country from internal and external threats – masculine patriots sons ... who won't stop in front of anything when the fatherland calls them to defend its supreme interests'.[36] The public discourse in the form of names of sports clubs is also indicative as the most popular names were Unak (Hero), Boretz (Fighter), Patriot (Patriot), Sokol (Falcon), and Brannik (Defender) symbolising strength and virility. The slogan of the Zveno Fascist political group which came to power in 1934 after a military coup was 'through sport for the fatherland', promoting further military tendencies in sport policy.

Historical circumstances and the construction of the sports policy domain predetermined the nature of structural relations and the ability of various groups to advocate changes in men–women relations in sport. All key individual and group state and voluntary actors in the domain were either male or male-dominated. Inevitably, they advocated virility, discipline, obedience, a modest and Spartan life and a readiness to fight. With some sporadic exceptions (mainly short references in Communist Party documents, or the 1931 Sport Law, for greater involvement), women were never recognised as a particular target group with its own needs, nor were practical policies devised for them.

Resource allocation to sports organisations was made by the state in exchange for subscribing and promoting masculine policies. Women in society, and in sport in particular, were poorly organised, enjoyed only modest participation, and were unable to reach standards of performance to qualify for national and international representation. Women's appearance in sport in this period was viewed more as a sensation than a token!

The New Man: Masculinity in Totalitarian Sports Policy

The period between 1944 and 1989 saw the rise and fall of Communism and was totalitarian in nature. Its key feature was the notion of the New Man, the builder of Communism who was determined to impose his will on the rest of the world. This new man, to use J. Hoberman's[37] description, was supposed to be a heroic male figure, larger than life, a brave and devoted family man and role model for idealistic youth.

The second, third and fourth of the quotations at the beginning of this chapter perfectly illustrate these key characteristics, and promote essentially masculine images. The task of creating 'perfect and beautiful people', healthy builders of socialism, ready for industrious labour and defence of the country was at the heart of the communist project. Moreover, general and area specific policies, sport included, were geared towards achieving these objectives. The image of the Bulgarian woman did not differ from the general picture, and even in the most feminine of all sports – rhythmic gymnastics – she was not portrayed as an individual character with specific needs, rather as a symbol of 'communist stubbornness' and 'socialist morale', a heroic athlete whose efforts should aim at 'fatherland prosperity'.

The communist project proclaimed equal rights and opportunities for men and women, so references to masculinity were ideologically obscured and sometimes difficult to discern. There were two powerful mechanisms for promoting masculine values in sports policy – general interest and representation. The general interest perpetuated masculinity by denying the signs of division between state and society and abolishing the signs of internal social division. What was rejected was the social heterogeneity of society, the existence of a variety of modes of life, behaviour and opinion, in so far as they contradicted the image of a society in harmony with itself. Individuals and groups were left very little chance of recognising and promoting women's specific interests, which were not on the agenda of the ruling Communist Party nor on the supreme sports governing body, the Bulgarian Sports Union (BSFS).

The concept of representation constituted the ideological matrix of the totalitarian state system by discerning four such key forms of representation: the *People-as-One image*, the *organisation*, the *social-historical creation*, and that of *society's transparency to itself*.[38] The first three have a particular bearing on shaping masculine values and policies in sport.

The image of *The People-as-One* portrayed the proletariat as identical to the people and the party, and the party with leadership, and the leadership with an ultimate concept. This image can be affirmed if what is different from it is denied. This process of double identification (with the people and the enemy) is best captured by the metaphor of the *body*. As the integrity of the body depends on the elimination of its parasites, so the pursuit of the enemy (in the form of regular ideological, organisational or ethnical purges) is seen as a form of necessary social profilaxis. In this period the strategic outcome of the first ideological representation was a justification for the introduction of the *Body Politic* – establishing by a supreme body (the Party) a uniform concept for every sphere of public life including sport, and performance criteria corresponding to it.

The novelty of this totalitarian project was in its attitude to the entire society as a vast *organisation* comprising a network of micro-organisations. This new society was simultaneously organised and organisable. It was organised in the sense that every individual or collective member's position and function was well predetermined and imprinted in this organisation. It was organisable because it was perceived as an amorphous matter which lent itself to the intervention of the constantly working organiser, the builder of Communism. Effective organisation also became the supreme criterion for gauging the action and knowledge of the leader. In sports policy, the criterion employed was the mythical Plan and quotas, where various groups' needs did not matter.

The third form of representation which complements the above image of the organisation was a *social-historical creation*. It derived from the myth of a social raw material offered to the power of the organiser, the creator of an already known future. As will be demonstrated in the rest of this analysis, the omnipresent organiser who determined the contribution of sport to shaping the new man, and the general interest in sport, that is, what and how sports are to be played and structured was, without exception, a man.

The notion of the body in the totalitarian period appears, in contrast to the pre-totalitarian sports visions, not as an explicit muscled figure, but as a physically strong individual, the member of a collective. In fact, until the mid-1980s body-building ('culturism') and martial arts were deemed to be exhibitionist activities undermining group morale, and were denied structural autonomy and other privileges. The need for healthy and fit citizens, capable workers and defenders of the country, participating in a collective effort to achieve common ends were used as strong arguments for introducing the body politics into sport. More specifically, three sets of arguments can be distinguished here.

1. The example of Soviet soldiers' endurance during the Second World War (a recycled argument from the pre-totalitarian period) and the Cold War (East–West rivalry) urged and sustained the military orientation of sports policy until the mid 1980s.

2. The general interest of society was applied in order to change the principle of the organisation of sport from 'territorial' to 'professional and departmental', which meant predominantly that people had to take part in sport, not where they lived, but where they studied and worked – in schools, factories and enterprises.

3. The need to assert Communism internationally highlighted the prominence of competition both as a major form of sport provision and for winning international support for the system.

Clearly the three arguments conveyed, and served to perpetuate, masculine values and images, and had an essential bearing on constructing sports policy. In principle, the sports policy domain was socially constructed by the Communist Party and the aspirations of its governmental agencies.

The structural centralisation of sport was inevitably accompanied by another essential step towards classifying sports organisations which shaped the core and the periphery of the domain, and effectively marginalised women's administrative involvement and participation. It has to be pointed out that all three major sports categorisations in 1949, 1958 and 1969 were instigated by BCP Politburo decisions.[39] The justification given for emphasising sports with well-established traditions does not bear scrutiny because, as will be demonstrated priorities changed according to increasingly rational criteria. Between 1949 and 1959 these were based on the capacity of team sports to organise large contingents and generate support for the Party's committees. Participation in most sports was mostly male. A reclassification in 1969 was provoked by two key factors: the capacity of sport to provide young people with the basic training and military skills for defence and to win international prestige. Team sports proved to be harder to administer and sustain and less cost-effective for the system.

The third, reshuffling of priorities, followed similar criteria and now included mostly individual orientated sports, although their numbers increased along the way. The restructuring of sports along these lines had a great impact on the distribution of resources and allocation of privileges as well as on the pursuit of strategies aimed at increasing women's participation. Aerobics emerged in the early 1980s as one of the most appealing female activities, but it was not given structural autonomy and was embraced within the remit of the BSFS Sport for All department led by men. Table 2 shows the changes in sports priorities.

TABLE 2

SPORTS CLASSIFICATION IN POLICY DOMAIN IMPOSED BY
THE COMMUNIST PARTY

1949	1958	1969	1988
Athletics	Basketball	Athletics	Athletics
Gymnastics	Football	Gymnastics	Gymnastics
Basketball	Volleyball	Swimming	Swimming
Volleyball	Wrestling		Wrestling
Boxing	Table tennis		Boxing
Football	Chess		Weightlifting
Cycling			Rhythmic gymnastics
Shooting			Rowing
Wrestling			
Equestrian			
Tourism			

Formal membership of sports organisations was supposed to be both individual and collective. The 'professional and departmental' principle of structuring the sports domain implied that sport clubs had to be set up in schools, factories and institutions. As clubs were not grounded in people's real interests, individual membership quickly turned into a fiction. This issue for the first and only time was acknowledged in the BSFS's founding Congress report[40] which stated that of the anticipated contribution from individual membership fees of 800,000 Leva only 70,000 Leva (5.6%) had been collected. In 1958 women collectively constituted 25 per cent of the BSFS members. Because of the principle of collective membership in sport, the main patterns of participation were also collective, and their value as a vehicle to promote and regulate sport consumption by women diminished.

Sports policy formulation was simultaneously determined by the domain structural composition, and which also determined the way it was shaped. Women's low participation in sport was always reluctantly acknowledged. In 1972[41] it was found that only 4.5 per cent of the active female population took part. The figure for women living in villages was even more alarming – only 0.25 per cent were recorded as having taken up a sport. In 1980 on average 80 per cent of school girls failed to reach the national fitness norms. Table 3 shows the sex difference in participation of Bulgarian athletes in the Olympic Games, and supports the view that women's sports were regarded as low priority. Despite these concerns, conceptual and structural of participation constraints continued, and women never gained recognition as a target group in any policy document of that period.

TABLE 3

BULGARIAN ATHLETES' FIRST PARTICIPATION IN SELECTED
SPORTS AT THE OLYMPIC GAMES

Sport	Men	Women	Gap
Athletics	1924	1980	36
Gymnastics	1896	1956	60
Swimming	1968	1968	0
Rowing	1968	1976	8
Canoe - Kayaking	1960	1964	4
Basketball	1952	1976	24
Volleyball	1964	1980	16

Another peculiarity of sports policy was the transformation of people's basic right to take part in sport into their duty as citizens. The rhetorical questions posed by the head of state, Zhivkov, 'What kind of builders of Socialism and Communism, or what defenders of the country would people be with their health undermined?' illustrate this change. A passage in the Politburo of BCP 1969 decision[42] urges 'every young boy and girl to become a swimmer', and to 'acquire the basic skills of at least one of the disciplines of gymnastics or athletics'. This is how the power of the organiser shaped women's participation in sport, by imposing on them large-scale activities and not responding to their preferences and needs.

Finally, essential for an appreciation of the workings of masculinity in sports policy were the structural relations established in the domain. Two such relations deserve mention. First is that between sport's collective production and consumption. As discussed earlier, grass roots club provision of sport was fictitious, and access to activities was offered by multisports societies (DFS) to various collectives and named pupils, workers or farmers. As a result, women's specific interests were never recognised and they were not allowed to organise themselves in one form or another. Second, the structuring of the sports policy domain produced a whole class of male policy-makers. Table 4 illustrates the composition of three principal sports governing bodies – strategic decision-making (BSFS Central Council), top-executive decision-making (BSFS Executive Board), and chairmanship of sports delivery units at municipal level (Sports Societies, DFSs). Clearly, women can be seen at best as marginal and with regard to leadership positions at municipal level, non-existent.

TABLE 4

FEMALE REPRESENTATION IN SPORTS GOVERNING BODIES
(members and chairpersons)

Period	BSFS Central Council			BSFS Executive Board			Sports Societies (DFSs)		
	Total	Women	%	Total	Women	%	Total	Women	%
1977	185	30	17	21	2	9	920	0	0
1982	195	26	13	23	2	8	324	0	0
1991	161	15	9	19	2	10	272	0	0

The picture was the same at international level. By the mid-1980s only 16 of 100 Bulgarian representatives on various international sports commissions and boards were women. Between 1964 and 1983 international sports relations with countries from Europe, Africa, Asia and America proliferated, but none of the 140 agreements and protocols (even at departmental level) was ever signed by a woman. The outcome of this continued marginalisation of women in sports policy-making bodies was an inhibited ability to advocate change – there were no conceptual grounds, structures, institutional or practical policies to support their views and needs.

The Europeanisation Project: Masculinity in Post-Totalitarian Sports Policy

The events of 1989 signalled the end of totalitarianism in East European countries. In Bulgaria, the new beginning was strongly associated with the Europeanisation project, which was supposed to set the country on the road to modern democratic development. The transition from a totalitarian to a democratic society, however, opened a deep ideological gulf revolving around the notion of restoration: objectives included for the builders of democracy the prevention of a return to Communism, while the communists were concerned to prevent the re-emergence of Fascism. Sports policy fell victim to this confusion, and 'don't throw the baby out with the bath water' became the slogan of totalitarian policy-makers whose supremacy was challenged.

The new sports policy promoted by the state Committee for Youth Physical Education and Sport (CYPES) abandoned the military rationale, and proclaimed the incorporation of common European values of human rights, freedom, choice and dignity in the sports' portfolio. This policy was based on the intention to enable every member of society to have access to sport. As many sports policy-makers lost their identification with the previous social system and its aims, the policy content became increasingly blurred and was nothing more than improvisation. The overriding theme of all policy discussions until late 1994 was that of 'survival'. BSFS's 9th congress report[43] is a perfect example of a 'revolutionary' situation, characterised by abundant heroic terminology, typical of the battlefield. Phraseology such as fight, 'clashes', 'impotence', 'fall out of line', 'chaos', 'destroying campaign', or 'debleeding' illustrate the point.

Subsequently, the state was constantly called to step in and save the achievements and the *status quo* of Bulgarian sport, thus effectively perpetuating its masculine features. This kind of rhetoric diverted individual and corporate attention and prevented them from seeing that in 1994, 60 per cent of BSFS expenditure was on salaries, and 0 per cent of its income came from services to the public.

President Stoyanov's address to victorious wrestlers and weightlifters makes a direct, yet covert, reference to the past. His appeal to create a 'new Bulgarian wonder' during the Olympic Games in Sydney 2000 rests on the notion of a heroic athlete capable of any physical achievement for the glory of his (and now her) country. More specifically envisaged was the success of the national Olympic team which came fourth with 35 medals including a bronze at the Seoul Olympics in 1988, and of the national football team at the 1994 World Cup in the USA. The discourse of totalitarian public policy-makers, whose supremacy was challenged, referred to both achievements as heroic and past and present politicians tried to capitalise on them. A similar attitude now tacitly supports the model of dominant sports policy-making and provides a justification for the slogans of past patriotism and the forces of conservatism. Following the general ideological rift, the pillar of voluntary sport, BSFS, because of its past history, was declared a totalitarian structure and its abolition recommended. The state CYPES pronounced itself a bearer of the new values in sports policy, which could not be asserted successfully before the demise of the BSFS. Naturally, the state agency used the ideological climate to advocate a firmer state grip on sport. President Stoyanov's second comment can be seen as an extension of this line of thought. He suggested that a Ministry of Sport would raise the status of sport, and would increase its chances for better treatment and support. Strengthening voluntary groups in society was not a concern.

So far, the construction of sports policy has been subordinated to the state's visions (BSFS was eventually abolished in 1998), which were also responsible for reshaping the sports policy domain. Domain membership is strictly controlled by the CYPES by means of three mechanisms – licensing, resource allocation and direct administrative intervention. This is not to suggest that registration of women's associations is not tolerated by the state, but the criteria set for licensing do not favour free association based purely on interests and needs. Grass root clubs do not get state subsidies which are allocated exclusively with the purpose of achieving élite results. It is not surprising that women's participation in sport remains low, as a national survey by A. Stoychev and S. Tzonev[44] has demonstrated. They found that, on average 73 per cent of men took part in competitive, and 61 per cent in non-competitive, sport, as opposed to 27 per cent and 39 per cent of women, respectively.

Virtually without exception, central policy-making positions in the sports domain continue to be held by men. Of 37 presidents of Olympic sports federations only two are female, and amongst 54 sports societies' (DFS) chairpersons, none is a woman. All executive positions in the CYPES since its inception in 1992, have been occupied by men. In addition, between 1994 and 1996, and with some incremental changes until 1999, 16 key positions in the domain, including the Bulgarian Olympic Committee, the Sport for All Association, the Confederation of National Sports Federations and the CYPES were shared by three males. The only organisation established and governed by women, and designed to provide services predominantly for women, is the Aerobic Union.

Ten years after political transformation there is a huge discrepancy between the proclaimed aims of the Europeanisation project and sports governing bodies' practical policies. As demonstrated above, policy making structures remain dominated by men and policy formulation exhibits masculine values. None of the three strategic policy documents – Conception for the System of Physical Education and Sports in Bulgaria,[45] the Government Programme for Developing Physical Education and Sport in Bulgaria 1997–2000,[46] and the National Programme for Physical Activity and Development, BULPHAR 2000[47] makes reference to women as a specific target group worth of attention. Only one of BULPHAR 2000's sub-programmes, the aerobic marathon, is advertised as particularly suitable for women.

Structural relations in the sports domain, its key actors and the nature of strategies promoted make changing women's position in sport a daunting task. On the one hand, women are denied support at grass roots level, where they are more likely to get involved in meeting their needs. On the other, they are grossly under-represented in sports governing bodies which devise policies. Despite the fact that the number of women groups and associations has grown significantly in the past ten years, this increase does not seem to have affected sports domain policy. The Bulgarian sports authorities were amongst 82 countries which voted for the Brighton Declaration on Women and Sport,[48] but so far they have made no serious effort to endorse its principles. It is clear that sports organisations cannot afford to ignore any longer the talents and needs of half the population, but women are lacking the organised voice and political mechanisms to put their concerns on the agenda.

Sports Policy's Course and Discourse: Residual and Emerging Masculinities

As demonstrated above, discourse and course of action in sports policy are intertwined. Popular discourse in sports policy has historically revolved around several key themes – heroism, virility, strength, productive labour, obedience, defence and choice. They have all been presented as grounded in the objective necessity of the country's unification, defence or civilised development, and in the main, have endorsed masculine contributions to these processes. Throughout the pre-totalitarian, totalitarian, and post-totalitarian periods, this male orientated discourse has been imposed on individual and collective actors by three principal institutions: the army, the Communist Party, and state agencies (head of state or government bodies), which have been dominated by men.

The typical image of sports policy in the first period was that of a muscled male body willing to fight for the cause of nationalism. The notion of the New Man, a heroic and dedicated powerful male figure, a member of an ideological collective exemplified the content of sports policy during totalitarianism. The post-totalitarian reality has not brought clear cut ideas on which to base sports policy but has employed under subscription to a modern, democratic and civilised Europe, old *and* new masculine discourses to promote past values and actions.

Analysts and commentators, who might offer corrective policies, have been ideologically trapped and have not effectively contributed to the issue of women in sport. Only two studies concerning women's patterns of participation in sport were published between 1959 and 1970,[49] and both reported positive developments. To date the number of female writers researching the topic is negligible – five out of 32. No study concerning policy on women's sports has ever been undertaken.

In the twentieth century the course of practical sports policies has been underpinned by masculine values and has aimed to support military training or to serve other male-orientated utilitarian purposes. Women's participation in sport has always been low and remains so. Despite various concerns about poor female participation, no strategic policy document in all three periods has ever identified women as a target group and accordingly devised policies to tackle inequality. The sports policy domain has always been dominated by men and women have been seen at best as marginal within the domain. Little has changed over time. Adequate sports policy conceptualisation, domain construction, sport production and consumption, arrangements and structural relations essential for empowering individuals and groups to advocate and promote change have never materialised.

Finally, the three periods considered provide ample evidence of mainly continuity rather than change in gender relations in sport. Furthermore, they illustrate the force of both residual and emerging masculinities in Bulgarian sports policy. For some 80 years residual practices have prevailed and been sustained. This may be reasonably interpreted as reflecting deep-rooted social stereotypes and norms, which have been and are reproduced in sport. Four specific masculine traits have been consistent in all three periods: 1. the existence of the political male athlete; 2. inconsistent and low female patterns of participation; 3. as a corollary, the marginalisation of women in the sports policy domain, and their absence from decision-making bodies, and 4. non-recognition of women as a target group subject to positive intervention.

There have been, of course, emerging practices, which have pointed towards new possibilities in sports policy for women. The lack of prominence given to the male body in the post–totalitarian conceptualisation of sport, and the association of national policy with common European values which recognise and actively promote gender equality entail a new twist for domestic policy-makers. Furthermore, women have successfully taken over and now exercise control over policy-making in aerobics. There are also now widespread examples of successful female sports managers in the private sector, a practice unknown in the pre-totalitarian or totalitarian periods. All is not gloom.

Nevertheless, given the history of sports policy-making in Bulgaria, radical changes are not likely to occur, unless women take a firm stance and mobilise political, social and economic resources, and work together with men to promote their needs and interests. The post-totalitarian reality clearly offers such possibilities but the difficulties as this chapter has made clear, should not be underestimated.

NOTES

1. K. Clatterbaugh, *Contemporary Perspectives on Masculinity: Men, Women, and Politics in Modern Society* (Oxford, 1990), pp.9–13.
2. J. Cagnon, 'Physical Strength, Once of Significance', in J. Pleck and J. Sawyer (eds.), *Men and Masculinity* (New Jersey, 1974), p.145.
3. J.A. Mangan and J. Walvin (eds.), *Manliness and Morality: Middle-Class Masculinity in Britain and America, 1800–1840* (Manchester, 1987).
4. J. Cagnon, 'Physical Strength', p.8.
5. M. MacNeil, 'Networks: Producing Olympic Ice Hockey for a National Television Audience', *Sociology of Sport Journal*, 13 (1996), 102–24.
6. M. Costa, and S. Guthrine (eds.), *Women and Sport* (Champaign, 1994).
7. C. Williams, G. Lawrence and D. Rowe, 'Patriarchy, media, sport', in G. Lawrence and D. Rowe (eds.), *Essays on Australian Sport* (Sydney, 1989), pp.215–29.
8. J. Hargreaves, *Sporting Females* (London, 1994).
9. C. Green, and L. Chalip, 'Enduring Involvement in Youth Soccer: The Socialization of Parent and Child', *Journal of Leisure Research*, 29. 1 (1997), 61–77.
10. S. Greendorfer, 'Sport Socialisation', in T. Horn (ed.), *Advances in Sport Psychology* (Champaign, 1992).
11. I. Lawrie, and R. Brown, 'Sex stereotypes, school subject preference and career aspirations as a function of single/mixed sex schooling and presence/absence of an opposite sex sibling', *British Journal of Educational Psychology*, 62, 1 (1992), 132–37.
12. D. Scully, and J. Clarke, 'Gender Issues in Sport Participation', in J. Kremer *et al.* (eds.), *Young People's Involvement in Sport* (London, 1997).
13. S. Greendorfer *et al.*
14. T. Kamphorst and K. Roberts (eds.), *Trends in Sports: A Multinational Perspective* (Voorthuizen, 1989).
15. G. Cushman *et al.* (eds.), *World Leisure Participation: Free Time in the Global Village* (London, 1996).
16. A. White and C. Brackenridge, 'Who Rules Sport? Gender Division in the Power Structure of British Sports Organisations from 1960', *International Review for the Sociology of Sport*, 20, 1–2 (1985), 95–107.

17. A. Doherty, 'Sex Differences in Managerial Leadership Perceptions of Sport Managers and Staff', *Proceedings, 3rd European Congress on Sport Management* (Budapest, 1995).
18. T. Kay, *Women and Sport: A Review Research* (London, 1995).
19. G. Whannel, 'Sport Stars, Narrativization and Masculinities', *Leisure Studies*, 18 (1999), 252.
20. Greendorfer *et al.*, p.217.
21. J. Rutherford, 'Who's That Man.', in R. Chapman, and J. Rutherford (eds.), *Male Order: Unwrapping Masculinity* (London, 1989), p.26.
22. N. Mandell, *Feminist Issues: Race, Class and Sexuality* (New Jersey, 1995), p.189.
23. R. Deem, 'The Politics of Women's Leisure', in Horne *et al.* (eds.), *Sport, Leisure and Social Relations* (London, 1987), p.210.
24. M. Talbot, 'Working together towards gender equity in sport – Challenges for sports organisations', *7th European Congress for Sport Management* (Thessaloniki, 1999).
25. E. Laumann and D. Knoke, *The Organizational State: Social Choice in National Policy Domains* (London, 1987).
26. B. Hogwood and L. Gunn, *Policy Analysis for the Real World* (New York, 1984).
27. M. Rush, *Politics and Society: An introduction to Political Sociology* (London, 1992), p.72.
28. V. Girginov, 'Bulgarian Sport Today: Is History Repeating Itself or is Real Change Occurring?', *European Physical Education Review*, 3, 1 (1997), 33–49.
29. V. Girginov and P. Bankov, 'Bulgaria Reborn: The Fascist Political Athlete and the Body Politic', in J.A. Mangan (ed.), *Superman Supreme: Fascist Body as Political Icon – Global Fascism* (London, forthcoming).
30. R. Williams, *Marxism and Literature* (New York, 1977).
31. V. Girginov, 'Bulgarian Sport Today', 33.
32. N. Sheitanov, *Kult na Tjaloto (Body Cult), Physical Education* (MNP, 1928).
33. Girginov, 'Bulgarian Sport Today', 33.
34. R. Bardareva, *Organizaciite za Physiceska Cultura v Balgaria: Prinosat in za razvitie na sportovete 1878–1944* (Sports Organisations in Bulgaria: Contribution to sports development 1878–1944) (Sofia, 1995), p.61.
35. N. Petrova, *100 Godini Obshtestveni Fizkulturni Organizacii v Balgaria* (100 years of Voluntary Sport Organisations in Bulgaria) (Sofia, 1978).
36. A. Vasev (ed.), *Zadaci i organisacija na fizkulturnoto dvizenie v Balgaria* (Tasks and Organisation of the Sports Movement in Bulgaria) (Sofia, 1950), p.89.
37. J. Hoberman, *Sport and Political Ideology* (London, 1984), p.196.
38. P. Lefort, *The Political Forms of Modern Society: Bureaucracy, Democracy, Totalitarianism* (Cambridge, 1986), pp.286–9.
39. BSFS, *Sbornik ot reshenija na Politburo i Sekretariata na CK na BKP za razvitieto na fiziceskata kultura i sporta v NRB* (A Collection of Politburo and Secretariat of BCP Central Committee decisions regarding Physical Culture and Sport in Bulgaria) (Sofia, 1986).
40. BSFS, *Materiali ot ucreditelnia kongres na BSFCS* (Founding Congress of the BSFS) (Sofia, 1958), p.77.
41. BSFS, *Otcet na CS BSFCS IV Kongres* (BSFS 4th Congress Report) (Sofia, 1972)
42. BSFS, *Sbornik ot reshenija*, p.43.
43. BSFS, *Otcet za Deinosta na BSFS v Perioda ot Osmia do Devetija Kongress* (BSFS, 9th Congress Report) (Sofia: BSFS, 1994).
44. A. Stoychev and S. Tzonev, 'Obshtestvenite subekti i sporta za vsichki' (Public subjects and Sport for All), *Sport and Nauka*, 6 (1995), 30.
45. CYPES, 'Conception for the system of physical education and sports in Republic Bulgaria' (Sofia, 1996).
46. Council of Ministers, Nacionalna programa za razvitieto na fiziceskoto vazpitanie i sporta v Balgaria za perioda 1997-2000 (National programme for developing Physical Education and Sport in Bulgaria ,1997–2000) (Sofia,1997).
47. CYPES, BULPHAR 2000 Balgarska Fiziceska Aktivnost i Razvitie 2000 (Bulgarian Physical Activity and Development) (Sofia, 1998)
48. Sports Council, *The Brighton Declaration on Women and Sport: Women Sport and the Challenge of Change* (London, 1994)
49. A. Stoychev and A. Daceva (eds.), *Sociologija na Sporta v Balgaria* (Sports Sociology in Bulgaria) (Sofia, 1970).

Epilogue:
'What Man has made of Man'[1]

J.A. MANGAN

In her recent novel *Manly Pursuits*, in part about 'Darwinism ... imperialism and "the white man's burden", and sexual ambivalence in a repressive era',[2] Ann Harris has drawn portraits of *fin de siècle* male characters depicting a range of European masculinities: Cecil Rhodes, ruthless Africa-obsessed homosexual; Alfred Milner, heterosexual ethnocentric-driven imperialist, and Francis Wills, gentle nature-enthralled paedophile. Masculinity comes in all shapes, sizes and forms! Nowhere is this point made more explicitly, incidentally, than in *Dislocating Masculinity: Comparative Ethnographies*, a collection by A. Cornwall and N. Lindisfarne. These sample chapter titles give a flavour of the collection as a whole, 'Gendered Identities and Gender Ambiguity among *Trevestis* in Salvador, Bahia', 'Variant Masculinities, Variant Virginities: Rethinking "Honour and Shame"' and 'Missing Masculinity? Prostitutes' clients in Alicante, Spain'.[3]

Reality is often flexible; idealism is often inflexible. Desirable male qualities in European history, and elsewhere, as mentioned in the Prologue, have more often than not have included aggression, assertion, strength and self-discipline – mental, moral and physical, in preparation for conflict of various kinds and for control in various situations. This has been the main recurring theme in *Making European Masculinities*. In pursuit of these perceived qualities, whatever variations have been condoned, accepted or even approved, there has been more continuity than change from the ancient Classical period to the modern Imperial period in European history.

Throughout that whole time and throughout Europe, recognised or unrecognised, sport in one form or another, for one group or another, has been a constant and consistent means of developing these required and respected male qualities. It has had a central place in the making of masculinity in preparation for confrontation in the world and with the world at both micro and macro level. Within Europe, literacy has not always been a male requirement, numeracy has not always been a male obligation, but frequently skill at sport has been a male asset – with sexual, social and martial advantages. Sport has been at the centre of male socialisation in the history of masculinity in Europe. That is the measure of its significance in European cultures. But what of the future?

This millennium moment is one of momentous change in European male and female relationships and this change is caught perfectly in sport. Sport makes modern men and women, to an extent, in the same image. The global espousal of modern competitive sports puts a premium on aggression, assertion, strength and self-discipline – for *both* men and women. The increasing access by women to the occupational world, especially of commerce, also ensures the public desirability of these competitive virtues in women. Furthermore, because of the association with the inculcation of these qualities, sport has historically been linked to war. It has been considered a valuable and appropriate training for war. And war in all its forms is increasingly the responsibility and the right of women.[4] These attributes, and these manifestations, are only part of the variety of cultural roles of men and women, but they are increasingly a relatively large part of their *ideal* cultural roles.

It is fully recognised, of course, that selective co-operation, cohesion and compassion have a place in the worlds of modern sport, commerce and war. Nevertheless, without aggression in particular, there would be no winners in these competitive activities!

In *Masculinities: Football, Polo and the Tango in Argentina*, Eduardo Archetti writes of the concept of 'hybridity' – the creation of modern diverse cultural mixtures.[5] He suggests that 'the existence of a clear boundary between "us" and "them" calls for the hybrid, the mixed … which is created by the transgression or the possibility of the transgression of this boundary'.[6] Since hybridity, in part, exists along the axes of inclusion and exclusion, it emerges 'from circumstances in which discontinuities have been produced'.[7]

Furthermore, hybridity is a permanent condition, a condition that challenges dominant cultural differences, that takes explicit forms of counter authority and exists in moments of political change.[8]

Archetti sees particular value in the use of the term by Garcia Canclini, who adopts a 'transdisciplinary framework which blends art, history and literature, folklore and anthropology, and sociology and mass communication.'[9] This, interestingly, was the approach adopted in J.A. Mangan's *Shaping the Superman: Fascist Body as Political Icon – Aryan Fascism* in the discussion of the Aryan Prometheus. It is considered of special value in any discussion of the androgynous future, with its comprehensiveness of perspective.

Archetti concentrates on football, polo and the tango – 'typical modern bodily practices', which 'in a world of increasing competition and trans-national exchanges ... are powerful expressions of national capabilities and potentialities – as powerful as art and literature'.[10] And not simply in the immediate present but, for example, in the recent past, '*homo ludens imperiosis*' – typical of the period of British late nineteenth-century imperialism underlines this point strongly.[11]

Archetti also favours an emphasis on sport (and dance) in 'hybridization' analysis because it makes possible an inspection of 'ways of classifying men and women and the relations between men and women'[12] within national and international global landscapes. This statement brings the discussion back to an androgynous post millennium.

The attractions of the concept of the hybrid in culture in the case of men *and* women of the post–millennium and sport as a component of culture, are at least twofold; first, hybrids are paradoxical – ideological constructions of social order, producers of tradition, and *symbols of continuity* and at the same time, transgressive talismen, classificatory subversives and *symbols of change*. As such they are valuable in an understanding of change. Second, and as a corollary, sport historically has been essentially a symbol of a masculine world – both a prescription and a privilege. It is so no longer. Symbolism has been extended. Tradition has been rejected; social order has been reconstructed: a *future* tradition has been demanded; a new social order has been put in place.

All this is germane to masculinity in the post-millennium global culture where women in part adopt traditional masculine attitudes and occupations and demand that men in part adopt traditional feminine responses and behaviour. Female emancipation has produced new cultural demands associated with perceived male and female qualities. For their part, men are required to adopt the perceived positive qualities of traditional femininity, while women, for their part, demand their adoption of perceived positive masculine qualities. The Androgynous Culture is in the making. As sport has been central to the definition of masculinity in the past, it will be central to the definition of androgyny in the future.

NOTES

1. William Wordsworth, 'Lines written in Early Spring'.
2. Ann Harris, *Manly Pursuits* (London, 1999), dustjacket blurb.
3. See A. Cornwall and N. Lindisfarne (eds.), *Dislocating Masculinity: Comparative Ethnographies* (London, 1994).
4. See J.A. Mangan (ed.), 'Epilogue: Continuities', in *Shaping the Superman: Fascist Body as Political Icon – Aryan Fascism* (London, 1999) and see also J.A. Mangan, 'Aggression and Adrogyny: Gender Fusion in and beyond Sport in the Post-Millennium', in *Revue française de civilisation britannique* (forthcoming, 2000).
5. Eduardo P. Archetti, *Masculinities: Football, Polo and the Tango in Argentina* (Oxford, 1999), p.24.
6. Ibid.
7. Ibid.
8. Ibid., p.26.
9. Ibid., p.16.
10. Ibid.
11. See J.A. Mangan, 'Prologue – Britain's Chief Spiritual Export: Imperial Sport as Moral Metaphor, Political Symbol and Cultural Bond', in J.A. Mangan (ed.), *The Cultural Bond: Sport, Empire, Society* (London, 1992), and J.A. Mangan, *The Games Ethic and Imperialism* (London, 1998), *passim*; J.A. Mangan (ed.), *Pleasure, Profit, Proselytism: British Culture and Sport at Home and Abroad, 1700–1914* (London, 1998), *passim*; and J.A. Mangan, *Athleticism in the Victorian School and Edwardian Public School* (Cambridge, 1981), Ch.6 'Oxbridge Fashions, Complacent Parents and Imperialism', pp.122–40.
12. Archetti, *Masculinities*, p.16.

Notes on Contributors

Evangelos Albanidis is Senior Lecturer in Sports History at the Department of Physical Education, Democritus University of Thrace.

Hans Bonde is Associate Professor at the University of Southern Denmark. He is currently writing a biography of the internationally renowned Danish youth leader Niels Bukh.

Remi Dalisson lectures in history at the University of Rouen.

Jean-Michel Delaplace is Professor of Sociology at the University of Montpellier.

Vassil Girginov is Senior Lecturer in Leisure and Sport Studies at Luton Business School, University of Luton.

Colm Hickey studied at the former Borough Road College and is a graduate of the University of London. He completed his MA at the University of London, Institute of Education. He is currently Deputy Headteacher of St Bernard's Catholic School, High Wycombe.

Jens Ljunggren teaches history at the University of Stockholm. He is currently doing research into masculinity in Sweden and Germany during the First World War.

J.A. Mangan is Director of the International Research Centre for Sport, Socialisation and Society at the University of Strathclyde, Glasgow.

Callum McKenzie is currently researching masculinity and field sports at the University of Strathclyde.

Frédéric Saumade is at the University of Montpellier.

Abstracts

The Ephebia in the Ancient Hellenic World and its Role in the Making of Masculinity
Evangelos Albanidis

The size of the ancient Hellenic world reached its peak during the Hellenistic period. From the second half of the eighth century BC onwards, a large number of colonies were founded in Gaul, the Italian peninsula and North Africa as well as along the coastlines of Thrace, Euxeinos Pontos and Asia Minor. Wherever the Hellenes founded new towns, they established educational, political, military and religious institutions. The ephebia was a school that provided military, gymnastic and intellectual education for young men of 18–20 years of age. This chapter is based on the collection and analysis of data related to the foundation and expansion of ephebia all over the Hellenic world. It examines the general goals of this institution as well as its specific role in the making of masculinity.

Fighting Bulls in Southern European Culture: Anthropomorphic Symbols of Aggression and Mythical Male Heroes
Frédéric Saumade and Jean-Michel Delaplace

This chapter examines symbols of virility in bullfighting by comparing the rituals of the Andalusian *corrida* with those of bullfighting in the Camargue. It analyses the anthropomorphic representations of the bull and the distinct cultural significance of bullfighting in the two regions.

Asserting Male Values: Nineteenth-Century Fêtes, Games and Masculinity – A French Case Study
Remi Dalisson

Prior to the gradual inclusion of women in sport and the acceptance of mixed sports, both to any significant degree phenomena of the twentieth century, sport was widely viewed as a male activity, with the role of inculcating and underlining masculine values, serving as an affirmation of masculinity, and reinforcing the segregation of the sexes to the advantage of man. This essay assesses to what extent the traditionally held view of sport as the domain of the male prevailed in France before the Third Republic and explains how the link between games and masculinity was displayed and conveyed.

The Other Side of the Coin: Victorian Masculinity, Field Sports and English Elite Education
J.A. Mangan and Callum McKenzie

The morality of field sports and their purpose in élite education were contentious issues during the nineteenth century. Field sports now symbolised aristocratic privilege and sustained the traditional code of the gentleman in a period when middle-class sensibilities were reconstructing his image and redefining his masculinity on games fields. This chapter considers the evolving relationship between masculinity, field sports and élite education during the nineteenth century and discusses field sports as both *complementary to, and in competition with* team games, in the making of period élite masculinity.

The Masculine Road through Modernity: Ling Gymnastics and Male Socialisation in Nineteenth-Century Sweden
Jens Ljunggren

Throughout the nineteenth century and for nearly half of the twentieth Ling gymnastics, devised by Per Henrik Ling (1776–1839). It was the predominant form of physical education in the Swedish school system. This chapter argues that Ling gymnastics evolved as an attempt to resolve some of the masculine problems with modernity. This it did by presenting a kind of masculinity that was a synthesis of traditional and modern. Ling gymnastics was designed to resolve a complex of problems in the first half of the nineteenth century. At the end of the century Ling gymnastics became heavily criticised. This can be explained by the process of modernisation and changes in the gender order.

Athleticism in the Service of the Proletariat: Preparation for the English Elementary School and the Extension of Middle-Class Manliness
J.A. Mangan and Colm Hickey

In 1888 the teacher training colleges of England and Wales had been subjected to a thorough examination and had been found wanting. One significant omission from their educational provision was the absence of any conversion to the playing of team games. Within a generation, however, athleticism was to dominate college life. For the first time in the academic community, the reasons why, and ways in which this ideological transformation took place, will now be considered. This chapter, in general, focuses on the process of diffusion and, in particular, on the way in which rituals were used to underpin the diffusion process.

Gymnastics as a Masculinity Rite: Ollerup Danish Gymnastics between the Wars
Hans Bonde

In the 1930s Niels Bukh was a celebrity and the most well-known Dane outside Denmark. He achieved this fame by developing his own distinctive *primitive* gymnastics at Ollerup Folk High School and demonstrating them throughout the world. This chapter explores the phenomenon of primitive gymnastics at Ollerup as a rite of passage and a feature of the ritual development of masculinity in Denmark.

Pre-Totalitarian, Totalitarian and Post-Totalitarian Masculinity: The Projection of the Male Image in Sports Policy in Bulgaria
Vassil Girginov

This chapter examines Bulgarian sports policy in ideas, conceptual apparatus and language, analyses the capacity of masculinity to produce a sports policy discourse and related practical policies in different circumstances and traces the residual and emerging forms of masculinity in sports policy.

Select Bibliography

The Ephebia in the Ancient Hellenic World and its Role in the Making of Masculinity
Evangelos Albanidis

T. Brady, 'The Gymnasion in Ptolemaic Egypt', *The University of Missouri Studies*, 3 (1936), 9–20.

C. Forbes, *Greek Physical Education* (New York, 1971).

I. Marrou, *History of Education in Antiquity* (Athens, 1961).

A. Mehl, 'Erziehung zum Hellenen – Erzierhung zum Weltbuerger. Bemerkungen zum Gymnasion in Hellenistischen Osten', *Nikephoros*, 5 (1992), 43–73.

M. Nilson, *Die Hellenistische Schule* (Munich, 1955).

J. Oehler, 'Ephebia', *Realencylopaedie der Classischen Alertumswissenschaft*, 5, 2, (1905), 2737–46.

E. Zierbarth, *Aus dem Griechiscen Schulwesen* (Berlin, 1914).

Fighting Bulls in Southern European Culture: Anthropomorphic Symbols of Aggression and Mythical Male Heroes
Frédéric Saumade and Jean-Michel Delaplace

J.M. de Cossfo, *Los toros. Tratado téchnico e historico* (Madrid: Espasa-Calpe, 1951).

J.M. Delaplace, 'Le marquis de Baroncelli-Javon et la course camarguaise: du maintien des traditions à la sportivisation', in S. Fauché *et al.*, *Sport et identités* (Paris: L'Harmattan, 2000), pp.193–200.

E. Désveaux and F. Saumade, 'Relativiser le sacrifice ou le quadrant tauromachique', *Gradhiva*, 16 (1994), 79–84.

A.G. Haudricourt, 'Note sur le statut familial des animaux', *L'Homme*, 99 (1986), 119–20.

F. Mistral, *Lou tresor dou felibrige* (Raphèle-les-Arles: M Petit, 1979).

F. Saumade, *Des sauvages en Occident. Les cultures tauromachiques en Camargue et en Andalousie* (Paris: Maison des Sciences de l'Homme et Ministère de la Culture et de la Francophonie, 1994).

M. Salem, *A la gloire de la Bouvino* (Nîmes: La Capitelle, 1965).

Asserting Male Values: Nineteenth-Century Fêtes, Games and Masculinity – A French Case Study
Remi Dalisson

G. Andrieu, *L'homme et la forme: marchands de la force ou le culte de la forme (XIX–XXième siècles)* (Joinville-le-Pont, 1988), p.43.

P. Arnaud and T. Terret, *Histoire du sport feminin* (Paris, 1994).

R. Caillois, *Les jeux et les hommes, le masque et le vertige* (Paris, 1967).

R. Dalisson, 'Activities sportives et Fêtes publiques, sociabilités et associationnisme dans la France du Nord L'exemple seine-et-marnais, 1815-1939', *STAPS* (1999).

A. Davisse and C. Louveau, 'Sport, école, société, la part des femmes', *Féminin, masculin et activities sportives* (Joinville-le-pont, 1991)

P. Duret, *Les jeunes et l'identité masculine* (Paris, 1999).

J. Durry and B. Jeu, 'La conquête du corps' in *Le sport dans la société française* (Paris, 1992), p.102.

J.M.L Hotte, *Le symbolisme des jeux* (Paris, 1976), p.70.

J. Thibault, *Sport et éducation physique en France, 1870–1970* (Paris, 1972), p.162.

G. Vincent and B. Camy, *Fêtes à Givors, Education, fête et culture* (Lyon, 1981).

The Other Side of the Coin: Victorian Masculinity, Field Sports and English Elite Education
J.A. Mangan and Callum McKenzie

J. Chandos, *Boys Together: English Public Schools, 1800–1864* (London: Hutchinson, 1984).

R. Hyam, *Godliness, Hunting and Quite Good Learning: The History of Magdalene College, 1792–1992* (Cambridge: Magdalene College).

J.A. Mangan, *Athleticism in the Victorian and Edwardian Public Schools* (Cambridge, 1981).

D. Newsome, *Godliness and Good Learning: Four Studies on a Victorian Idea* (London: John Murray, 1961).

The Masculine Road through Modernity: Ling Gymnastics and Male Socialisation in Nineteenth-Century Sweden
Jens Ljunggren

H. Bonde, *Mandighed og sport* (Odense, 1991).

C. Florin, *'Där de härliga lagrarna gro-': kultur, klass och kön i det svenska läroverket 1850–1914* (Stockholm: Tiden, 1993).

M.S. Kimmel, *Manhood in America: a cultural history* (New York: Free Press, 1996).

T. Laqueur, *Making Sex: Body and Gender from the Greeks to Freud* (Cambridge, MA: Harvard University Press, 1990).

J. Lindroth, *Idrottens väg till folkrörelse: studier i svensk idrottsrörelse till 1915* (Uppsala, 1974).

P.H. Ling, *Gymnastikens allmänna grunder* (facsimile published by Svenska gymnastikförbundet, 1979).

J. Ljunggren, *Kroppens bildning: Linggymnastikens manlighetsprojekt 1790–1914* (Eslöv: B. Östlings bokförl. Symposion, 1999).

H. Meinander, *Towards a Bourgeois Manhood: Boys' Physical Education in Nordic Secondary Schools 1880–1940* (Helsinki: Societas scientiarum Fennica, 1994).

G.L. Mosse, *The Image of Man: The Creation of Modern Masculinity* (Oxford: Oxford University Press, 1999).

B. Söderberg, 'P. H. Ling – Heron, vetenskapsmannen och gudsbelätet: Något om Lingbilden under 1800 – och tidigt 1900-tal', *Idrott, historia och samhälle* (1995).

Athleticism in the Service of the Proletariat: Preparation for the English Elementary School and the Extension of Middle-Class Manliness
J.A. Mangan and Colm Hickey

T. Adkins, *The History of St. John's College Battersea. The Story of a Noble Experiment* (London, 1906).

G.W. Gent, *Memorials of St. Mark's College* (London, 1891).

G.F. Bartle, 'Staffing Policy at a Victorian Training College', *Victorian Education*, Occasional Publication no.2 (1976), 16–23.

G.F. Bartle, *A History of Borough Road College* (Kettering, 1976).

C. Hibbert, *No Ordinary Place: Radley College and the Public School System 1847–1997* (London, 1998).

D. Leinster-Mackay, *The Rise of the English Prep School* (London, 1984).

J.A. Mangan, *Athleticism in the Victorian and Edwardian Public School: The Emergence and Consolidation of an Educational Ideology* (Cambridge, 1981).

J.A. Mangan, *The Games Ethic and Imperialism* (London, 1998).

J.A. Mangan and Colm Hickey, 'English Elementary Education Revisited and Revised: Drill and Athleticism in Tandem', *European Sports History Review*, Vol.1 (1999), 63–91.

F.C. Pritchard, *A History of Westminster College 1851–1951* (London, 1951).

Gymnastics as a Masculinity Rite: Ollerup Danish Gymnastics between the Wars

Hans Bonde

H. Bonde, 'I.P. Muller, Danish Apostle of Health', *The International Journal of the History of Sport*, 8, 3 (1991), 347–69.

H. Bonde, 'Farmers' Gymnastics in Denmark in the late Nineteenth and Early Twentieth Centuries: A Semiotic Analysis of Exercise in Moral Action', *The International Journal of the History of Sport*, 10, 2 (1993), 193–214.

A. van Gennep, *The Rites of Passage* (Chicago, 1960).

M.M. Hart (ed.), *Sport in the Socio-Cultural Process* (Dubuque/Iowa, 1972).

R. Holt, *Sport and Society in Modern France* (London, 1981).

J. MacAloon, *This Great Symbol* (Chicago, 1981).

J.A. Mangan, *Athleticism in the Victorian and Edwardian Public Schools* (Cambridge, 1981), pp.141–78.

S. Moore and S. Myerhoff (eds.), *Secular Ritual* (Amsterdam, 1977).

V. Turner, *The Ritual Process* (Chicago, 1969).

V. Turner, 'Liminal to liminoid in play, flow and ritual', in C. Harris *et al.*, *Play, Games and Sports in Cultural Contexts* (Champaign, IL, 1983), pp.136–66.

F.W. Young, *Initiation Ceremonies* (New York, 1965), p.152.

Pre-Totalitarian, Totalitarian and Post-Totalitarian Masculinity: The Projection of the Male Image in Sports Policy in Bulgaria
Vassil Girginov

M. Costa and S. Guthrine (eds.), *Women and Sport* (Champaign: Human Kinetics, 1994).

V. Girginov and P. Bankov, 'Fascist Political Athletes and the Body Politic: Bulgaria Reborn', *The International Journal of the History of Sport*, 16, 4 (1999) 82–103.

T. Kay, *Women and Sport: A Review of Research* (London: Sports Council, 1995).

J.A. Mangan and J. Walvin (eds.), *Manliness and Morality: Middle-Class Masculinity in Britain and America, 1800–1940* (Manchester: Manchester University Press, 1987).

D. Rowe (ed.), *Power Play: Essays in the Sociology of Australian Sport* (Sydney: University Press, 1989), pp.215–29.

D. Scully and J. Clarke, 'Gender Issues in Sport Participation', in J. Kremer *et al.* (eds.), *Young People's Involvement in Sport* (London: Routledge, 1997).

M. Talbot, 'Working Together towards Gender Equity in Sport – Challenges for Sports Organisations', A key note address, 7th European Congress for Sport Management (Thessaloniki, 1999).

A. White and C. Brackenridge, 'Who Rules Sport? Gender Division in the Power Structure of British Sports Organisations from 1960', *International Review for the Sociology of Sport*, 20, 1/2 (1985), 95–107.

C. Williams, G. Lawrence and D. Rowe, 'Patriarchy, Media, Sport', in G. Lawrence and J. Hargreaves, *Sporting Females* (London: Routledge, 1994).

Index